TSAR AND COSSACK, 1855–1914

Robert H. McNeal

St. Martin's Press   New York

Printed in Hong Kong

Published in the United Kingdom by
the Macmillan Press Ltd.
First published in the United States of America in 1987

ISBN 0–312–82188–3

Library of Congress Cataloging in Publication Data
McNeal, Robert Hatch, 1930–
  Tsar and cossack, 1855–1914.

  Bibliography: p.
  Includes index.
  1. Sociology, Military—History—19th century.
  2. Sociology, Military—Soviet Union—20th century.
  3. Cossacks—History—19th century. 4. Cossacks—
  History—20th century. 5. Civil–military relations—
  Soviet Union—History—19th century. 6. Civil–military
  relations—Soviet Union—History—20th century.
  I. Title.
  UA770.M38   1987   306′.27′0947   85–1942
  ISBN 0–312–82188–3

In memory of
Thorley Hatch McNeal

Contents

Contents

List of Maps and Charts

Acknowledgements

E. Willis Brooks, John S. Bushnell, Mary Schaeffer Conroy, Gregory P. Tschebotarioff, William C. Fuller, Jr, Richard Gregor, Robert E. Jones, Jean Konkoff, Joseph Lake, Maurice Levin, Philip Longworth, Timothy Mixter, Norman Naimark, Marvin Rintala, Robert and Galina Rothstein, K. F. Shatsillo, Marc Szeftel, and, I must regretfully admit, others whom I probably have overlooked contributed generously to my work on the Cossacks. Without diminishing my gratitude to them, a special word of thanks to Bruce W. Menning is obligatory for sharing so much of his expertise, especially on the Don Cossacks.

Research grants from the University of Toronto, University of Massachusetts at Amherst and the International Research and Exchanges Board made an indispensable contribution to the project.

During a brief visit to the Library of Congress the hospitality of the Kennan Institute for Advanced Russian Studies was very helpful.

R. H. McN.

Note on Translation and Transliteration

Although most Russian words used in this study appear in translation, certain military and civil-administrative terms appear in Russian because there is no equivalent in English (e.g. voisko, ataman, zemstvo, uezd). Because some of these words appear frequently in the study, it is simplest to treat them as if they were English words, omitting italics and Russian soft or hard signs and forming the plural by adding 's'.

Units of measure appear in pre-revolutionary Russian form (excepting indication of the size of voiskos in Chapter 1). A table of equivalences follows:

1 desiatina	2.7 acres	6.67 hectares
1 versta	3500 feet	1.07 kilometres
1 sazhen'	7 feet	2.13 metres
1 pud	36 pounds	16.33 kilogrammes
1 chetvert'	5.96 bushels	210 litres
1 vedro	21 pints	9.93 litres

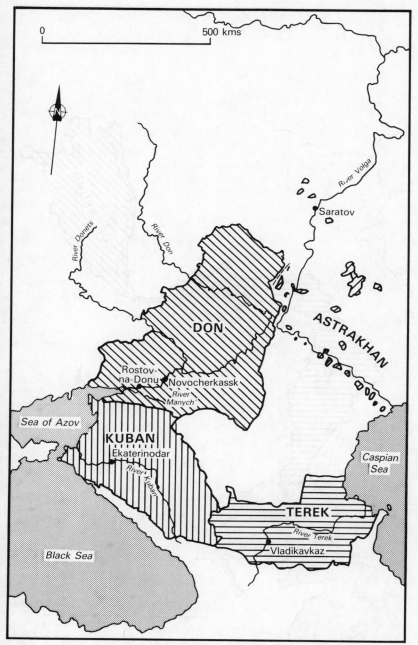

Map 1   Don, Kuban, Terek and Astrakhan voiskos

Map 2 Ural and Orenburg voiskos

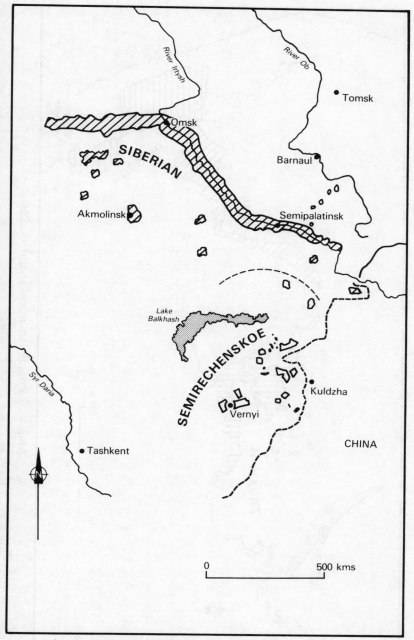

Map 3   Siberian and Semirechenskoe voiskos

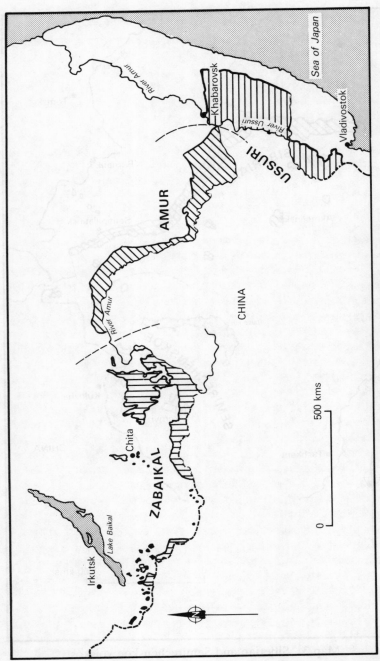

Map 4 Zabaikal, Amur and Ussuri voiskos

1 Loyalties

THE TSAR

In the land of the quiet Don in the city of Novocherkassk on the great square before the cathedral of Saint Alexander Nevsky, stands a statue of the Cossack Ermak Timofeevich, his hand outstretched to offer the crown of Siberia to (the unseen) Tsar Ivan the Terrible. This monument, inscribed 'To Ermak from the Dontsy' (that is, the Don Cossacks), was erected in 1904 as an obvious effort to reinforce the official myth of tsar and Cossack, of mutual loyalty and generosity, the warrior-caste providing self-sacrificing valour and the monarch rewarding them with land and privilege.[1]

Certainly the tsars and their minions, especially in the last century and a half of the Empire, worked assiduously to propagate this myth. Granted, the tsar was supposed to be the benevolent, if stern, father of all the people of his realm, but with the Cossacks he cultivated a special relationship. Nicholas I emphasized this in 1837 when he bestowed the newly-contrived title of 'Most August Ataman of All Cossack Voiskos' on his heir, beginning a succession of heir-atamans that extended to the son of the last tsar, Alexei Nicholaevich.[2] When Nicholas I appointed the first most august ataman he journeyed with his son to Novocherkassk, the Don Cossack capital, for the presentation. Thenceforward visits of the tsar and/or heir were an important ingredient in the myth of the special relationship, treated not merely as an inspection but a kind of personal communion. Each successive tsar from Nicholas I managed to make at least one ceremonial visit to the Don, the largest and senior surviving Cossack community. Because the other Cossacks resided in territory stretching across the expanse of Eurasia, from the Sea of Azov nearly to the Pacific, it was impractical for Nicholas I, his son or grandson to call on all the Cossacks, and the Don served symbolically for the rest. But his heir, the future

Alexander II, managed to get to the Cossacks of the Ural and Alexander III to those of the Kuban and Terek. Nicholas II was the first tsar who, as heir and most august ataman, was able to visit almost all of the Cossack voiskos in Asia.[3]

Since it was not practical for the tsar or heir to travel frequently to the far-flung lands of the Cossacks to reinforce the idea of a personal relationship, a symbolic handful of Cossacks could be brought to the precincts of the imperial family to serve as household guards, the 'convoi'. This not only put the tsar in direct contact with 'his' Cossacks, it provided an occasion to imply that he was one of them, beginning with the enrolment in the convoi of the future Alexander III in 1859. Alexander II himself joined in 1861 and Nicholas II at birth, 6 May 1868.[4]

Out in the regions of Cossack settlement, various ceremonies and artefacts sustained the myth of tsar and Cossack. To list the 'regalia' of the various voiskos as they had accumulated by 1902 required almost 100 pages in the centennial history of the War Ministry.[5] The most important and sometimes substantive kind of item in this inventory was the 'gramota'. This kind of document, which may be translated 'charter', in the era of Cossack autonomy resembled a formal diplomatic communication from the tsar via the pre-Petrine equivalent of a foreign office. Later, as the Cossacks fell under the sway of the Empire, it became an official monarchial assurance of the privileges of the estate, corresponding to the 'Charter of the Nobility' of Catherine the Great. Granted, Cossack charters were usually fairly vague about what was being guaranteed and in the early twentieth century were little more than thank-you notes for counterrevolutionary service. But because the charters expressed the patronage of the tsar towards his deserving warrior-estate, often using the verb/noun 'zhalovat'/zha- lovanie' (literally 'compensation/to compensate'), this kind of charter became known as a 'zhalovaniia gramota'. By the end of the nineteenth century the various Cossack voiskos treasured 141 documents that were regarded as charters of some sort. During and after the threat of revolution in the early twentieth century, Nicholas II issued a round of charters to all the Cossack voiskos, including some that had never been honoured thus.[6] Of all the charters, the two most celebrated were from 1792 and 1793 respectively, in which Catherine the Great awarded the two most populous Cossack voiskos, the Kuban and Don, their land, the crucial privilege of the estate. In keeping with the spirit of the myth, the Kuban voisko spent 150 000 rubles on a statue of Catherine in 1894 to honour the centennial of the charter.[7] In the Don, the documents themselves were, after the Napoleonic Wars, kept in caskets made of silver captured from the French, like the relics of saints. In the less wealthy Astrakhan voisko they were carried on pillows for public display. Public readings of the charters were the focal point of the civic ceremonies of the Cossacks by the nineteenth century, a priest carrying out this reverend function in the Don.[8] The occasion for this ritual was the meeting of the 'krug', once a rough but more or less democratic assembly, but by the nineteenth century merged with the legal holidays of the Cossack community. In the Don, which had five such holidays by 1890, the choice of occasions emphasized the myth of tsar and Cossack: 1 January (in honour of the first charter); 6 May (birthday of the heir/august ataman); 30 August (in honour of the rights and privileges granted by the tsars); 1 October (in honour of the naming of Alexander Nicholaevich as august ataman); 17 October (in honour of the narrow escape of Alexander III in a railway accident).[9]

Next to the charters the most respected kind of artefact was the inscribed banner, donated by this or that tsar as a token of thanks. For example, 'a white banner bearing the monarchial coat of arms and the inscription "to the truly loyal Don voisko for the service rendered at the time of the war with the Persians" '. Only the Don had received a peculiar species of banner from the tsars, one from Peter I and one from Catherine II. This was the bunchuk, or horsetail on a staff, evoking the early Tatar connections of these Cossacks. And until the twentieth century only the Don, Terek and Ural voiskos rejoiced in the possession of another kind of gift of the tsars, the 'naseka' of the ataman, a decorated staff. After the onset of the Russo-Japanese War, Nicholas II awarded this symbol of authority to all the atamans of voiskos. Following the revolution of 1905, he issued another round of nasekas. In addition to these mainstays of the regalia, a variety of voiskos had an assortment of bric-a-brac that the monarchs had bestowed on them at one time or another. There were some maces, a kind of decorated staff called a 'pernach', kettledrums, silver tuning-keys for same, the odd salt-cellar and silver dish, sabre and uniforms worn by Nicholas I or Alexander II.[10]

Such were the formalities. What can one say of the vitality, the sincerity, of the myth of tsar and Cossack? On the Cossack side there is evidence of real respect, along with consciousness of various grievances, such as the burden of military service and the loss of bygone freedom. The most persuasive signs of deep-rooted 'naive monarchism', as Soviet historians call it, probably concern the charters and the Cossacks' wish to believe that the monarch had promised them major privileges. Not only were the real charters treated with respect, the people of the Don, Ural and Terek all were attached to legends of charters that supposedly were issued to them even before any of the authentic ones. In the Don it was an imaginary charter from Ivan the Terrible, celebrating the capture of Kazan in 1552 by promising those Cossacks their namesake river and its tributaries.[11] The Terek Cossacks also attributed their legendary charter to Ivan the Terrible, dating it 1555. The Cossacks of the Ural believed that the first Romanov, Mikhail Fedorovich, had granted them their river 'from the headwaters to the sea, with all its tributaries'.[12] The rebel Pugachev, appealing to the Ural Cossacks in particular as the 'Amperator Peter III', exploited this myth by repeating just this promise and adding to it 'the cross and the beard' – that is, the customs of the Old Believers.[13] Belief in these legends weakened by the twentieth century, eroded by various problems that this book discusses. No doubt there was less than unanimous enthusiasm for the officially contrived 'Don Hymn':

It stirs, it moves,
The Orthodox quiet Don,
And obediently answers
The summons of the Monarch.[14]

Yet many defended his throne, and as late as the 1960s a handful of surviving *émigré* officers in Paris and New York were lovingly keeping alive the myth of tsar and Cossack in small, private museums.[15]

On the side of the tsars, sincere commitment to the myth of tsar and Cossack was from the first alloyed with political interest. The Cossacks, properly handled, could be useful, even if they could also be obstreperous, particularly before the nineteenth century. It seems fair to surmise, however, that with the increasing success of the policy of domesticating the Cossacks, the tsars became more disposed to believe the myth in which they played a beneficent role. Such seems to have been the self-image of Alexander II when he reversed the legal opinion and policy judgement of his bureaucrats to give the Don officers personal title to their land in honour of the tricentennial of the Don Cossacks.[16] Alexander III on two notable occasions overrode considerable bureaucratic opinion to make substantial awards of territory to the Cossacks, and his son likewise opposed the ministerial consensus in preventing the subtraction of a large plot of land from the

Cossacks.[17] That the last tsar felt some real attachment to the myth emerged at a time when he had no need to dissemble concerning the Cossacks, nor to mention them at all. Wearing the uniform of the Kuban Cossacks, Nicholas II, on the point of abdicating, expressed one regret: 'The Cossacks whom I hurled at the front will blame me.'[18]

THE SOSLOVIE

For the Cossacks there was an alternative myth, contrasting with that of tsar and Cossack. This was the myth of the free Cossack. It was rooted in the origins of the Cossacks, men who fled the serfdom of the Polish–Lithuanian and Muscovite states to the free steppe, the land between the Slavic states of the north and the Turkish–Tatar sphere along the Black Sea littoral. By 1500 small clusters of population, fugitives from the north with some admixture of the Turkish–Tatar population, had appeared, called Cossacks (kazaki), the name probably derived from a Turkish word for 'brigand'. These communities, although culturally rudimentary and violent, took real pride in their independence and democracy. Their assemblies, called the 'krug' (circle) among the Don Cossacks, elected their leaders, the 'ataman' and his deputy the 'esaul' (both names reflecting Turkish–Tatar influence), among others. Those elected held office at the pleasure of the krug and returned to the ranks when replaced. Apart from fishing and hunting, the Cossacks lived by plunder (mainly of the Tatars and Turks) and by the sale of their military services as guards, escorts and auxiliary troops to the Polish–Lithuanian and Russian monarchies. The proceeds of these ventures the Cossacks distributed among themselves with some idea of equity, and there were no private fortunes in land in the first period of Cossack life. On this basis arose the image of the free warrior, which survived even into the twentieth century, when there were some efforts to merge it with modern liberalism.[19] But the era of Cossack liberty could only be transitional, declining as the power of the Slavic states, and especially Russia, gradually expanded over the steppe. The Cossacks were too few and economically dependent to resist this trend in the long run, and the main theme of Cossack history became the decline of Cossack liberty and the rise of tsarist control. Gradually absorbing the land and population of the Cossacks, the Empire of the tsars also had to find a place for these people in its legal social order, for such martial communities were in most cases considered too useful simply to be disbanded. The southern frontier zone of the Russian Empire was settled and consolidated only gradually, and in some areas a Cossack population of colonist–fighters remained useful until the twentieth century – granted, only in Asiatic Russia by that late date. In short, the Cossacks had to become a legal estate (soslovie) of the Russian Empire.

The system of estates that evolved in eighteenth- and nineteenth-century Russia was by no means a simple matter of nobles and commoners or three estates. By the time the first Russian code of laws appeared in 1832 it was difficult to say just how many estates there were, owing to the complexity of the subdivisions that existed within the main divisions laid down by the code: dvorianstvo (nobles), dukhoventsvo (clergy), gorodskie obyvateli (city residents), sel'skie obyvateli (rural residents), inorodnie (aliens – that is, members of officially-recognized non-Russian ethnic groups), Finnish citizens and foreigners. The code perhaps recognized two subspecies of nobles, three of clergy, five of urban residents, seven of rural residents and eight of aliens.[20] But this count is debatable as well as inconstant, for it is not always clear when a subdivision within a category should be considered an estate. For example, the three subcategories under clergy in the version above count two kinds of Orthodox clergy ('black' or monastic and 'white' or secular) and non-Orthodox, but should the latter be subdivided by sect, such as Roman Catholic, Lutheran, Jewish, Moslem, Buddhist, and even others? As we shall see, the Cossacks might well be counted as more than one legal class.

In any case, the Russian Empire assumed that its subjects all belonged to some estate and so had to place the Cossacks in this order as the formerly independent communities were absorbed by the Empire. For many years, this process did not proceed in a systematic fashion. The Russian law code of 1649 made only a few allusions to the Cossacks, and the first law thereafter that dealt with them appears to be an order dated 1659 appointing Yurii Khmelnitsky, son of the famous Bohdan, as Hetman of the Ukraine.[21] Certainly by the beginning of the eighteenth century there was a steady stream of legislation that treated the Cossacks as some kind of social category within the population of Imperial Russia, but no law actually defined this estate. In the Legislative Commission of Catherine the Great, 1767–8, a proposal attempted to define the Cossacks as a social order, but nothing was decided.[22] Speransky's *Code of Laws,* completed in 1832, finally established the Cossacks as an estate (the 'kazachestvo'), placing them along with the peasants in the broad category of 'rural residents'.[23] But it did not go into much detail on the characteristics of the Cossacks as an estate, because it happened that a commission headed by General A. I. Chernyshev had been at work since 1819 preparing a major statute for the Don Cossacks, and its work was not promulgated until 1835.[24] This 'Statute [polozhenie] on the Administration of the Don Voisko' was the first systematic attempt to define the Cossacks as an estate, setting down their rights and obligations.[25] Indeed, it was the only time that the Russian Empire ever adopted a comprehensive law on the Cossacks, integrating in one document military obligation, civil government and economic matters. Originally issued for the Don Cossacks only, in the 1840s it was adapted to five other Cossack voiskos with local modifications.[26]

But in the very process of defining the Cossacks as an estate, the Don statute of 1835 introduced complexities and ambiguities into the matter. Without intending to do so the statute approximately reproduced under the rubric 'Cossack' the main elements in the Imperial social order as a whole: nobles, clergy, urban residents, rural residents and aliens. The largest subcategory within the Cossack estate was the ordinary Cossack, the approximate counterpart of the largest subdivision of 'rural residents', the peasantry. Both were the bottom layer in their respective contexts. The Cossacks never experienced serfdom, but there were recurrent signs that the St Petersburg policy-makers regarded them as a species of peasant, which is not surprising considering that the *Code* placed the Cossacks beside the peasants in the broad category of 'rural residents'. Like the emancipated peasant, the Cossack participated in a system of communal land tenure, but unlike the peasant he never rendered obrok (money dues), barshchina (labour dues), or land redemption payments. Above all, the Cossack did not pay the podushnaia podat' (soul tax or capitation). This was probably the most precious 'privilege' that separated the Cossack from the peasant. One basic distinction within the entire system of legal estates in the Empire was between the podatnye (taxed) and nepodatnye (untaxed). The nobility was the most notable category among the untaxed, which endeared this privilege to the Cossack. The value of this distinction diminished with the abolition of the soul tax in 1883–6, just as freedom from the obligation of the taxed estates to provide recruits who served in the army for 25 years meant less after this obligation was transformed into shorter-term conscription in 1874. The peculiar system of Cossack military obligation, which is one of the main themes of this book, at all times distinguished the

Cossacks from the peasantry, even if the distinction was more a burden than a privilege.

Certainly the law recognized a difference between the ordinary Cossack and the noble Cossack, just as it distinguished the peasant from the noble. Despite the myth of democracy in the independent Cossack communities, social differentiation began to appear among them when they were in their prime as independent polities. Among the Don Cossacks, the tendency for some individuals and families to gain repeated election to powerful and lucrative offices became well established in the eighteenth century. This elite was first called the 'starshina' (elders) and later 'chinovniki' (literally holders of rank). In their original form, the starshina had no definite legal status, but they nevertheless developed a firm sense of class interest, and from an early date there was serious conflict between them and the ordinary Cossacks. The starshina not only tended to monopolize the choice offices, they were also highly susceptible to the blandishments of the Empire. The decline of Cossack independence and democracy was greatly assisted by the inclination of the starshina to exchange Cossack liberty for class privilege.[27] In the first phase of this development, the starshina placed the Cossacks under their command at the service of the tsars in return for 'compensation' (zhalovanie) and support for their tenure in office, which ended free elections. By the time agriculture began to appear in the last third of the eighteenth century as a substantial part of the Don economy, the main ambition of the starshina was to become nobles with land and serfs. Such was their main proposal to the Legislative Commission of Catherine the Great.[28]

The response of the Imperial regime to this development was ambivalent. They found the starshina extremely useful in mobilizing troops and subjecting the Cossack population to state control, but they had reservations about the desirability of creating nobles too freely, especially after the Charter of the Nobility in 1785 exempted this estate from military or civil service.[29] This sufficed to scuttle proposals that the solution to the problem of integrating the Cossacks into the estate order should be that all receive nobility. Moreover, there was a growing awareness in St Petersburg that the appearance of a wealthy nobility in the Don would mean the loss of much of the land required for the maintenance of ordinary Cossacks as self-supporting troops. These conflicting impulses concerning the Cossack nobility, which clearly existed *de facto* by the late eighteenth century, led to vacillating and muddled policy towards the establishment of a legal status for this class. Military expediency helped the starshina towards the objective of noble status. By the late eighteenth century a considerable number of the Don Cossack starshina had received regular army officer rank, and in 1789 Paul I generously promulgated a law equating Don Cossack officer ranks, which by tradition had peculiar names below the rank of colonel, with regular army ranks. According to the Table of Ranks established by Peter the Great, officers assumed nobility automatically, and the Cossack officers definitely counted on this. But the War Ministry, and especially General Chernyshev, who laboured so long over the Don statute of 1835, had other ideas. At one point the ministry proposed that the 1798 law did not confer nobility on all officers, but was willing to compromise and award it to all but the three bottom ranks.[30] Against this, the *Code of Laws* of the Empire accepted the notion that all officers of voiskos to which the 1798 law applied did have nobility, and this remained in place.[31]

Although they had achieved noble status, the Don chinovniks did not obtain the corporate institutions of the Russian nobility in their standard form. When in 1816 the ataman petitioned that they be permitted to elect a 'marshal of the nobility' as in normal guberniias, the regime refused, and only in 1870 was this office finally established.[32] And although the Don nobility did have their assembly for the whole of the Don Cossack territory, they lacked any assemblies on the subordinate level, the uezd, which played a significant role in the normal guberniia. As for Cossack voiskos other than the Don, they never had any assembly of nobles.

In sum, there was a confusing legal situation. Cossack nobles were in some ways Cossacks, not only in name but also by virtue of their participation in the communal life of the ordinary Cossacks. Cossack nobles could hold office in and receive land allotments from local Cossack communities, which was not the case with respect to the generality of nobles and peasant communities. At the same time, the Cossack nobles enjoyed most of the privileges pertaining to the noble estate in the Empire. Considering both aspects of the situation, one might regard the Cossack nobility as a special estate in its own right, even though the *Code of Laws* did not recognize this explicitly.

Before 1851 there was similar ambiguity concerning the status of Cossack clergy. When the Don Cossacks were independent, they elected priests from within their midst, partly because they were remote from the Russian state and its ecclesiastical department. Even after the subordination of the Don area to the Eparchiate of Voronezh in 1718, clergy were often drawn from the Cossacks. This resulted in a peculiar situation in which there were men who were Cossacks and yet enjoyed the legal status of clergy. Their sons were considered Cossacks and subject to military service unless, as was common, they followed their fathers' vocation. A law of 1851 forbade further enrolments in the clergy by Cossacks, making priests of Cossack descent simply members of the clerical estate, with one distinction: that their sons reverted to Cossack status if they did not become clergymen.[33] This, and the reputation of having Cossack roots, was all that distinguished them from the non-Cossack clergy.

Strictly speaking, there was no separate estate of Cossack merchants. According to the tsars' charters, all Cossacks enjoyed the right to engage in trade on Cossack territory, but in the Don some had come to specialize in commerce by the opening of the nineteenth century. They tended to hire substitutes to fulfil their military obligation, a practice that the administration objected to in uncontrolled form. In 1804 ataman Platov proposed to regulate such matters by establishing a 'Society of Merchant Cossacks', and in the course of preparing the legislation he even suggested that members of the society become a separate estate. This would have paralleled the kuptsy (merchants, the leading estate among the 'urban residents'). But the government rejected Platov's proposal, and instead there were for many years after 1804, among the Don and most other Cossack voiskos, 'societies of merchants', dues-paying, regulated in number and exempt from military service – an estate in all but name.[34]

The counterpart of the aliens (legally-recognized ethnic minorities) among the Cossacks is a curiosity: the 2000 Kalmyks (Mongol, Buddhist), migratory people whom the government quite arbitrarily defined as Don Cossacks in 1798,[35] and who enjoyed legally specified rights to land, and peculiar cultural institutions, including religious practices that involved a clergy. The latter in the strictest sense constituted one of the most exotic legal social categories in the entire system of estates and their subdivisions.[36] There were indeed other non-Russian ethnic groups who were enrolled as Cossacks, such as about 1000 Chinese, who joined the Semirechenskoe voisko in 1869,[37] but only the Kalmyks enjoyed legal recognition as a subdivision of the Cossacks.

Finally, one must mention another category that definitely existed in the Cossack perception of social relations, even though it was not a legal estate. This was the group that the Cossacks called 'inogorodnie', literally 'people from a different town', in practice any non-Cossack settled in Cossack territory. By 1910 slightly over half the population on Cossack land was non-Cossack, the inogorodnie. Of course these people belonged to some estate, noble, peasant or whatever, but in their relation to the Cossacks they all shared a common degree of exclusion from Cossack society. Increasingly, the numbers and sometimes the prosperity of the non-Cossacks was one of the most galling matters in the Cossack view of society. To deflect such animosity from influential non-Cossacks, such as estate-owners who lived among the Cossacks, some local Cossack administrations took to awarding the title of 'honorary Cossack' (or honorary starik-elder), a practice that was recognized in law in 1895. But these people enjoyed no special rights and were not a legal estate.[38]

In the late nineteenth century the great Russian scholar of jurisprudence N. M. Korkunov wrote: 'it is not rare to meet among us a person who does not know himself what estate he belongs to'.[39] By that time many influential Russians, including some conservatives, believed that the concept of the estate was outworn. But, as the question of 'inogorodnie' suggests, a large number of Cossacks disagreed. Among the Don Cossacks, who were mainly of Great Russian ancestry, it remained common even in the twentieth century to refer to 'Russatskie' or 'katsapy' (from the Ukrainian) to distinguish Cossack from Russian. It is characteristic too that many Don Cossacks as late as 1900 wore their military uniform in daily life.[40] Unlike most other estates of the Russian Empire, the Cossacks lived a life that was in many ways visibly controlled by their estate as an institution, involving a special system of military, political and economic institutions. Moreover, with the exception of a rather brief, aberrant period, the laws made it extremely hard for Cossacks to leave this estate and join another, or even to leave their native locality.[41] Like many questions of mass consciousness, proof is difficult, but it seems reasonably clear that even in the early twentieth century the Cossack knew he was a Cossack, and probably took some pride in the fact.

THE VOISKO

Cossack self-consciousness concerned not only the estate as a whole, but more specifically the 'voisko'. The general usage of this Russian word means any army or armed force, but by the nineteenth century it had assumed a special meaning with reference to the Cossacks: a voisko was the highest administrative unit or community among the Cossacks. Such a unit produced troops, but a voisko was not any sort of operational category and it included men, women and children – the entire Cossack society dwelling on a specific territory that was supposedly set aside for them. One was not simply a Cossack but a Don Cossack (the 'Dontsy'), Ural Cossack ('Ural'tsy') and so forth. The tsars recognized this distinction in their charters, which were never addressed to the Cossacks in general but only to specific voiskos. Much as the bureaucrats were inclined to attempt to produce standard law for all Cossacks, they never considered dropping the concept of separate voiskos, recognizing that a great many Cossacks were strongly attached to this tradition. In any case, the bureaucrats accepted that the far-flung voiskos lived in varying circumstances and that special legislation for individual voiskos was often a practical necessity. There is even some case for the argument that each voisko represented a separate estate, in that its privileges and obligations were distinctive. The *Code of Laws* implied as much by breaking down its treatment of subjects such as civil administration into a separate section for each voisko.[42] And this was the *Code* as it stood in the early twentieth century, reflecting many years of efforts to standardize Cossack administration. Such an argument probably goes too far, for many of the differences between the law of one voisko and another were minor, and some important laws on Cossacks were almost uniform.[43] But, as we will see repeatedly, the arrangements that applied to the Ural voisko were highly distinctive.

The power to make and unmake voiskos was fundamental to the authority of tsar over Cossack. In the eighteenth century the two major Cossack formations of the western steppe, the Zaporozhian and Malorossiiskii, were abolished.[44] Others were created, abolished, amalgamated and partitioned.[45] The result of this process, by the late nineteenth century, was eleven voiskos.

By all odds, the most important was the Don. It was the senior surviving voisko with a formidable tradition of independence.[46] The government dated the founding of the voisko from 1570 when the first charter from a tsar was sent to the Don Cossacks, but their community predated this. Although they valued the charter and banners that successive tsars sent them, the Don krug stubbornly resisted efforts to exact from them an oath of allegiance to a tsar until 1672, just after the first great Don Cossack rebel, Stenka Razin, had raised many of the Don Cossacks against the regime.[47] Crushed by Muscovite regular troops, the Don Cossacks capitulated and took the oath, to be repeated for all subsequent tsars. In the early eighteenth century Peter the Great dealt a series of additional blows to Don independence, crushing the second major rebel, Kondratii Bulavin, establishing a substantial fort on the site of the future city of Rostov-na-Donu, eliminating the power of the krug to elect the ataman of its choice, and transferring business between the Don and the Imperial government from the office responsible for foreign affairs to the military department.[48] There were still signs of resistance among the Don Cossacks. In 1772 many Don Cossacks objected to their assignment to the forts near the mouth of the Don and nearly murdered the general who had been sent to reprove them.[49] Only after regular troops made their appearance and the Don ataman of the time was arrested and exiled did the regime prevail. It was just after this that the third great Don Cossack rebel, Emilian Pugachev, posing as tsar, aroused his tens of thousands, although not many in his native voisko, which he approached only when in retreat near the end of his career.[50] There was one further episode of Don Cossack mutiny; a show of resistance in 1792–4 to plans to resettle some from this voisko in the line facing the hostile Caucasian mountaineers. Again Imperial regulars overawed the recalcitrants.[51]

Meanwhile, in 1775 Prince Potemkin dictated the first formalized legal order for the internal governance of the voisko, concentrating authority in the appointed ataman.[52] It remained in place until the substantially more elaborate Don Statute of 1835 came into force. The statute of 1835 succeeded to a considerable extent in fulfilling one of its objectives, the restraint of the acquisitiveness of the Don starshina, but these magnates still held substantial power over the affairs of the voisko. According to the statute, they elected from their own midst the public officials of the Don under the appointed ataman, although from 1848 that vital post always went to a non-Cossack career officer. This elite remained an influential force in the affairs not only of the Don Cossacks but of all Cossacks until the end of the Empire. The St Petersburg regime might regard them as 'a restless element', but their opinion counted more than that of any other Cossack group.[53]

Peter the Great encompassed the Don Cossack land in his Empire, but it remained for Catherine the Great to order a survey to determine the specific extent of its territory. When this was complete she presented, with much official pomp, her charter of 1793, accompanied by a map, defining the 'Land [zemlia] of the Don Cossack Voisko'.[54] This land was supposedly granted for eternity, and, with minor modifications and one considerable addition (the Rostov and Taganrog regions in 1887), it lasted at least until the end of the Empire. It was a handsome endowment, larger than England and Wales or the state of Michigan, about 15 million desiatinas (over 63 000 square miles or almost 165 000 square km).[55] Almost 90 per cent was officially classified as 'good' for agriculture, with a moderate climate. The grape flourished in part of the area. There were important fisheries on the Don River and in the Sea of Azov, and large coal deposits. The capital of the 'Land of the Don Cossack Voisko' was originally Cherkassk, the most important city of Cossack provenance in the Empire, situated about 60 km upstream from the Don delta. Because of the spring floods there, the centre was transferred in 1805 to Novocherkassk (New Cherkassk), which was located on higher ground in the same vicinity.

The Don was the largest voisko in Cossack population, about 610 000 in 1860 and 1 427 000 in 1912. This constituted about 23 per cent of all Cossacks in 1860 and 34 per cent in 1912. In addition to the Cossack inhabitants of the voisko land there were the 'inogorodnie'. In the Don there were about 320 000 non-Cossacks resident in 1860, or 34 per cent of the total population; by 1910 this had grown to 1 783 000 or 56 per cent.[56]

Most of the Don Cossacks were Great Russian in origin, but they mixed with Turco-Tatar people (including captured women), and the pioneer ethnographer Kharuzin maintained that the Cossacks of the southern Don tended to be swarthier than those in the north.[57] In addition there were fugitives of Ukrainian origin and the sizeable body of Kalmyks (physically oriental in appearance) whom the government decided to define as Don Cossacks. Officially the Don Cossacks were Russian Orthodox believers, apart from the Buddhist (Dalai-Lamist) Kalmyks, but from the time of the Nikonian reforms in the mid-seventeenth century some of the fugitives who joined the Don Cossacks were Old Believers, and a significant minority of the earlier arrivals held to the old ways, too. The regime was uncomfortable with the existence of these 'schismatics' among the Don Cossacks, and the Eparchiate of Voronezh conducted continual efforts to overcome this dissidence. Officially, only 11.2 per cent of the Don Cossack population was reported as Old Believers in 1910 but this was surely an understatement.[58]

By virtue of its tradition, self-consciousness, military contribution and sheer size, the Don voisko dominated the Cossack system as a whole. Official concern with the Don overshadowed the attention paid to other voiskos, and in many ways the Don served as the model. Information concerning the Don is far greater in volume and more accessible than material on the other voiskos, so it is impossible to prevent the present study from leaning heavily on this material, running some risk of underrating the peculiarity of the affairs of the other voiskos. But such an imbalance is not entirely misleading, for it reflects the perception or misperception held by the tsars and their military and civil administrators.

The Kuban and Terek voiskos, which were officially bracketed as the 'Caucasian Cossacks', came into being only in 1860, but they had long and complex antecedents.[59] Many were descended from the Zaporozhian Cossacks, whose early origins and martial traditions rivalled those of the Don. Peter the Great disbanded this Ukrainian community but Anna permitted its revival in 1734 to participate in renewed fighting against the Turks. Catherine the Great did not want to reserve part of 'New Russia' for the obstreperous Zaporozhians and dissolved them once again in 1775. To reduce Cossack displeasure, which was great enough that some defected to the Ottoman Empire, and to colonize territory along the Kuban River, many of these Cossacks in 1787–92 were transplanted to become the Chernomorskoe (Black Sea) voisko.[60] In the early nineteenth century additional Cossack settlers of Ukrainian origin arrived: some of those who had gone to the Turks and some of the former Malorossiiskii (Ukrainian) Cossacks.[61] The land of the Chernomorskoe voisko Catherine II guaranteed forever in a charter in 1792.[62]

Further east and south in the isthmus between the Black and Caspian Seas, along the valley of the Terek River, small Cossack communities existed in the seventeenth century, and they were amplified by Peter the Great through the transplantation of others, under state control. By 1800 there were three tiny voiskos (Grebenskoe, Terskoe Semeinoe and Terskoe Kizliarskoe), four separate groups merely organized as 'regiments', and one 'command'. Nicholas I, who was using Cossack troops in his war to subdue the Caucasian mountaineers, personally imposed his plan for the consolidation of these small entities into a single 'Caucasian Line Voisko' in 1845.[63]

With the end of serious fighting in the mountains the regime sought to reorganize and expand the Caucasian Cossack voiskos. In 1860 two new voiskos, the Kuban and Terek, appeared, the former including the Chernomorskoe Cossacks and approximately the western half of the Caucasian Line, the latter the eastern half. Thus the Kuban voisko became the second largest in population, growing from 384 000 Cossacks in 1860 to 1 183 000 in 1910, which meant that they had almost overtaken the Don. The area of the Kuban was about 8.6 million desiatinas (over 36 000 square miles or 94 000 square km), somewhat more than half the size of the Don but still the second or third largest voisko in area.[64] This was for the most part extremely desirable land, fertile, well-watered and temperate, and in due course oil was discovered. At mid-century the area was still sparsely populated, which made it all the more attractive. As a result the Kuban experienced an exceptionally rapid influx of settlers, some officially sponsored, others not. Some of the settlers enrolled as Cossacks, which assured them land allotments but, in the words of a war minister, failed to make them Cossacks 'not only in name but also in spirit'. Because of the presence of the former Zaporozhians and also additional settlers from the Ukraine, a majority of the Cossack population of the Kuban (57 per cent in 1897) were Ukrainian-speaking.[65] But not all the settlers became Cossacks. While only 1 per cent of the population of the Kuban was non-Cossack in 1860, 57 per cent was in 1912 (1.26 million Cossacks out of a total population of 2.94 million). The name of the administrative centre of the voisko honoured the myth of monarchial beneficence to the Cossacks: Ekaterinodar ('Catherine's gift').

With its administrative centre in Vladikavkaz, the neighbouring Terek voisko was smaller, about 6.6 million desiatinas (almost 28 000 square miles, over 72 000 square km), but it was exceptionally attractive land, mild enough in climate for the grape to flourish in many places. The foothills of the Caucasus range in its boundaries contained popular mineral spas, and a major oil field was discovered. By 1912 80 per cent of the total population of the Terek voisko (1 235 000) was non-Cossack, by far the highest proportion among the voiskos. The basic Cossack population here had arrived before the nineteenth century, Great Russians except for one locality which had a number of Ukrainians. But many of the early settlers had been Old Believers, and around 1870 about a fifth of the Terek Cossacks openly professed this faith.[66]

The Astrakhan voisko was an anomalous and minor affair. Its antecedents were fairly old, but it lacked any tradition of independence. The first Cossacks in the area were 'gorodovie' (city or town) Cossacks, a small class of hired guards who had served the Russian state from the fourteenth century.[67] Such groups had been scattered along the lower Volga in various places when it was a frontier, one such group planted near the mouth of the great river at Astrakhan in 1737, including some baptized Kalmyks. Just after 1800 some of the small groupings further upstream were attached to this command, and in 1817 a larger collection of scattered Cossack settlements from

Astrakhan all the way to a point significantly north of Saratov, a distance of over 700 km (more if one follows the course of the river) with enclaves some distance west or (especially) east of the Volga River. A detailed map published in 1911 shows perhaps 30 pockets of Astrakhan voisko land (difficult to enumerate because some are barely contiguous with others).[68] Though numerous and dispersed, these enclaves did not add up to much territory, about 800 000 desiatinas (over 3000 square miles, almost 400 square km), slightly more than only one other voisko. Its population, 18 000 Cossacks in 1860 and 38 000 in 1912, was also minute compared to the largest voiskos, but it pretty well occupied the small tracts of land allotted to this voisko, so non-Cossacks accounted for only 11 per cent of the total population even in 1910.

The 'sur'eznoe' (serious – not to be trifled with) voisko some Ural Cossacks called their community, when the writer Korolenko travelled there around 1900.[69] And he indeed found widespread evidence of attachment to the voisko and disgruntlement towards the regime among these people. Their name itself implied testimony to their capacity to be a serious discomfort to St Petersburg. In the late sixteenth century the first Cossack settlers on the frontier between Europe and Asia southwest of the Ural Mountains took their name from the river that flows from these mountains to the Caspian Sea, the Yaik. So outraged was Catherine the Great at the general adherence of the Yaik Cossacks to the rebel Pugachev that after the harsh suppression of the uprising she ordered the name of the river, the voisko and its capital to be changed from 'Yaik' to 'Ural' ('Yaitskii Gorodok' to 'Ural'sk' in the case of the administrative centre).

But this was neither the first nor the last rebellious outburst among these Cossacks. They had supported Razin's revolt and in 1677 again attacked the authorities. Their dissident attitude was reinforced by the schism in the Orthodox Church, many Old Believers fleeing to this voisko, which remained heavily committed to the old ways until the end of the Empire. Official figures for 1910 showed that 44.8 per cent of the Ural Cossacks were Old Believers, but there was reason to believe that this greatly understated the position. A specialist on this question wrote in 1878 that 92 per cent were Old Believers and in 1862 the official data showed 82 per cent Old Believers and fewer than 1 per cent Orthodox.[70]

Like the Don, the Yaik/Ural Cossacks produced their own elite, the starshina, who cooperated more closely with the Russian state than did the rank and file. Class struggle between the rank and file Cossacks and the starshina was an integral part of the rebelliousness of this voisko. Indeed, a typical rising against the starshina had occurred and had been suppressed just before the arrival of Pugachev, preparing the mood for the larger revolt.[71] In 1837 there was a major scandal, treated by the authorities as a mutiny, when a group of Cossack delegates stopped the carriage of the heir (Alexander Nicholaevich) at the end of a formal visit in order to present a petition charging voisko officials with malfeasance.[72] As we will see, this was not the last time Ural Cossacks actively ran foul of the tsar's government.

Despite its recalcitrance, the Ural voisko was allowed to remain, along with the Don, the only once-independent voisko to survive intact to the twentieth century. Even well into the nineteenth century the regime needed Cossacks in this thinly-settled area, which was mostly arid, and not very attractive for grain agriculture. To its east and south lay Central Asia and its fractious, wandering tribes, such as the Kirghiz. To move regular troops all the way to the borders of this area and maintain them there was expensive, and the Ural Cossacks could do the job both on their own territory, along the Ural River, and when on active duty further east in Turkestan. To obtain this service it seemed worthwhile to turn over to the Ural voisko the rich fisheries of that river, which sustained most of the population. This was not true, however, of the voisko territory upstream from the city of Ural'sk. Here, in the so-called Iletsk area, the Cossacks lived by farming and were excluded from the fishing rights of the rest of the voisko, in fact a quite separate group.

With almost 6.5 million desiatinas (over 27 000 square miles, 71 000 square km), forming a deep strip along the western banks of the Ural River, this was a relatively large voisko. But with so much of the land lying on the edge of arid Central Asia, the Ural population remained fairly small among voiskos, rising from about 77 000 Cossacks in 1860 to 159 000 in 1912. The non-Cossack population, negligible in 1860, reached 43 per cent of the total by 1912.

To extend the loose cordon that was supposed to check the wanderings of the Kirghiz and others, in the eighteenth century the Empire constructed the Orenburg voisko on territory lying along the higher reaches of the Yaik/Ural River. The land awarded to the voisko was but a thin strip along the river as it ran east, then became a large bulge as the river ran north, from which another arm reached out to the east along the River Ui. This was a thinly populated region, with few enough Russians, and the state sought to establish a military presence by enrolling a motley variety of people as Cossacks. Small numbers of 'town Cossacks' from points east of the Volga, such as Ufa and Samara, were transplanted to the Orenburg region, along with Kalmyks from Stavropol (on the Volga) and peasants from the Cheliabinsk district, all enrolled as Cossacks and in 1755 placed under an ataman. This process of promiscuous Cossackizing continued well into the nineteenth century, encompassing retired soldiers and their sons, soldiers in military colonies, peasants, Tatars and a few Mordvins and Chuvash. Most of the Kalmyks, who had remained in a separate subdivision of the voisko, were, however, returned to civilian status in 1842.[73]

The result of this protracted build-up of the Cossacks in the Orenburg area was a relatively large voisko in population and territory, even if not a community with much sense of common tradition. It stood third in numbers of Cossacks, behind the Don and Kuban: 214 000 in 1860 and 508 000 in 1912, with almost seven million desiatinas (over 29 000 square miles, 76 000 square km) of land.[74] The Cossack population was dominant in this area, the non-Cossacks negligible in 1860 and constituting only 17 per cent in 1912.

A similar pattern prevailed in the process by which the five more easterly voiskos were formed. In the case of the Siberian voisko a few of the Cossacks were reputedly descendants of Ermak's adventurers of the sixteenth century. In the eighteenth and nineteenth centuries, convicts, exiled Zaporozhian Cossacks, local and imported peasants and soldiers' children were added to the mix. Known as the Siberian Line Cossacks before 1800, they received the status of a voisko in 1808. By 1860 there were about 90 000 members of this voisko, stretched in a thin line along the northern rim of Central Asia, with eight enclaves scattered to the south of the line and thirteen small enclaves running north to form a picket along the foothills of the Altai range. In 1867 this population was reduced by the detachment of some of the Siberian Cossacks to form the new Semirechenskoe voisko. The name means 'Seven Rivers', the biggest of which was the Ili. This was part of the Russian Empire's thrust into the eastern fringe of the Chinese Empire. The War Ministry considered expanding the voisko towards Kuldzha, but this never came to pass.[75] The Semirechenskoe voisko was always a minor affair, occupying a large number of enclaves in eastern Central Asia west of Kuldzha. In their haste to improvise this presence of military settlers the regime even recruited about 1000 local 'Chinese'.[76] The state gave the voisko bits of land from time to time, and no thorough survey ever existed.[77] By 1912 the Siberian voisko contained 164 000 Cossacks and the Semirechenskoe 42 000, non-Cossacks constituting 44 per cent and 31 per cent, respectively, of the total voisko population. The partition of the Siberian voisko involved people rather than land, and its territory remained around five million desiatinas (21 000 square miles, 55 000 square km). The collection of enclaves that constituted the Semirechenskoe voisko made it the smallest voisko at 671 000 desiatinas (2800 square miles, over 7000 square km).

While the cordon of voisko land reached from the Caspian Sea around the northern rim of Central Asia, with scattered settlements trailing north and south near the Chinese border, there was a long gap of Cossack settlement from the Siberian voisko, along the border of Mongolia, until one came to the vicinity of Irkutsk. True, there had been some scattered Cossack settlements in this area, but well north of the international boundary as it was determined in the nineteenth century. In 1871 the regime, finding these Cossacks few, poor and not very useful, transferred most of them to civilian status. But some of the descendants of town Cossacks of several generations' standing did not want to give up their status, and the regime therefore made a special arrangement for the 'Cossacks of Enisei and Irkutsk Guberniias' in the new legislation. Legally they remained members of the Cossack estate, provided just over 200 troops for guard duty, and (unlike other Cossacks) were subject to civil administration.[78] In reality, these small and anomalous groups were more like a separate estate than Cossacks, not constituting a voisko and not obliged to provide military service on the same terms as Cossacks.[79] This book will not deal with them again.

South of Irkutsk (a little southwest of Lake Baikal) the line of voisko territory resumed, following the Chinese border with only a few small breaks all the way to the vicinity of Vladivostok. The Zabaikal (Transbaikal) voisko, consisting of a considerable number of large and small enclaves, covered approximately the western third of this enormously long cordon, the Amur voisko the centre and the Ussuri the eastern third, which ran north–south along the river of that name. All were established in the second half of the nineteenth century, as the interest of the Russian Empire in the Far East grew. The Zabaikal voisko was formally constituted in 1851.[80] A few city Cossacks, discharged soldiers, local peasants and natives (Buriats and Tungus) filled the ranks, which numbered 107 000 by 1806 and 241 000 by 1910. In 1860 some of these Cossacks were detached to form the Amur voisko further east; in 1889 the process was repeated, to complete the extension of Cossack settlements virtually to the Pacific with the establishment of the Ussuri voisko.[81] In the latter two cases, the problem of finding people to fill out the voiskos was solved partly by the transfer of Cossacks from the Don, Orenburg and Zabaikal voiskos.[82]. But neither the Amur nor the Ussuri voiskos ever became particularly populous. By 1912 there were 43 000 Amur and 32 000 Ussuri Cossacks. But they had a plentitude of land, even if nobody knew exactly how much. In 1912 the territory of the Zabaikal voisko was reported at a round ten million desiatinas (over 42 000 square miles, 109 000 square km), which made it second only to the Don in area. Non-Cossacks were slow to settle in this remote area. By 1912 they constituted only 6 per cent of the total Zabaikal population, 4 per cent of the Amur and 19 per cent of the Ussuri voiskos. The Amur officially had 5.2 million desiatinas (22 000 square miles, over 57 000 square km), the Ussuri over 9 million desiatinas (39 000 square miles, 100 000 square km).

In 1862 there were almost 1.6 million Cossacks in the voiskos that were destined to survive until 1914, and in 1912 there were just over 4 million.[83] Considered as separate voiskos, the Cossacks in the late nineteenth and early twentieth centuries were a mixed lot. In population they ranged in 1912 from over 1.4 million in the Don and 1.2 million in the Kuban to less than 40 000 each in the Astrakhan, Semirechenskoe, Amur and Ussuri. The balance between this population and non-Cossacks resident on voisko territory varied vastly, from 5 per cent non-Cossacks in the Zabaikal to 80 per cent in the Terek. The territory allotted to them ranged from about 15 million desiatinas (Don) down to 0.8 million (Astrakhan). The natural wealth, and especially resources per capita, varied enormously in the immensely long chain of voiskos stretching from the Sea of Azov almost to the Sea of Japan, variations that included by the early part of the twentieth century some of the most modern, industrialized parts of the Empire and the rudest frontier regions. The history of the different voiskos, and especially their historical relation to the Russian state, were equally diverse. The Don and Ural voiskos survived as communities (with greatly altered institutions) from the era of independence to the end of the Empire, and they undoubtedly possessed a much higher level of Cossack self-consciousness than did the voiskos that were merely recent creations of the St Petersburg bureaucracy. Somewhere in between with respect to the question of *esprit de corps,* lay the Kuban (with its important element of Zaporozhian ancestry) and the older state-created voiskos, such as the

Terek, Astrakhan and Orenburg (probably in descending order of loyalty to the voisko). Corresponding to the variation in antiquity and independence was the varying importance of the voisko elite – the starshina. Although the state manipulated the Don, Ural and Zaporozhian/Chernomorskoe/Kuban elites, it did not create this class, which was troublesome to the state as well as useful. Therefore the state took no pains to create just such a class in the voiskos that it constructed entirely on its own. True, it needed and found officers and civil administrators, who enjoyed various perquisites in common with the officers of, say, the Don. But the newer and more artificially-created the voisko, the weaker the role and the self-consciousness of the noble/officer class.

Less striking but significant variations concerned ethnicity and religion. Although the Cossacks were primarily Great Russian in background and the majority spoke that language (even if with a regional dialect), they had throughout their history mixed actively with diverse groups, including their fellow Slavic/Orthodox Ukrainians and a variety of non-Slavic/non-Christian peoples – Mongols, Turkic peoples and others. Most of these non-European peoples did not retain legally separate status after Cossackization, so it is impossible to determine from official statistics just how great was their impact on the Cossack population. Nor can one determine just how numerous were the Old Believers (or various sectarians) among the Cossacks, for the official figures surely did not reflect the true situation. The Old Believers may be considered merely a subculture of Orthodox Russia, but the cleavage was intense in its way. It is clear that a good majority of Ural Cossacks were dissidents in this sense, with significant numbers among the Don and Terek.

Despite their diversity, to which this book cannot do justice, the Cossacks in the later Russian Empire were all part of a single system. This is a book about that system, an anachronistic military–civil–economic order that emerged in its final form in the last half of the nineteenth century and struggled on, increasingly beset by the travails of modernization, until the crisis of the First World War.

2   The Martial Estate

А-ой да, вот и, засиротила,	A-oi da, and thou has orphaned,
Ей, ты, служба царская,	Thou, service of the tsar,
Ей, много, много малых де...	Thou, many, many little chi ...
Много, скажем, малых детушек	Many, we say, many little children.

Don Cossack song[1]

In the latter years of the Russian Empire, the Cossacks were often called the 'martial estate' (voennoe soslovie), and with reason. No other estate was defined by its military obligations, while the Cossacks survived as a legal entity because of their special contribution to the armed power of the Empire. Every substantial issue involving the Cossacks revolved around the military service that they rendered.

Because the terms of military service for the Cossacks always differed from those applied to other citizens, it is difficult to compare the weight of service on Cossacks and others, but it is clear that the martial estate carried by far the heavier burden. Before the reform of law on military service under War Minister D. A. Miliutin in 1874, only 'the taxed estates', mainly peasants and lower-class townsmen (meshchanstvo), were subject to conscription. Thus a substantial minority of the populace, including the nobility, merchants, clergy and most ethnic aliens, was completely exempt. Of those who were liable to conscription only about one in 26 were actually called in the peacetime years of the mid-century period. In contrast, almost all male Cossacks served, the only exceptions being a small number of clergy, the seriously unfit, a small guild of Cossack merchants, and some Ural Cossacks who were permitted to hire substitutes. After the Miliutin reforms, the entire non-Cossack population was in theory subject to military obligation, but, in addition to the unfit, many were excused because of their family status and smaller numbers benefited from other exemptions. In the first seven years of the new system, the percentage of those in the eligible age group who were actually called ranged from just over 20 per cent to just under 30 per cent.[2] The Cossacks, operating under reformed rules of their own, continued to render not much less than truly universal military service. The Cossacks in 1878 constituted about one fortieth of the population of European Russia, but constituted about one fourteenth of the active duty forces in peacetime. This proportion fluctuated over the last decades of the Empire, but the direction of imbalance did not.[3]

THE REFORM OF COSSACK MILITARY SERVICE

Before 1855 the principal attempt to regulate the military service of the Cossacks was the statute of 1835 that was issued to the Don and adapted to most of the voiskos during the remainder of the reign of Nicholas I.[4] It required each Cossack to serve for 30 years (25 for a small number who served in guards' units and for all officers). It would have been impossible to sustain the domestic economy of the Cossacks if all eligible men remained on active duty for such a long time, nor did the state desire such a large force in peacetime. The Don statute accommodated this situation by alternating Cossacks between 'field' and 'internal' service. The former meant active duty and the latter a form of reserve status in which the Cossack lived at home and supposedly kept himself (and his horse in most cases) in a state of readiness, subject to annual inspection. Official writers acknowledged that they did not know much about what actually happened in internal service and that the state of readiness was in reality not very good. In border areas, where unfriendly natives were a factor, there was some local patrolling to be done, but in the Don or other well-settled regions there was little to occupy this form of service. In the Kuban in 1868 some 1641 Cossacks on internal service were assigned in small numbers (e.g. four) to serve as guards, mainly at prisons or ferry-crossings.[5] The Don statute treated all manner of civic offices as internal service, and this usage of the term continued long after the reforms of the 1870s abolished the distinction between field and internal service among the Cossacks. A contemporary expert considered that internal service had 'little in common with military service in general'.[6]

The specific systems of rotation between field and internal service varied considerably among the voiskos at the accession of Alexander II. One pattern applied to the Caucasian Line, Astrakhan, Novorossiisk, Orenburg, Bashkir, Siberian Line and Zabaikal Cossacks. A given unit, such as a numbered regiment, remained permanently on active duty, and responsibility for manning it was assigned to a particular district within the voisko. Men of serving age from a district rotated on and off field service to maintain the unit. But in the Don, Black Sea and Ural voiskos (representing a large majority of Cossack effectives), specific regiments and other units alternated between field and internal service. Each of these three voiskos had its own method of allocating the call-up when a particular unit was mobilized. In the Don there were two levels of subdivision, the okrug and the stanitsa. Each maintained a roster of eligibles; those coming off a tour of field service were placed on the bottom of the list, moving towards the the top as those ahead of them rotated onto active duty along with those who had just come of age. When a particular regiment was re-mobilized in its turn, the levy to man it was distributed among the okrugs and within them the stanitsas, so that the burden did not fall too heavily on any one area. In contrast, among the Black Sea Cossacks each particular unit was manned by residents of a district, who went on and off field service together, along with the unit. Finally, the Ural Cossacks had their own system, which caused the state many difficulties and must be treated separately. Suffice to say that when a Ural unit was mobilized, it was staffed by volunteers and a lottery, and that those who served were paid ('hired' in the traditional expression) by those who stayed home.[7]

Just how the official norms worked out for individual Cossacks is uncertain. The actual service rosters were maintained only at the okrug or stanitsa level, and were unavailable to writers of the second half of the nineteenth century. If the Don statute were followed literally, the Cossack would begin a three-year tour of field service at the age of 20, then rotate to internal service for five years. This implies that he would serve three terms in the field before reaching the age of 40, at which time he would go on internal service to complete his obligation, according to the norm that was in effect after 1856 in the Don (25 years rather than the former 30). But a Cossack was not called up automatically five years after his previous term of field service. The fortunes of war and peace, the diverse means described above to activate individuals in various voiskos, meant that he could not count on a completely regular rotation. The War Ministry apparently did not know how many turns the average Cossack served, and the expert Khoroshkhin' was probably as accurate as anyone now can be when he said that under the norm of 1856 'almost every Cossack was once, twice or even three times in the combatant units', meaning field service.[8]

At the beginning of the reign of Alexander II, then, the system of Cossack military service was far from uniform and rather primitive, but it did permit the mobilization of a large part of the male Cossack population in time of need. The Crimean War was such a time. Faced with an Anglo-French invasion in the peninsula, a threatening Austrian attitude in the West and a Turkish front behind which simmered a long-term struggle with Caucasian mountaineers, the tsar had to amplify his regular forces with as many Cossack irregulars as could be raised. In addition to the 80 188 officers and men on active duty at the opening of 1853, enough Cossacks and their officers were mobilized during the war to provide 160 177 by 1856, the final year of the war. Most of these were from the Don, which not only activated the 54 regiments called for in its prewar table of organization, but with a mass levy added 29 regiments. This was more than a quarter of the entire male Don Cossack population, an emergency level that was not sustained for long. Indeed, part of the emergency levy that was guarding the shores of the Sea of Azov was dismissed after that body of water iced over in the winter of 1855–6, eliminating the threat of invasion.[9]

In the aftermath of the Crimean War, the new tsar and his advisers were deeply concerned with the reform of the armed forces, which had failed to crush the invader. The main concern was, naturally, the regulars. Not only were the Cossacks irregulars, they were a form of irregular that seemed to represent the primitiveness that was widely blamed for the Crimean failure. It is hardly surprising that the military reformers, in the early postwar period, seemed to treat the Cossacks as a peripheral and to some extent expendable military force. General O. N. Sukhozanet, the first War Minister appointed by Alexander II, did not seem particularly interested in enhancing the Cossacks' role in the army. In a major report of 1859 he merely noted that they were needed for border service.[10]

His successor, Miliutin, was still less inclined to value the Cossacks, whom he had seen during the war in the Caucasus where many Cossacks served. In the lengthy diary covering his years as War Minister, the only mention of Cossacks concerns an epidemic among their horses, which Miliutin may have considered more important than the Cossacks themselves. Miliutin lost little time in stating his rather unenthusiastic attitude towards the Cossacks. In a speech to the Committee of Ministers on 22 February 1862, and in his first secret annual report to the tsar later that year, he took the same position. First, the Cossacks were useful as irregular cavalry, guarding the frontier and conducting partisan warfare. But they were costly. Even though they partially equipped themselves, the state had to spend 8 million to 9.5 million rubles per year on them. In the early Alexandrine period, the need for economizing in the wake of the calamitously expensive Crimean War was a matter of urgency, and Miliutin favoured reduction of the Cossack establishment. Indeed, he noted with approval that the peacetime active duty forces had already been reduced. With respect to the longer-term prospects, he said that it was now pointless to raise the general question of the political and economic usefulness of the Cossacks, inasmuch as they were needed to hold down border areas against 'Asiatics'. 'This is not the time to raise any general questions relating to the eventual future of our Cossacks.' Surely this was a hint that he did not envisage them as a permanent fixture. But as a practical reformer, he was not going to start his career as War Minister with a bold proposal to abolish the Cossacks. Meanwhile, it was necessary, according to Miliutin, 'to harmonize, as much as possible in the present state of things, the way of life of the voiskos with the population as a whole with regard to the general conditions of civil and economic life'.[11]

Efforts in this direction were already underway when Miliutin became War Minister in November 1861. In 1856 the ataman of the Don Cossacks, Gen. M. G. Khomutov, petitioned the War Minister Sukhozanet to permit the preparation of a new edition of the Don statute. He argued that, in the 20 years since the original version, many new laws and regulations had appeared but were nowhere consolidated. Evidently aiming mainly at improved administrative efficiency rather than any fundamental reform, Khomutov suggested that his office submit for approval by the War Ministry sections of the revised statute as quickly as they could be prepared.[12] Sukhozanet, who was not noted as an active leader, did nothing definite about this proposal until 10 October 1859. Perhaps he thought it necessary first to establish an appropriate office to deal with Cossack affairs. Since 1833 they had been consigned to the Department of Military Colonies of the War Ministry, which was primarily concerned not with Cossacks but with those settlements of farmer–soldiers established by Alexander I. With the beginning of the liquidation of the military colonies in 1856, it was necessary to find a new administrative centre for the Cossacks. To meet this need the Main Administration of Irregular Forces was established on 1 January 1858, a bureaucratic agency in charge of Cossack affairs as well as those of a few small additional groups, such as the Greek Battalion of Balaklava.[13]

With this office in place, it was deemed inappropriate to deal with the Don statute in sections. A review of the whole was necessary, and not only with respect to the Don but also the other voiskos. Five regional 'special temporary committees' were to be named, meeting in Novocherkassk (dealing with the Don), Stavropol (Caucasian Line and Black Sea voiskos), Orenburg (Orenburg, Ural and Bashkir), Omsk (Siberian Line and the Tobolsk infantry battalion).[14] At the request of the regional governor–general, the Orenburg and Ural committee was divided into two, and the War Ministry decided to replace the Stavropol committee with one in St Petersburg.[15] In several voiskos, including the Don, the special temporary committee was supplemented by the convocation of a consultative assembly of deputies from the ordinary Cossacks, nobles and landless officers.[16] With almost frivolous optimism, these committees were ordered to complete within one year a review of all enactments concerning their voisko, submitting drafts of a reformed statute by 1 January 1860. When the committees failed to meet this deadline, it was extended to mid-1863 and then to January 1865.[17]

This review and reform was intended to deal with Cossack life as a whole, but it was the question of military service that came to preoccupy and finally undo this first reform-era attempt to restructure the Cossacks. Fundamental to this attempted reform was the belief that there were too many Cossacks for the military needs of the state. The figures in the first volume of the annual report of the War Ministry, covering the year 1858, show that there was a marked surplus of Cossacks who were eligible for service compared to the number that the army wanted. The official list of eligibles showed 237 373, not including officers. Even if there were an emergency, it would require only 176 495 Cossacks (exclusive of officers) to staff the table of organization of the units that were considered to be the full force of Cossacks, leaving a surplus of about 60 878 eligibles.[18] By 1860 the surplus was approaching 80 000, thanks to the birthrate and the enrolment of new Cossacks, especially in the fertile lands of the Kuban.[19] But the War Ministry thought that it would want fewer rather than more Cossacks in the future. They were still regarded as irregulars, of limited value to the army. In the Caucasus the major campaign to suppress the Murids virtually ended in 1859 when Shamyl was captured. This war had occupied a large share of active-duty Cossacks in 'peacetime', not only all the active Black Sea and Caucasian Line Cossack units but also most of the Don regiments (on the eve of the Crimean War, 21 out of a total of 36 active regiments).[20] What would the army do with these irregulars when they were no longer needed in the Caucasus? For years Don Cossacks had been travelling the relatively short distance from their homes to the Caucasus on their own mounts. If they were not needed so close to home, how could they be utilized elsewhere? At the opening of the 1860s there was no railway to the Don country, and to move large numbers of Don Cossacks to and from the European frontier of the Empire was no simple or economical matter.

The policy-makers in St Petersburg therefore embarked on a number of piecemeal measures to deal with the presumed surplus of Cossacks even before Miliutin became minister. The first step came on the coronation of Alexander II in 1856. The Don, Black Sea and Caucasian Line Cossacks were rewarded for their efforts in the Crimean War with a reduction of their service obligation from 30 years to 25, of which the final three were to be within their voiskos. For guards units and officers, the obligation was reduced to 20 years. In 1866 this norm was extended to the other voiskos in honour of the marriage of the heir to the throne, the Most August Ataman.[21] In 1857 the War Ministry ordered the chiefs of the voiskos to establish three or more groupings for rotation onto active service, each called a 'turn' (ochered'). The Don statute of 1835 had recognized the existence of such 'turns' but had not specified any number. The point of the new rule was to encourage the voiskos to stretch out the interval between tours of active duty for the individual Cossack, providing that the size of the manpower pool permitted this.[22]

In 1858 another option was introduced for the Don and Orenburg voiskos and later extended to several others. It now became legal for a Cossack to change places with another on the service roster or to hire a substitute when his turn came up, subject to certain limitations. A Cossack could skip only two call-ups by means of substitution, and he assumed the military and civil obligations of the man he exchanged with or hired. The authorities in St Petersburg seem not to have learned whether this option was exercised by (or even known to) the Cossacks in their scattered villages.[23] In any case, neither this regulation nor the one permitting additional turns reduced the surplus of eligible manpower. The new options simply aimed at 'the

improvement of the way of life of the Cossacks and the facilitation of
their domestic economy', as one order put it. This was all very well for
the Cossack, but it did not exploit his presumably increased ability to
pay taxes.[24]

The committee dealing with the Caucasus produced a memorandum
in 1861 which summed up the problem of the surplus supply of
Cossacks and the economic interests of the state. In the Caucasus the
question of over-supply was especially acute, because the end of the
war against the mountaineers abruptly reduced the need for troops,
and the richness of the land could be expected to support a
substantially increased population. As the memorandum noted, even
the mountaineers themselves were being placed on guard duty, and it
was hard to imagine when large numbers of irregular cavalry would be
needed again. Therefore, it was argued, the time had come to reduce
Cossack forces by encouraging departures from the martial estate,
settling this population in 'work that is more productive for the state
and society'. The counter-argument, that Cossacks were cheap troops
and would be needed in time of protracted war, was rebutted with the
unsupported assertion that the state had to contribute a great deal to
the support of the Cossacks. 'If one takes into account all the data, the
maintenance of Cossack troops hardly seems as cheap as it might
appear on first glance.'[25]

This was precisely the point that Miliutin affirmed in his first year as
War Minister, and he soon attempted to move the regional committees
on reform in this direction. In 1862 he issued to the temporary
committees a 'General Programme of the Main Bases of the Statutes
of the Voiskos'. It offered a fundamentally new concept of the
Cossacks and their military service:

> in place of the obligation of each male to military service to entrust
> this predominantly to 'volunteers', who devote themselves to the
> warrior's life, thus to offer some portion of the population the free
> choice of occupation and business. The same goal suggests the
> possibility of permitting free entry into the martial estate and exit
> from it, ...[26]

Aware that this proposal was radical, Miliutin sent it to the heads of
the voiskos as a secret document, to be shown to the local commissions
on legislative reform only if the atamans considered this appropriate.
With premature optimism, the War Minister proclaimed in his report
to the tsar that the absence of negative replies from the 'commanders'

of the voiskos (a usage that showed little awareness of Cossack sensitivities) indicated that his proposal was 'appropriate for the actual demands of Cossack society, in the expression of some [atamans] even beneficent'. But in the same report the minister noted that the preliminary draft from the Don, composed before his own programme, called for no major changes in the *status quo* other than a reduction in the term of service. When the full draft arrived the next year, he could no longer avoid the realization that the largest voisko opposed his idea. The Don committee wished to retain obligatory service for all Cossacks, but with only one-third of the eligibles on active duty in a given peacetime year. This, said Miliutin in his report for 1865, showed 'a false understanding of historic right'. It paid no attention to the War Ministry programme, and retained 'all the conditions of the former martial estate, sealed off from and alienated from other estates'.[27]

The upshot of this clash of opinion was that the War Ministry, presumably Miliutin himself, wrote off the previous six years' work and started anew. This time the authorities in St Petersburg sought to meet some kind of timetable and to impose their ideas about a rational order for the Cossacks by keeping the drafting committee in the capital and under the chairmanship of the head of the Administration of Irregular Forces. The regional committees were disbanded, and on 2 October 1865 a 'Temporary Committee for the Review of Cossack Statutes' was established under the Administration of Irregular Forces. The 'Temporary Rules' established for this body specified that the separate voiskos should be represented in the committee by 'persons of Cossack ancestry who know their needs', chosen by the atamans of their respective voiskos: three from the Don, one each from the Kuban, Terek, Astrakhan, Ural, Orenburg and Siberia, and one for all the Far East. However, the Administration of Irregular Forces was to have an unspecified number of its staff on the committee, which was to be chaired by the head of this office, who was never a Cossack. Moreover, a chancellery of the committee was established, entirely from the personnel of the Administration of Irregular Forces, and was permitted to begin work even before the arrival of the delegates from the voiskos. This organ lasted until 1872 and for a time was in practice a standing sub-department of the administration, finally transferring its functions to another sub-office whose work it really duplicated.[28]

The centralist spirit of the new approach was stressed in a report from the head of the Administration of Irregular Forces to Miliutin, which the latter approved on 29 October 1865. It began by rejecting as impractical the examination of proposals from the former local committees, went on to propose that the committee first draft rules which could be uniform to all voiskos, and in the military sphere set the goal of establishing uniform service obligations for all Cossacks. Although the report did not mention the War Ministry's previous proposal of voluntary military service for Cossacks, it hinted that something of the sort was still favoured, in as much as it mentioned the establishment for all citizens of the right of entry to and exit from the estate. The kind of reform envisaged by Miliutin was drafted by the chancellery of the committee in the year following (November 1865–November 1866). At the end of this time, the delegates from the voiskos appeared and on 5 November 1866 Alexander II personally addressed the gathering, an attempt to throw the weight of his prestige on the side of Miliutin's policy. The tsar spoke briefly and did not go into detail, concluding that:

> ... I want their [the Cossacks'] military significance to be harmonious with civil life and economic well-being, in so far as possible. The Cossack population, while rendering as before its military obligation, at the same time can and should enjoy the benefits of civil well-being in common with all sectors of the Empire.[29]

With a committee consisting of bureaucrats who were under his control and delegates largely from small voiskos with little sense of independence, Miliutin's representative Gen. N. I. Karlgof (chairman of the committee and head of the Administration of Irregular Forces) was able in about six months to push through a radical reform of the system of Cossack military service. Initially the committee considered simply reducing the term of service further, but rejected this as harmful to the military readiness of the Cossacks. Instead, it proposed a scheme that continued the assumption that the Empire would need far fewer Cossack troops than the growing population of the voiskos could provide. It therefore intended to divide Cossacks into two basic categories: those who would perform military service and those who would be excused. All Cossack males between the ages of 19 and 25 were to have the option of volunteering for service, and if this did not produce enough men to fill the units required by the War Ministry, the balance would be conscripted by lot. The total term of service remained 22 years. One-third of the units thus raised would be on active duty in peacetime and two-thirds on the status called 'l'gota' (literally 'exemption'; in this context it may be translated as 'off-duty status').

Those Cossacks who did not serve (because they did not volunteer and did not draw an unlucky lot) would be enrolled permanently in what amounted to a new estate – 'voisko citizens' (voiskovie grazhdaniny), This category would enjoy the rights of the Cossack estate but would render cash payments to the voisko instead of military service. These payments would continue as long as the voisko citizen was of serving age and would be used to sustain the military readiness of his comrades in the armed forces. Children of voisko citizens would be liable to the same chance of military service as those of other Cossacks. Service for officers would be voluntary.[30]

Despite the dissenting votes of the Don delegates, this general plan was approved by the Military Council in May 1867, with the proviso that each voisko should prepare its own variant on the model.[31] Orenburg quickly fell into line, adopting the reformed plan of service as of 1 July 1867. Its provisions were illustrative of others that followed. The voisko agreed to provide three artillery batteries, nine infantry battalions and fifteen cavalry regiments, of which one-third would be on duty at any given moment in peacetime, the units rotating on and off active service at intervals of two and one-half years. Those not serving were to pay four rubles per year to the voisko and 56 and 2/3 (!) kopeks to the stanitsa. Similar statutes were adopted by the Kuban and Terek (1870), Siberia (1871), Astrakhan and Zabaikal (1872).[32] The question of free departure from the Cossack estate was dealt with separately in a law of 1869, which applied to all voiskos. Henceforth all Cossack officers and civil servants with rank could enrol in other estates at will, and ordinary Cossacks would do so after fulfilling their military obligation.[33]

Thus began a period in which the Don and Ural voiskos clung to their traditional norms for military service, while all the others except the Amur adopted the new Miliutin scheme.[34] The implementation of the reform cast some doubt on the conviction of the War Ministry that they needed fewer Cossacks than previously. Only in the case of the Kuban was the total force actually reduced, and the obligation of the Orenburg voisko even increased substantially: nine infantry battalions in place of six and fifteen cavalry regiments in place of twelve. Elsewhere the quotas remained unchanged.[35] But the official belief that there was a surplus of eligible manpower was sustained by the numbers of those who entered the new class of 'voisko citizens'. By 1880 a total of just over 30 000 Cossacks had entered this status and presumably were paying a fee to their voisko. Over half of these (almost 18 000) were in the Kuban, where the rich and underpopulated land was attracting new recruits at a brisk rate. Here one eligible Cossack in three was able to avoid military service, which must have made the region all the more attractive to immigrants.[36] In the Astrakhan, Siberian and Zabaikal voiskos, the proportion of eligibles who avoided service was between 20 and 30 per cent, in the Terek 13 per cent and in Orenburg (with its increased quota of manpower) only 7 per cent. With increasing populations it was predictable that these percentages would increase, and in the Kuban it was possible to anticipate a time when only a minority of Cossacks would actually serve. The opinion of rank and file Cossacks is inaccessible, but one expert argued that the economic contribution that was paid by those who did not serve was far outweighed by the burden on those who did.[37]

Burdensome as military service may have been, the option of leaving the Cossack estate was rarely practised. The framers of the new system were risking the possibility that there might be a mass exodus, but in actuality there was no significant reduction in the Cossack population through transfers to other estates. One reason for this was that the process was not easy. The Cossack first had to apply to his voisko administration, which might or might not be cooperative. In 1886 the central authorities overruled local officials who had rejected the application of some retired Cossacks to become clergy, as was their right.[38] But few would have bothered to push an appeal to the War Ministry in such cases. Then there was the problem of finding another, more attractive estate that one could enter – no easy matter. Above all, there was the loss of the Cossack's right to a land allotment. Statistics for the period 1871–9 show a total of only 40 373 departures from the Cossack estate, but this includes women, some of whom married into other estates, and a significant number of disciplinary expulsions.[39]

While the new system of military service was following its questionably successful course in most voiskos, the Don, with its weight of population and tradition, strongly resisted pressure from the War Ministry to conform. It is hard to know what popular opinion existed in this matter, but it is clear that the Don aristocrats were strongly opposed to the proposed reform, and that they made their opinions heard in Petersburg. In 1867 the Don delegates to the Temporary Committee submitted a strong memorandum of protest, contemptuously rejecting the idea of 'conscription' or a 'landwehr' or 'even the system of the Ural Cossacks' (which involved selection by volunteers and by lot). Such a system would introduce 'an entirely new class of voisko citizens', who would be close to the taxed estates, dividing the Cossacks into 'two hostile camps'. The only change that was needed in the system of military service, they said, was the one proposed by the Don regional committee: the introduction of a system of rotation that would place a third of the forces on active duty in peacetime. Finally, they appealed to 'the Imperial charters and the Imperial Word of Four Monarchs'. 'Any change in this tradition would be received by the Don with regret, as the destruction of the privileges accorded them and as a departure from the path which their ancestors laid out for them.'[40] The Don could not overcome the determination of the War Ministry to apply its new programme to other voiskos, but the War Ministry was unwilling to impose its wishes on the Don. The matter was allowed to rest until 1871.

In that year Miliutin began his major effort to reform the system of military service for the population at large, leading to the adoption of the law on universal military obligation on 1 January 1874.[41] In the course of the discussion that was involved in this basic revision, a number of points emerged which gave the War Ministry cause to reconsider its Cossack policy. The fundamental change that faced the security of the Russian Empire was the emergence of a united Germany, the largest military force in the world. The defence of Russia's western frontiers was now a much more immediate concern, and the only economically feasible way to meet the need for expanded forces was the adoption of some variant on the method used by Prussia in its victories over Austria and France: conscription and a trained reserve. The traditional pattern of Cossack service could quite easily be adapted to this end, and was especially advantageous concerning cavalry. It was extremely expensive for the state to maintain a large stock of mounts for reservists to use in time of mobilization, but the Cossack kept his own horse in readiness when he was not on active duty. The strategic analysis prepared by General N. N. Obruchev, on orders from Miliutin, called for a large force of cavalry along Russia's western frontier. This was intended to prevent an invader from concentrating his forces in the first days of a war, thus providing time for the mobilization of the large reserve of trained forces.[42] The Cossacks obviously could make a substantial contribution to this force. Whatever Miliutin had said about costs, there was a case for the view that Cossacks could be regularized more economically than fresh contingents of ordinary citizens could be equipped and trained for this purpose. Moreover, it was now possible to envisage the routine deployment of Cossack cavalry in Russia's western borderlands. The railway revolution was beginning in earnest in Russia in the 1860s. Obruchev's report underscored the need to expand the country's rail network, and stressed the importance both of those lines that would support a western front and of those that would reach into the region of the Don Cossacks.[43] In fact, Rostov-na-Donu was joined to Moscow and thence the western areas by a line completed in 1869, making it possible to move Don Cossacks to European Russia. They were no longer superfluous in the absence of an unpacified frontier or a war in their own section of the Empire.[44]

Faced with these considerations, Miliutin reversed his attitude towards the reform of Cossack military service and particularly the previously-scorned proposal from the Don that they continue universal service, with a peacetime active-duty force of one-third and a reserve of two-thirds.[45] Some contemporary writers mentioned another argument in favour of the Cossack tradition of universal obligation. If the non-Cossack population was subject to universal obligation, it was argued, it was unfair for Cossacks, under the reform of 1867, to operate a system in which many were able to avoid service.[46] But this argument was specious, considering that the majority of the non-Cossack eligibles were exempted from service by lottery. The most persuasive reason for reinstating universal military service among the Cossacks was not equity but military expediency.[47]

As late as the beginning of 1870, when he filed his annual secret report for the previous year, Miliutin was on record as favouring the adoption of the Orenburg model to all voiskos.[48] But the following year he said that the main military concern was the adequacy of the Don, as the westernmost voisko, in case of a war on the European frontier. With this new outlook Miliutin, in a letter of 15 May 1871, informed the Don ataman that the system of Cossack military service was to be reviewed by a War Ministry commission which was undertaking a study of the organization of the entire army. Adopting a much more conciliatory tone, he asked that the voisko staff, with the participation of experienced regimental and other unit commanders, should consider the problems involved and send their responses to him. Miliutin sketched the questions that needed to be resolved, such as the shortfall in filling out the wartime personnel complement of the units (here a reversal of emphasis in policy on the numbers of Cossacks needed), the shortness of the period of active service, the absence of a regular rota of service for officers, and other technical problems. His new position said nothing about a reduction of numbers of serving Cossacks, voluntary service or other aspects of the unfulfilled reform plan.[49]

On 28 May 1871 the completeness of the reversal at the War Ministry became clear in a letter from the head of the Main Administration of Irregular Forces (this office having taken on a modified name in 1869), which stated that the Don did not have to adopt any particular system of military service, that the Don staff was simply being asked to consider the question 'thoroughly and in detail'. Although some new kind of draft was sent from Petersburg to the Don in November 1871, this was regarded as merely advisory. With the authorization to rewrite the rules of military service on their own terms, the Don leadership now produced a modified version of its traditional system, which they submitted to the War Ministry at the opening of 1871. The 'main principles' of the new law were approved by the tsar with considerable dispatch in February 1873, and only then went to the Main Administration of Irregular Forces for a thorough review. In this process it was decided to divide the forthcoming enactment into two separate parts: a 'Regulation (ustav) on the Military Obligation of the Don Voisko' and a 'Statute (polozhenie) on the Military Service of the Don Cossack Voisko'. The regulation was regarded as analagous to the general regulation on military obligation for the populace as a whole, the famous Miliutin reform. It covered the obligations of the individual citizen, Cossack in this case, with respect to military service, and it could be adapted with little change to the other voiskos, excepting the eccentric Uralt'sy. The statute, on the other hand, dealt with the size, organization and training of the troops provided by the Don, and was peculiar to them. This statute was approved first, on 14 October 1874, while the regulation on military obligation was signed on 17 and 24 April 1875.[50]

Not only had the Don succeeded in resisting the model of 1867, they even had their own reformed system of military service adopted as the model for all the other voiskos except the Ural. As early as 1873 the decision to replace the model of 1867 with the new Don scheme had been taken in the Main Administration of Irregular Forces, and in 1876 the Military Council approved this decision.[51] The basic idea of using the Don, by far the largest voisko, as the pattern for the others with respect to military service had, of course, been the policy of 1835. It had been criticized by General Karlgof at the opening of the attempted reforms of the 1860s and discarded in the work of the Petersburg committee under his chairmanship. But by the mid-1870s the new Don system appeared to be the easiest way to satisfy both the largest Cossack voisko and the War Ministry's new perception of its need for substantial numbers of Cossacks on active duty and in reserve. Statutes based on the Don model were issued for Orenburg (1876), Zabaikal (1878), Amur and Semirechenskoe (1879), Siberia (1880), Astrakhan (1881), and Kuban and Terek (1882). In the last two cases the Russo-Turkish War had delayed the change.[52]

The new system of Cossack military service rested on the principle of universal military obligation for non-nobles. No longer was it possible to escape service by leaving the estate, by good fortune in a lottery or by hiring a substitute (except in the Ural voisko).[53] This was a system designed to maximize the capacity of the pool of Cossack manpower to provide soldiers. Even those who were physically unfit for field service but able to work had to make a contribution to the voisko (cash or labour) in lieu of active duty. Until standardized in 1906, the specific obligation varied, but in the Don it was the significant sum of 15 rubles per year until one's class reached retirement age after 20 years.[54] And the concept of physical fitness was not applied tender-heartedly. In general the judgement of fitness was left up to the regional military command. The only specific physical requirement stated in the law was that the Cossack had to be just over five feet tall, although a subsequent regulation of 1876 listed 83 specific defects (e.g. loss of two fingers) that disqualified a Cossack from service.[55] Only those who claimed a medical exemption received any professional examination. The Don voisko exempted only about 3 per cent in 1878–9, much lower than most modern systems of conscription, but with the coming of real medical exams the figures rose to 15 per cent in 1894 and 24 per cent in 1906.[56]

In harmony with the law on military obligation that had been issued in 1874 for the non-Cossack population, the new Cossack regulation offered relief on grounds of family need, education or occupation, but the benefits were limited. If a Cossack was the only male worker in the family (a 'kormiak' in popular usage), or the only one not on active duty, or a member of a family in which two were on active service, he could pass directly into off-duty status. But this exempted him neither from basic training nor membership in a trained and supposedly equipped reserve.[57] Moreover, advocates of Cossack interest maintained that the standards that local officials applied in determining eligibility for exemption were harsh. For example, a writer on the Kuban in the early twentieth century cited cases in which lads of 12 and 16 in families with no adult male surviving were classified as able-bodied workers so that their elder brothers would not be excused as kormiaks.[58] Apart from kormiaks, it was legally possible to gain an exemption on grounds of economic hardship, which included victims of fire and simply 'extreme poverty'.[59]

Men with various levels of education were entitled to a reduced term of active service: as little as six months for the exceedingly rare (non-noble) Cossack who finished a first-rank institution (university or institute) and as much as three years for the graduate of a third-rank institution (sub-gymnasium school). But all of these were to serve in the ready reserve for 12 years. Physicians, teachers and even officially approved artists were exempt from active service in peacetime, but had 12 years of ready reserve obligation. Various government officials and the Orthodox clergy were wholly exempt from service.[60]

Some Cossacks might avoid extended active service if the pool of eligibles exceeded the requirements of the War Ministry. Each year the ministry told each voisko the size of its levy, and the voisko command broke this down for its subdivisions, where quotas were distributed to each stanitsa. Here the assembly assigned each Cossack who was 20 and had no claim to an exemption a place on a numbered list. The quota was filled from the top of the list, and those who were fortunate enough to hold places 'below the cut-off number' did not have to go on active duty. They were placed on off-duty status and became part of the reserve force. It was possible, with the consent of the ataman of the voisko, for a Cossack who was called to duty to exchange places with a 'volunteer' who had a low number. The law did not specify any financial transaction in such cases, nor did it forbid it. In practice it seems that the Don Cossacks used the same term for this form of substitute-hiring that the Ural Cossacks had long applied in their somewhat different arrangement: 'naemka' (a diminutive of 'hiring'). In the early years after the adoption of the new law on military service the pool of Cossacks who were not called up was relatively small, and the practice of 'hiring' seems to have been infrequent. But in time the population increased more than the levy, and by 1912 the War Ministry regarded substitution as a problem. The Duma defence commission reported that 'rich Cossacks hire in place of themselves poor ones, often less educated and often sickly'. At this late date the War Ministry proposed the abolition of substitution.[61]

There was another way that a few prosperous Cossacks were able to buy their way out of part or all of their active service. Cossack officers were entitled to batmen, who were excused from other duty. In the Terek voisko, at least, there were officers (no doubt impoverished) who would nominally take on a batman and then require little or no service, in return for payment.[62]

The great majority of non-noble Cossacks who did not benefit from any form of exemption began their military careers at the age of 18 in the 'preparatory category' (prigotovitel'nyi razriad), which lasted three years.[63] At the age of 21 the Cossack began 12 years in the 'combatant category' (stroevyi razriad), which was divided into three 'turns' (ocheredi) of four years each. The 'first turn' (aged 21–4) served on active duty in peacetime, usually at a considerable distance from the Cossack's home. If there was no war or revolution before he reached the age of 33, this was the only lengthy period of active military service that he would face. In practice it was likely to be less than four full years, because the army command assumed in peacetime that no war would begin in European Russia during the winter. Therefore the new replacements joined their units in late winter or spring. The men whom they replaced had already departed for home on about 1 October, leaving the regiment short-handed in the winter and, depending on the travel time from the place of active duty to the home area, cutting the actual time on service to about three and a half years.[64] At the end of his four years in the first turn the Cossack, now back at home, entered the 'second turn' for the next four years (aged 25–8), maintaining his horse and equipment and attending an annual training camp of about a month. In time of war this second turn would be the first to be mobilized, ahead of the 'third turn' (aged 29–32), which, however, was also supposed to be in a state of armed and trained readiness. The third-turn Cossacks, however, did not have to maintain their horses.

The three turns each had their regiments or other enumerated units, which (unlike the earlier Don system) did not rotate on and off active service in peacetime. Thus, at the time the new system took effect (1875), Don Cossack regiments 1–20 (plus two guards' regiments) were on permanent active service, numbers 21–40 were on 'off-duty status' in the second turn, and 41–60 in the third turn. After finishing his four years in, let us say, Don Cossack regiment no. 10, the Cossack was enrolled for the next four years in a second-turn regiment such as no. 25, and after four more years a third-turn regiment such as no. 45.[65]

At the age of 32, the Cossack was transferred to the 'reserve category' (zapasnyi razriad) for five years, with no very specific obligations unless a general mobilization occurred. Thereafter he was merely enrolled in a 'general levy' (opolchenie), which had very little practical significance. Despite minor variations among the different voiskos and some ameliorations of the burden of service in the course of time, this system remained the foundation of Cossack military service for the duration of Imperial Russia.

The departure and return of Cossacks for active duty played a major role in the life of the local community. Only a small minority of peasants were actually conscripted, so in their villages there was nothing comparable to the annual departure of almost all the 21 year-olds, usually mounted and serving together in the same unit. Nor was there anything like the return of this group. According to the ethnographer Kharuzin, who visited the Don around 1880, the ceremony of departure sometimes lasted two days, usually occurring on a hill near the village and involving a church service and serious eating and drinking. But it seems to have been less dramatic than the return. As the group approached its village, scouts would announce to the village elder (ataman) that Cossacks of a particular regiment were on their way, bearing an icon or banner. The entire community would drop its work and prepare for the entry of the troops, met first by the ataman offering them bread and salt.

For many of the wives (and most young Cossacks married before departing for active duty) this was a particularly crucial time, for it was understood that many of them had not spent over three of their best years in perfect celibacy. Kharuzin was impressed by the rich store of synonyms for 'illegitimate child' in the local patois and the well-established practice of liaisons between fathers-in-law and daughters-in-law. The young wife was expected to greet her husband on his return, kneeling before his horse, in some cases specifically thanking the mount for the safe return of the Cossack. If she did not appear for the ritual, it usually meant that she not only had been unfaithful but was unrepentant, which would be the worse for her. On the other hand, she might greet him and at once make a public confession, which might help to spare her a severe beating, especially if the confession was supported by bystanders' comments, such as: 'the green grape isn't sweet, young reason isn't strong, don't punish this harshly'; or 'what can you do, my lord? ... they're young'; or 'only God is without sin, we're all sinners'. But if the Cossack, who sometimes had learned by letter what his wife was up to, ignored her greeting and rode past her, she could expect little mercy. It may have helped in some cases that a church service, followed by a feast and copious vodka, occurred before the troops disbanded to go to their homes.[66]

THE TROUBLESOME URAL COSSACKS

The Ural Cossacks were sufficiently eccentric and obstreperous that it is next to impossible to integrate the history of the regulation of their military service into that of the other voiskos. Constituting only about 4 per cent of all Cossacks in the period of the reforms (93 000 males and females in 1881), the Ural Cossacks presented the tsar with more difficulties than any other voisko. This was by no means a novelty. As we have seen, the Pugachev rebellion drew heavily on the Ural Cossacks (then called the Iaik), and a majority of these people were Old Believers.[67]

Relations between the tsar's government and the Ural Cossacks were aggravated by the commitment of these Cossacks to a peculiar system of military service, which they had practised for about two centuries prior to the Miliutin era. This was called 'naemka,' literally 'hiring'. It enabled the wealthier Ural Cossacks to render very little military service in person, but it was far from a simple matter of purchasing the services of a substitute when one was called to duty. It was instead a customary (not statutory) and communal practice, which rested on three assumptions: that the Ural Cossacks as an estate owed the tsar a certain levy of cavalry; that the Cossacks could determine how this force was raised; and that it was legitimate for some members of the estate to make their contribution wholly or mainly in cash. It was possible to envisage such a practice because considerable numbers of Ural Cossacks regularly obtained a considerable income as a result of their special rights to the fisheries of the Ural River and the Caspian Sea at its mouth. The sale of sturgeon and its caviar brought in a substantial money income, a situation without parallel for most other Cossacks.[68] The richer Ural'tsy paid a substantial annual fee to their poorer comrades to persuade the latter to volunteer for service, fully equipped, in the active units required by the tsar. This was worked out annually in an informal convention of almost all serving-age Cossacks when they gathered at the principal city of the voisko, Ural'sk, to share in the catch of the sturgeon during the annual migration upstream. A minority of considerably poorer Ural Cossacks, about one-sixth of the whole, did not come to Ural'sk and met in Iletsk, further upstream.[69]

At the fishermen's convention, the levy necessary to meet the state's requirements was announced and volunteers came forward. If there were not enough, then the remainder drew lots to make up the deficit. According to the chief specialist on the Ural'tsy around 1890, N. Borodin, it was only in 1883 that records were kept of the balance between volunteers and lottery-conscripts. In that year 40 per cent of the levy was voluntary, but this reflected a new system (described below), and it is safe to say that for many years a substantial majority of the Ural Cossacks on active duty were relatively poor Cossacks who volunteered for the money. Under the old system there was virtually a class of long-service Ural'tsy, along with a richer class that served scarcely at all. Certainly the money was substantial by the standards of the place and time. In 1875 it ranged from 240 rubles to 350 rubles, depending on the burdensomeness of the service, which was most costly in the guards squadron, and least expensive in the steppe fortresses. The funds to pay this fee were raised by the non-serving, who outnumbered those serving in normal peacetime years. The larger the levy in proportion to the pool of eligibles, the higher the fee that each non-server had to pay, and pay personally, to the man he 'hired'. In the decade before the authorities abolished this system, the annual sum paid by a non-server ranged from 54.55 rubles in 1873 to 191.20 in 1879, a considerable sum, well beyond the reach of almost all peasants of that time. A further negotiation among those serving determined the actual amount that was paid for assignment to a particular duty, closer to home or further away, less or more expensive. This involved a second form of actual payment between individuals, as those with the least burdensome service contributed to the stipend of those with harder duty.[70]

In 1803 the War Ministry had attempted to abolish the Ural custom of 'hiring'. Such a degree of local autonomy was distressing to the administrators in St Petersburg, who argued that the complex negotiations involved in hiring slowed the mobilization process in time of war. But most of the Ural Cossacks clung to their traditions. Rich and poor made common cause in defence of the old ways because the richer Cossacks, who benefited by avoiding military service, were regarded as religious leaders among the Old Believers. In 1804 there were widespread disturbances in the Ural, as orators denounced the violation of their ancient rights, granted by the (legendary) charter of Tsar Mikhail Fedorovich, the first Romanov monarch, in 1613. This document, the Ural'tsy believed, was lost in a fire, but its imagined contents gave an aura of sanctity to the traditions of the voisko. Failing to intimidate or persuade the protestors, the government in 1806 relented and restored the custom of hiring, but not without sentencing 44 Cossacks to the knout and exile at hard labour.[71]

Some observers thought that the hiring system worked well. August von Haxthausen, who visited the Ural region during his famous trip through Russia in 1843, wrote:

> And what excellent troops they are! All of them depart cheerfully and willingly because it is their own decision and they are paid. Their families are provided for, they are well equipped, and it does not cost the government a penny. Clearly the government could not commit a more serious political error than to attempt to modify this system even slightly.[72]

But the administrators in St Petersburg did not share this opinion. When Miliutin sent out to the various atamans his 'General Programme' for the reform of the Cossacks (with its concept of free entry into and exit from the martial estate), he evidently assumed that it could be adapted to the Ural voisko as well as others. The ataman, one General A. D. Stolypin, who seems to have been as independent-minded as his son, the future Chairman of the Council of Ministers (1906–11), did not oblige Miliutin by accepting the War Minister's ideas. Instead he presided over the preparation of a draft that Miliutin described as 'extremely peculiar', which probably means that it reflected the traditional practices of the Ural'tsy. Worse, Stolypin had the draft printed, and when the War Ministry rejected it, he was so 'offended' that he resigned as ataman.[73] In the following ten years a compromise was reached in drafting a new law on the military obligations of the Ural Cossacks, signed by the tsar on 9 March 1874. Reporting on this outcome, War Minister Miliutin said that the state had made all possible concessions to the Ural'tsy. 'It is impossible to go further in this direction.'[74]

It was indeed true that the new law allowed hiring to continue in some form, and with it some other peculiarities.[75] At the age of 17 the Ural Cossack was enrolled in the 'underage category' (maloletki), in which he merely paid a fee of six rubles a year. At 19 he entered the 'internal service' for two years, the first of which was simply devoted to the assembly of the necessary equipment. In the second year of this status the Cossack had to participate in a short summer training assembly, along with older men of service years. Then, at the age of 21, he joined the 'field category' (polevyi razriad) for 15 years. It was from this age-group that the active-service troops were drawn. The terms of this service were a compromise between the abolition of hiring and its retention in the old form. On the one hand, every Ural Cossack in the field category was obliged to serve at least one year in person. On the other hand, this service could be either in a conventional unit or in a special 'instructional sotnia'. The latter was in fact a privileged establishment in Ural'sk, in which a small number (136 in 1885) of wealthy Cossacks received officer training. Hiring was ostensibly continued in that volunteers were invited, and every Cossack on active duty was to be paid 'assistance' (podmoga) to defray the cost of his equipment. This fund was to be raised by payments from other field-category Cossacks. The active service levy could thus consist partly of volunteers who would receive a payment from their non-serving comrades. But the wording of the new law in fact permitted the authorities effectively to destroy hiring in its previous sense. A non-serving Cossack in the field category had to attend a summer training assembly, along with those on internal service, and in time of war he could be called to active duty. At the age of 36 the Cossack (even if he had served only one year in person) joined the ranks of the internal service for five years. Here, along with the Cossacks of age 20 and the non-serving members of the field-service category, he was merely a reservist, attending a short inspection and training assembly in his home area.

The vestiges of the traditional system that the authorities included in the new law on military service for the Ural voisko were insufficient to placate the great majority of the Cossacks. The contents of the new system had not been public for long before the ataman of the voisko received a petition asking that the new law be rescinded. According to the secret report of the War Minister on the year 1874, the adherents of the 'heresy' (of the Old Believers), which was 'disseminated everywhere' in the voisko, were spreading the rumour that the new law required conversion to official Orthodoxy. An old man named Guzikov was arrested for preaching that those who accepted the new statute received 'the mark of antichrist'. Other agitators claimed that charters issued by the tsars of the seventeenth and eighteenth centuries were being violated. In the opinion of the minister, however, the crucial problem was the requirement that every able Ural Cossack serve one year in person.[76]

To combat this propaganda the authorities sent a staff officer and the members of the Temporary Committee, which had written the new law, into the countryside to explain its provisions. In vain. In the autumn of 1874 the Ural Cossacks were to elect delegates to a 'general congress' (obshchii s'ezd') or voisko assembly. This was under the terms of a new law on civil administration, which had been adopted along with the new military service regulation.[77] The Cossacks demonstrated their resistance by boycotting the elections to the new assembly in 20 of the 29 stanitsas of the Ural voisko, sending instead a petition addressed to the tsar, calling for the retention of the traditional system. The tsar's reply was the dispatch of a battalion of infantry (soon reinforced by a company), which was quartered in the homes of the more active protestors at their expense. When the government tried to collect for the cost of the upkeep of the troops, the Cossacks responded with passive resistance. They would not pay, but invited the police to sell their goods to raise the funds. Threatened, four of the recalcitrant stanitsas capitulated in 1874 and elected delegates as required. But 16 remained obdurate, and at the opening of 1875 the War Minister secretly reported to the tsar that local commanders 'fear for the tranquillity of the region': 'it is impossible to guarantee that there will not be difficulties in the spring when the time for training assemblies arrives.' He was right. Only 1403 of 2556 Cossacks who should have reported to the training assemblies did so.[78]

By this time, the regime was already embarked on a campaign of punishment for those who had displayed resistance when the new law was first introduced. By the end of 1874, 28 dissidents had been sent to Siberia, and in December of that year the regime decided to make the newly-conquered region of the Amu-Daria a place of exile for a much larger number of trouble-makers. Beginning in May 1875 about 2500 were arrested and dispatched without their families and stripped of their legal status as Cossacks. This punishment also had its impact on the remaining Ural Cossacks, who were suspected of sympathy for the protest. By reducing the pool of Cossacks who were eligible for service, while maintaining the same requirement for troops, the ratio between those receiving assistance to those providing it was altered, so that each non-server would have to pay more. Before the deportations began (1874), the annual contribution of the non-servers was 57.55 rubles. In 1879 it reached 191.20. In 1882 the government, perhaps fearing that it would destroy the economic base of the voisko, reduced this penalty by lowering the size of the force required, so that the percentage of eligibles on active service declined from about 20 to 16.[79]

The deportation saw repression countered by passive resistance. About 2500 male Cossacks were designated (without trial) for deportation. A few of the old and feeble were sent to Orenburg, a few others to Siberia, but about 2000 were taken under military escort to the region of the Amu-Daria, where they were supposed to build themselves settlements in the wilderness. The Ural voisko was assessed the sizeable sum of 50 000 rubles to pay for this. The deportees repeatedly tried to avert their fate by refusing to cooperate. They would lie down on the road and on one occasion refused to mount camels that had been provided for their transportation. Some were persuaded to go along by others who believed that it was prophesied that they would go to the East to spread the Christian faith. On arriving near the Amu-Daria, they refused to build settlements, firm in the belief that they would be permitted to go home. The regime tried to deal with this by sending the wives and children of the exiles to join them. But the Cossacks would not capitulate. Almost 400 illegally made their way back to the Ural region, where they spread dissent. At least ten different groups, with pathetic trust, struggled to St Petersburg, attempting to present petitions to the tsar or tsarevich. Unable to crush this opposition entirely, the government took advantage of the accession of the new tsar in 1881 to issue an amnesty to any Ural exiles who would repent and obey. About a quarter of the surviving exiles accepted, but the majority would not (and 212 were reported dead). A pardon, in return for obedience, was offered in 1883 in honour of the coronation of Alexander iii, but only 16 accepted. In 1891 the offer was extended on the tricentennial of the voisko. By this time only a few surviving dissenters had not been brought to heel or their graves, although a few petitions continued to appear early in the reign of Nicholas ii. This whole episode may demonstrate the brutality of the regime, the hollowness of the supposedly special nature of the relationship between tsar and Cossack. On the other hand, both the persistent belief of the victims that they could approach the tsar with their petitions and the continued willingness of the tsar to offer amnesty to this insignificant number of people attest to a kind of vitality in the official myth of tsar and Cossack.[80]

The repression of the exiles had the desired effect on the majority of the Ural Cossacks. They accepted the new law, grudgingly, and even put up with subsequent steps that eroded the vestiges of the traditional order. At first the annual meetings of the fishermen continued to set the fee to be paid by those in the field category who did not go on active service. But in 1877, it was agreed by the assembly of delegates in the voisko that it was no longer convenient for almost every Cossack of serving age to travel to Ural'sk for the autumn fishery, partly because of the need to pay increasing attention to agriculture. The fixing of the fee was handed over to a meeting of delegates from the stanitsas. Then in 1883, on the initiative of the ataman, Prince G. S. Golitsyn, the voisko administration took over the fixing and collecting of the contribution of the non-servers and the payment of the assistance to those on duty. The scholarly Cossack writer Borodin observed bitterly that this fiscal system was simply a local tax (podat'). One has to appreciate the traditional pride of the Cossacks that they were not, like peasants, one of the 'taxed' estates to understand the seriousness of this charge.[81]

As a result of this shift in fiscal responsibility, the role of volunteers diminished. As soon as the new law was implemented, a considerable part of each annual levy was filled by 'obligated Cossacks' ('obiazatel'nie'), who were serving their mandatory year on active service. In 1883 40 per cent of the levy still consisted of volunteers, but in that year, as it took over the management of the financial side of military service, the voisko administration began to conscript any poor Cossacks who had fallen into arrears in their payment towards the 'assistance' that was being paid to those on active duty. Under the old system arrears were not a problem, because the richer Cossacks were the only ones who avoided service by paying the hiring sum. But under the management of the voisko authorities, an annual levy was placed on all Cossacks in the field category, rich and poor. The effect of this method of fund-raising was that many Ural Cossacks who were not legally obliged to serve were conscripted because of arrears, and by 1887 there were no more volunteers in the levy. Borodin, quite plausibly, believed that the replacement of the volunteer system with complete conscription was highly detrimental to morale. He also observed that the new system was increasingly unable to cover the costs of equipping the levy. The poorer Cossacks could not afford the costs, even with the official assistance, and the rich were no longer making up this difference. In a general mobilization the contribution of each non-server might reach 800 rubles, an economic impossibility. In their eagerness to reform the Ural Cossacks, the War Ministry had transformed a working system, albeit eccentric, into a calamity.[82]

It was therefore hardly surprising that the authorities wanted to dispose of the problem by applying to the Ural voisko the same rules that had been installed elsewhere on the Don model of 1874. As early as 1881 the War Minister reported that this was his goal, but said that it was agreed that this should be done gradually. The process turned out to be exceedingly gradual, no doubt owing to the record of the

Ural Cossacks as trouble-makers, and it was only in 1910 that they were finally subject to the standard rules for Cossack military service.[83]

THE MAKING OF A REGULAR MILITARY FORCE

In 1879 the 'Main Administration of Irregular Forces' became 'The Main Administration of Cossack Forces'.[84] This formal recognition of the altered status of the Cossacks in the Russian military establishment reflected accurately the evolution of policy concerning the purpose of the Cossacks. Granted, the transition from irregular to regular had not come about strictly as a result of the reforms in the system of military service in the Miliutin era. For many years there had been a creeping regularization in War Ministry policy. This was not the result of a conscious decision to alter the basic conception of the Cossacks, but a natural tendency of professional military leaders to diminish the undisciplined character that the irregular Cossack tradition displayed. There were modest, piecemeal steps, such as the award of military rank to Cossack officers in 1798, the authorization of standard army pay and allowances for Cossacks serving over 200 verstas from home the following year, and the issuance of the first rule on Cossack uniforms in 1801. And there were some major, fairly systematic efforts, most notably the Don statute of 1835 and the issuance of the first field regulations for Cossacks in 1838.[85] The latter resulted from the horror with which Nicholas I reviewed Don regiments during his visit in 1837. Accustomed to think that the guards regiments represented Cossack cavalry in general, he fumed, 'I expected to see 22 regiments of Cossacks and I saw some sort of peasants. No one had any understanding of a [straight] front. And the horses. These were not Cossack horses but a peasant sort.'[86] The publication of field regulations, including a section setting standards for plunder (a realistic recognition of the irregular Cossack tradition), did not by any means complete the task of regularizing these troops. According to a Don officer, writing of the situation in 1863, the Cossacks mobilized to fight the Polish rebels appeared at inspection 'in old, patched clothing with rusty guns and sabres, with rope instead of leather in their horses' equipment'.[87]

After 1870 the new strategic perspective of Russia required that, if Cossacks were to play a serious role in the defence of the Austro-German frontier, those deployed with the army in the West must become in effect regulars. This meant, above all, the Donsty, whose numbers and geographical location marked them as the core of the Cossack contribution to the regular army cavalry. To a lesser extent this applied to other voiskos whose forces might be used in the West or the Caucasus: the Kuban, Terek, Orenburg, Ural and miniscule Astrakhan. Some of their units, however, and all those that were raised in the East, were intended mainly for the traditional business of patrolling a loosely-held border against Asiatics, and were subject to less intensive regularization.

In 1869 two administrative reforms that Miliutin established for the regular army had a major impact on the Cossacks. First, in the newly established military okrugs (districts), Cossack cavalry was placed under the command of the district cavalry commander, with the exception of the Warsaw district. Second, the standard cavalry division was reorganized to consist of three regular regiments and one Don Cossack regiment. Once these steps had been taken, it was obvious that the Cossack cavalry needed to be regularized in its quality, as was decided in 1870.[88] Implementing this decision was no small task, especially considering the limited financial means of the War Ministry, and even a generation later the Cossacks were in some respects behind the regulars. But the War Ministry clearly regarded this as its major goal in Cossack affairs for about 25 years following 1870, and much was accomplished. A fundamental step, enacted in 1870, was the subordination of all active-duty Cossacks to the regular army code of discipline.[89]

The process of regularization implied some limitation on the size of the Cossack force that the army wanted. The number of Cossacks that was to be integrated into army division was controlled by the size of the regular army, and the question of finance limited the numbers of both Cossacks and regulars. In 1882, 5 out of 20 regiments of Don cavalry were removed from the active-duty list as an economy measure. Two Don regiments were restored in 1889, and the new total, 17, remained static until the mobilization of the Russo-Japanese War of 1904–5.[90] The total number of Cossacks from all the voiskos on active service in peacetime initially declined as a result of the reform of the service obligations. On the eve of the Crimean War, in 1853, the figure was down to 56 314. A decade later, in 1883, after the Don model of service obligation had been applied to all the voiskos except the Ural, it was down to 45 055, and a low point for the period from the Crimean to the First World War came in 1886, with 43 610. Thereafter the active force recovered to 56 802 in 1890 and then settled into a plateau which it maintained until the eve of the Russo-Japanese War, fluctuating between 50 000 and 60 000. There was no durable increase in this period: the figure for 1903 was only 53 563.[91]

Because of this stable level of demand for conscripts, along with a substantially increasing Cossack population, the regime was able to man the units that it wanted with little difficulty. In 1873 the active-duty Cossack force was almost 3 per cent of the population of the estate, while in 1903 a mere 1.7 per cent constituted a force that was only slightly smaller.[92]

It is true that during the early 1880s, when the new laws on service obligation were just settling into effect on all the voiskos, there was a shortage of men. In 1880 the War Ministry annual report showed a shortfall of 6799 men against the full wartime complement of units on the table of organization.[93] In 1885 it was still considered possible that it might be necessary to hold 25-year-olds from the Don on active duty at the end of their term to keep units up to strength, and the voisko was authorized to do this, although it does not appear that they did so.[94] But by the following year, the War Minister was able to report that the population situation was sufficiently comfortable that it was possible to excuse the neediest cases from active duty in wartime in case of economic hardship in the family, and the law on military obligation was thus amended.[95] By 1890 there was a surplus of 32 549 men in the combatant category, even after those excused for physical or other reasons had been taken into account, and this over-supply remained until the end of the decade, despite some increase in the table of organization.[96] Granted, there sometimes was a problem in finding enough men in a particular voisko, and the regulations did not permit a unit in any one voisko to be manned partly by Cossacks from a different voisko in case of need. In 1898, for example, there were shortfalls of available men in three voiskos against the table of organization for full wartime mobilization of the three turns. But in only one of these cases, the Siberian voisko, did the high command consider the shortage, 1052, to be significant. The minister noted that in case of mobilization it would have to be made up from the reserve category.[97] As for the excess of available manpower in time of full mobilization, it was regarded as a pool of replacements for possible casualties.[98] The possibility of utilizing this surplus by systematically creating new units on the table of organization was not pursued, presumably because of the cost. Even though the Cossacks were to a considerable extent self-financing, the War Ministry budget had to contribute to their upkeep, particularly on active service, and this restrained any plans for expansion. The army increased its Cossack force modestly, approximately on a par with increases of the rest of its forces, in the last quarter of the nineteenth century. In 1881 the Cossacks represented about 5 per cent of the active-duty army, and this figure was the same on the eve of the Russo-Japanese War.[99]

The Cossacks were mainly cavalry, armed with rifle, sabre and pike. These troopers were formed into basic units called the 'sotnia'. Although this literally means 'hundred', the actual table of organization varied. The Don 1874 model included 110 ordinary Cossacks in wartime and 112 in peacetime, plus a few noncoms, trumpeters and clerks. Sometimes a sotnia was maintained as a separate command, but usually they were grouped by four or six to form a regiment. On the regimental level, sotnias were normally combined only with others from the same voisko, although there were a few 'composite' regiments that mixed sotnias from different voiskos.[100] On the divisional level in the western military okrugs, the War Ministry frequently combined three non-Cossack cavalry regiments with one Cossack regiment, although there were a few all-Cossack divisions. The integration of Cossack cavalry regiments into regular army divisions required, for tactical reasons, the matching of the Cossack regiments to the regular norms with respect to the number of 'ranks' (riad) per platoon (vzvod). Each Cossack regiment in such a division had to add 96 men for this purpose, a seemingly modest task that taxed the fiscal resources of the War Ministry. It took three years (1885–7) for them to trim some other expenditures before the minister could report that all 18 Cossack regiments that were assigned to regular divisions had been expanded to the desired size.[101]

But not all Cossacks were in the cavalry. Apart from a few specialists who served in such work as railway technology and gunsmithing, there were combat units of artillery and infantry. In 1895, a representative year, 20 Cossack horse artillery batteries of six or four guns each were on active duty. The Don led the way with eight batteries, one of which was a guards unit. These, like most Don cavalry regiments, were assigned to regular cavalry divisions. The Kuban voisko had five batteries, Orenburg three and Terek and Zabaikal two each. Because of the cost of artillery, only the Don units maintained second- and third-turn batteries in reserve, excepting the guards unit, which had none. The rest had only a second turn, permitting them to double but not treble their force in wartime.[102]

Infantry was still less common. The Zaporozhian Cossacks who were transplanted to the Kuban area brought with them a tradition of maintaining infantry called 'plastun' and after 1892 they maintained a peacetime strength of six battalions of about 600 men each. Evidently the War Ministry esteemed these troops, because they ordered expansion of their numbers in 1888 and 1892, trebling the peacetime force that had existed previously. For the rest, there were but two battalions of infantry in the Zabaikal voisko and one in the Ussuri. The Cossacks did not maintain their own engineers or other branches of the service.[103]

Two categories of units were consistently based on the capital because of their honorific status. One of these was 'His Imperial Majesty's Own Convoy', a mounted household guards unit. Because this was essentially a decorative detachment, it was chosen only from picturesque peoples from the Caucasus and Crimea after the early nineteenth century. Its make-up was altered a number of times, and it became exclusively Cossack only after 1890, when a small detachment of Crimean Tatars was removed from the convoy. But from the early nineteenth century, Cossacks from the Caucasian Line and Black Sea voiskos (reorganized as Terek and Kuban) played a prominent role in the organization, and in 1861 they were reorganized as the first, second and third Caucasus Cossack Squadrons of His Imperial Majesty's Own Convoy. At the opening of the reign of Alexander III they were reorganized as two Kuban and two Terek lifeguards squadrons, renamed 'sotnias' in 1891. Until this date half of the force was off active duty in the second turn at any given moment, but afterwards the whole force was on duty continually and the second turn or reserve was abolished.

The approximately 500 Cossacks of the convoy were an elite, selected by the atamans of their native districts for their appearance, character and skill in trick-riding (dzhigatovka), singing and dancing. After medical examination and inspection at the voisko headquarters, the annual replacement force was sent by rail to begin its four-year service in Tsarskoe Selo. Not all those sent were new conscripts. Some were volunteers who had served the mandatory four years of active service, including non-commissioned officers, who served in the convoy as ordinary Cossacks, while keeping their rank. On duty at the imperial residences, including the royal family's trips to the Crimea and elsewhere, the Cossacks of the convoy enjoyed various perquisites in return for their presumed devotion and discipline. They had to report for service with their own uniform and horse, which had to be a bay. But, unlike ordinary Cossacks, they were given a uniform and various emoluments, such as a tip for every parade and payment for 'a second horse'. This custom dated from the days before rail transport, when Cossacks had to ride to St Petersburg from the Caucasus. In the later nineteenth century they came by rail and did not have to pay for a second horse. They stood to earn about 130 rubles per year, which was banked for them during the four years of their service, giving the Cossack a small fortune by his standards when he returned to his village. His arrival in Tsarskoe Selo and return to the village were celebrated with various ceremonies, the tsar greeting the new contingent each year and the voisko ataman welcoming the returnees at the borders of the voisko territory to thank them for their service to the sovereign. In the reign of Nicholas II some of the Cossacks of the convoy enjoyed another privilege: many of them, especially from the Terek, were Old Believers, and despite the regime's official disapproval of this heresy, they were allowed to have an Old Believer priest administer the oath.[104]

The other type of Cossack unit that was stationed in the capital in peacetime was the lifeguard. The Don had the main share of this honorific assignment which was not purely decorative. In time of war, the lifeguards fought. All the guards units' personnel were especially selected by the local authorities at the time of each annual call-up, and only those who were at least five feet ten inches tall could qualify. The oldest Don Cossack lifeguards regiment had been given this status in 1798, although some smaller Cossack guards formations had existed as far back as 1775. This was His Majesty's Lifeguards Cossack Regiment. The junior Don regiment to enjoy this status was the 'Ataman Regiment', which was nominally under the command of the Don ataman. But after the heir to the throne became Ataman of all the Cossacks in 1827 the Ataman Regiment was taken into guards corps, and began sending a sotnia to the capital. Later the whole regiment was stationed there, and in 1856 the regiment was renamed 'His Imperial Highness the Heir Tsarevich Ataman Regiment'. The Don service statute of 1874 required that each of the two guards regiments in peacetime should provide two squadrons, which constituted one of the two 'divisions' of the 'Lifeguards Composite Cossack Regiment'. Each regiment also maintained second and third turns on inactive service. But in the Russo-Turkish War of 1877–8, it proved expensive and cumbersome to assemble the reserve and active components of such a regiment. In 1884 these regiments therefore dropped their second or third turns. In time of war, a reserve guards regiment would be created from the surplus of eligible Don Cossacks to provide replacements for the two guards regiments.[105]

The only other voisko to participate significantly in guards service in the latter half of the nineteenth century was the Ural. Despite their record of trouble-making, there was a tradition dating back to 1798 that they would provide a sotnia of cavalry for the guards. For a mere two years, 1880–2, the Siberian Cossacks sent 30 men a year to serve with the Lifeguards Grenadier Regiment in order to produce qualified personnel to return to Siberia as instructors. But this proved unsatisfactory and was quickly disbanded. With this minor exception, the voiskos other than the Don, Kuban, Terek and Ural did not participate in convoy or guards service until 1906, when, as will be discussed later, a new Composite Lifeguards Cossack Regiment was established.[106] To the present day one monument to the presence of the Cossacks in the imperial capital still stands, the Cossack Barracks, a massive, redbrick, prison-like structure, quite unlike the elegant neo-classical barracks of the guards regiments near the Winter Palace. Dilapidated but too solid to be demolished easily, it still stood in 1982 across the park of the St Alexander Nevsky Monastery, occupying a long stretch on the Obvodnyi Canal embankment.

As for the Cossack formations that were not in convoy or lifeguards, their deployment was far-flung, from the neighbourhood of Warsaw to that of Vladivostok. The regiments that were integrated with the regular army in European Russia constituted the largest share of the total Cossack force. These were mainly Don cavalry regiments and horse-artillery batteries, for in the last quarter of the century only one of the 15 or 17 active-duty Don regiments were stationed elsewhere. This was a single regiment that in 1884 was posted to the Don region capital of Novocherkassk at the request of the voisko ataman, who was becoming increasingly concerned about the security problem among non-Cossacks who were working in Rostov-na-Donu and the Donets basin mines.[107] There had been some Don Cossacks in the Warsaw area for many years, but until the pacification of the Caucasus it was not possible to spare more than roughly half the Dontsy for other areas. The phasing-out of Don regiments in the Caucasus began at the opening of the 1860s and was completed by 1866.[108] Meanwhile the Polish uprising of 1863 and the associated tensions in Russian relations with the West had evoked a major mobilization of the Dontsy. By early 1864 they had 43 regiments on duty in Poland and also the Odessa and Vilno military districts.[109] When the emergency was over, most of this force went home, but a large part stayed on in the same areas, where they were integrated into regular cavalry divisions. When the new law on military service was implemented in 1875, the largest number of Don regiments, five, was assigned to the Moscow military okrug, four to the Warsaw military okrug, three to Vilno, two each to Odessa, Kharkov and Kiev and one each to Finland and the Don. With the exception of a regiment in Odessa, these units were not quartered in the principal city of the district, but in minor places such as Torzhok and Mekhov.[110]

In the next decade there was a significant change in the deployment of Cossacks in European Russia, reflecting the integration of the Cossacks with the regulars and the growing concern for the security of the western frontier. The internal military okrugs, Moscow and Kharkov, were stripped of all but one Cossack regiment, which remained in Moscow guberniia. The Warsaw okrug contingent was increased from 9 regiments in 1889 to 12 in 1894–1903. Kiev okrug was assigned a steady eight regiments over the same period, Vilno and Odessa two regiments, Vilno having had three until 1894. Of the 24 regiments on duty at the end of the century, 16 were from the Don, the remainder coming from the Kuban, Terek, Orenburg and Ural voiskos. The latter two also contributed a small force (between 3 and 13 sotnias during 1889–1903) that was regularly stationed in the Kazan and Perm military districts for police purposes.[111]

Far as they were from the Don and other Cossack regions, various garrison towns of Poland, Ukraine and Lithuania became a regular part of the life of Cossacks, as annual contingents of 21-year-old troopers arrived in the spring to replace the 25-year-olds who were returning to their homes. Some of the garrison towns and Cossack stanitsas had a continuing link, even if not a particularly pleasant one, over more than a generation. Beginning in 1888 the active duty regiments of the Don were each based on one of the six okrugs within the voisko. Thus successive call-ups of Cossacks from a given part of the Don tended to be assigned to the same western post, sons following fathers in due course.[112] As late as 1936, a musicologist found Cossacks in Kalach singing a traditional song that began, 'Ai, who has not been in Poland', and continued to recount the amorous exploits of the Cossacks in Mlawa among the 'nice, nice, nice' Polish women and 'stupid Polish pany'.[113] But the War Ministry saw to it that permanent ties did not grow up, forbidding Cossacks to marry while on active duty.[114]

The Caucasus military okrug, facing Turkey and Persia and containing mountaineers who still needed some watching, absorbed almost the entire contingent raised by the Kuban and Terek voiskos, although they also contributed to the force (13 or 14 sotnias, a little over 2 regiments) in Transcaspia. The size of the force in the Caucasus ranged from 94 to 98 sotnias in the 1890s, the equivalent of about 16 full-sized regiments.[115]

Thus the European frontier absorbed about half the active Cossack force, the Caucasus and Transcaspia about a third, and the remainder was dispersed across Central Asia and Siberia. This line was manned by the Orenburg, Ural, Semirechenskoe, Siberian, Transbaikal, Amur and Ussuri voiskos. By far the largest part of this force was stationed in Central Asia (the Omsk and Turkestan military okrugs). During most of the 1890s there were about 40 sotnias there, a small force compared to the vastness of the tsar's recently-won empire of desert and mountain. But this was still a much larger force than the one patrolling the Mongolian border of the Irkutsk military okrug in the 1890s: a mere two sotnias. Most of the duty assigned the Cossacks in Asia had little in common with that of the regiments that were integrated with cavalry divisions. Indeed, the Amur and Ussuri Cossacks in 1897 were ordered to provide crews for steamers and barges on the riperian frontier with China.[116] In the Far East, the government particularly wanted to increase the number of Cossacks who could support its expansionist policies, but this proved difficult. In 1889 there were only eight sotnias on duty in the Priamur military district, which included the maritime province, and in 1901 it was at the same level, not counting six sotnias from the region which had been added in the 'Kwantung military district' in Manchuria.[117]

The popular image of the Cossacks emphasizes their role as mounted police, especially against demonstrators or strikers. This is not without foundation, but it misses the main point of government policy in the late nineteenth century. It is true that until the 1870s a number of Cossack units that were not assigned to border patrol or combat units were used for police work in European Russia, where the regime always lacked any substantial professional constabulary. The corps of gendarmes, although it figures prominently in the history of the intelligentsia, was too small for routine police work. To deal with major disorders, all the armed forces were the government's ultimate weapon, but the War Ministry was never comfortable about this role, and it was still less enthusiastic about routine police duty of the sort that some Cossack units had performed for many years.[118] So it was that when the ministry decided that the Cossacks were to play a major role in the regular cavalry, they attempted to reduce the Cossacks' police function as much as possible. A memo of 1868 from General

Staff stated that they had noted repeatedly that Cossack units in the western region were not there 'exclusively for police service and as personal servants of commanding personnel, but as much as possible to be trained for actual military service'.[119]

To make a force of regulars out of irregular soldiers and amateur policemen required training, weapons, leadership. Before the Miliutin era, basic training had been rather informal. The stanitsa ataman was entrusted with responsibility for 'striving by all means to renew and imbue the ancient martial games of the Cossacks', utilizing Sundays and holidays for the retraining of veteran Cossacks and gathering the young ones for an unspecified period of local instruction.[120] By the 1860s the War Ministry began to take some steps to systematize preinduction training. In 1865 the Don voisko was ordered to assign one instructor to each stanitsa to teach marksmanship, and in 1869 a regulation specified that the trainees should all spend the month of May prior to induction at a camp in their stanitsa, learning riding, marksmanship and other skills with a maximum of 65 students per instructor. Meanwhile, the Kuban had been ordered in 1867 to establish an 'instructional division' for the whole voisko, which was to provide a 4½-month summer training programme.[121]

It was only with the introduction of the new law on service obligation, first in the Don and later in other voiskos, that a systematic and general programme of pre-induction training began. This was in theory a three-year process (except in the Ural voisko), but in practice it amounted only to something more than a month of formal instruction. In the first year the main object for each inductee was to acquire equipment and a horse. To lighten this burden, he was absolved of all taxes while in the preparatory category. In the autumn of the second year he was to attend an unspecified number of training sessions in his village. Only in the spring of the third year did he have to attend a training camp for one month. Granted, the official mythology about the glorious martial tradition of the Cossacks and the transmission from father to son was probably not entirely groundless, but informal military training in the village could scarcely have amounted to much, considering that firearms were normally locked up in arsenals and that horses suitable for service were a luxury which most Cossacks obtained only when required by law to do so, if then.[122]

The more serious part of the Cossack's military training occurred after he had gone on active duty. Although the regular cavalry field regulations were applied to Cossack cavalry regiments, the principal statement of policy on Cossack training acknowledged that the demands imposed on them would be 'lower than the regulars'. In particular they need not practice formal or *manège* horsemanship, nor attain high standards in infantry drill. They should be excused from the standards of the regulars with respect to the condition of their uniforms. On the other hand, the authorities hoped that the Cossack cavalry would be better than the regulars when it came to saddling-up quickly, covering long distances, riding in dispersed formations, and in scouting. They also hoped that the Cossack units would benefit from the fact that each had a district regional basis, each sotnia usually coming from one particular stanitsa. The War Ministry believed that this was beneficial in combat and urged the preservation of these ties. In 1878 the ministry extended to the Cossacks an important part of Miliutin's plan for the reformed training of all troops: the teaching of literacy. This does not, however, mean that all Cossacks emerged from their term of service able to read and write. A generation after the introduction of this training only 43 per cent of all male Cossacks were officially reported to be literate.[123]

After four years of active service, the Cossack was considered trained, and the goal of the War Ministry was to maintain his competence through the eight years of service in the second and third turns. Regulations on this training varied among voiskos, but the basic Don model of 1874 permitted the Cossack to skip the reserve training period during the first year of his second turn. After that he was required to appear with horse and equipment for three weeks in each of the remaining years of the turn. In the third turn, Don Cossacks had to report for this assembly only once, in the third year of the four-year turn (excepting those who had been allowed to skip active duty on grounds of family hardship – the kormiak, who had to appear each year). These assemblies met jointly with those of the preparatory category on land allotted by the voisko.[124]

An observer of these training assemblies, writing in the 1890s, did not have a high opinion of their value, complaining that they taught 'only what was required for inspections', omitting almost entirely any tactical exercises. He estimated that marksmanship occupied about half the training, and considered this excessive.[125] On the other hand, they may have needed it; in 1874 in Finland the regular infantry scored 35–56 per cent hits on the target, the Cossacks only 9 per cent.[126] The official judgement was more favourable in 1891. The Don was deemed satisfactory in its training assembly, the Terek, Orenburg, Ural, Astrakhan and Siberian voiskos good. But the Kuban was considered highly unsatisfactory in riding, marksmanship, uniform and equipment; the Semirechenskoe, Zabaikal, Amur and Ussuri all poor in uniform and equipment.[127]

For the Cossacks to become regular troops, they not only had to be properly trained but also properly equipped. The tradition of self-equipment by the individual Cossack was fiscally useful to the War Ministry, but from a military point of view it became important to standardize the items that the Cossack acquired, approximately on the lines of the regular army. Only in 1879 did the authorities begin systematic efforts to achieve this in the Don voisko, authorizing the establishment in each of the six okrugs of the voisko an officially approved, privately-owned, commissary. In addition to maintaining permanent shops (only three in the voisko in 1900), these merchants also appeared at local bazaars. Even though the ataman could fine owners of commissaries in case of poor performance, every writer who commented on this operation complained about the quality of the goods, and especially the riding tack, sold to this captive market.[128] In other voiskos the supply of mandatory items was left entirely to private enterprise, and the official historian of the Semirechenskoe voisko recounts unsatisfactory attempts to deal with the problem by loaning or granting Cossacks money that they were supposed to use to buy suitable fabric for uniforms or to pay to a tailor in Vernyi.[129] The actual listing of what the Cossack had to buy appeared in an oblique way in 1882, when for the first time the Don Cossacks were obliged to have identity papers, in the form of a small booklet that not only listed the holder's name, past service, fines and pay received, but also various items of equipment, such as shirt and gloves, that he was implicitly obliged to have. But this list had never received formal legal sanction, and a commission under the Main Administration of Cossack Forces was established to investigate the problem. In 1885 it produced an official list covering all voiskos, which took effect the following year. This left little to the imagination, specifying such items as 'three sets of underclothes', 'two sets of horseshoes', 'one gymnastic shirt and tie', 'scales for hay' and 'one lasso'. To maintain this array of equipment while on active duty, the ordinary Cossack cavalryman received 21.45 rubles per year 'repair money' and the infantryman 11 rubles (above the miserly equivalent of private's wages: 3 rubles per year).[130] The uniform, except for the Kuban and Terek voiskos, reflected the regularization of the Cossacks, for it was essentially the same as the regulars, apart from a distinctive red stripe on the breeches. In honour of their traditional links with the Caucasus, the two voiskos of that region were permitted to retain the 'cherkeska', a black coat with its wide skirt and dramatic cartridge-pockets on the breast. In 1900 some unromantic general even sought to abolish this colourful tradition, but it was restored in 1904.[131]

The state provided the Cossack with firearms, but not pike and sabre. And the state did not pay the entire cost of the firearms. In the 1860s, the state paid two-thirds of the cost of the Tenner six-line (15.24 mm) rifle that had been introduced at the beginning of the decade, the voisko paying the rest.[132] But with the advance of the regularization in the following decade this weapon was replaced with the four-line (10.67 mm) Safonov. This represented a major financial undertaking, and the ever-parsimonious War Ministry decided to charge not a third of the cost to the voiskos but half.[133] Moreover, the voiskos had to pay for the construction of armouries in which to store the weapons that would be issued to the second and third turns in time of mobilization or for training assemblies. Previously, the Cossack of serving age had kept his own weapon at home when on off-duty status, but after the 1870s he was disarmed except for cold weapons when off active service. A writer who knew Don Cossacks of the generation that fought in the Turkish War of 1877–8 maintains that they were unpleasantly surprised when, on returning from the war, their rifles were taken from them.[134] Because of the cost, the process of rearming the Cossacks lasted from 1873 to 1880.[135] The Safonov rifle was issued only to Cossacks, the regular infantry and cavalry using different weapons, but in 1893 the War Ministry began to reequip regulars and Cossacks alike with the Mosin three-line (7.62 mm) model-1891 rifle, a task completed in 1895.[136] While most Cossacks were armed with rifles, artillerymen and some other personnel received revolvers. In place of obsolete pistols (often handmade by villagers in the Caucasus), over 11 000 Smith and Wesson revolvers were purchased in 1875 at a cost of 250 000 rubles, half paid by the voiskos and half by the War Ministry. These were replaced by the Russian-made Nagan revolver beginning in 1895.[137]

Leadership remained a difficult problem in the regularization of the Cossacks, although this was not usually considered to be the case with respect to non-commissioned officers. They were obtained by the same, rather rudimentary, methods that were applied in the regular army, although the Cossack noncom was called an 'uriadnik' rather than an 'unter-ofitser'. In either case there were principally two grades, junior and senior. The uriadnik was promoted from the ranks of the ordinary Cossacks after at least 16 months' service. Literacy was required in theory, but there was no systematic test, nor was there any formal training programme other than a course of unspecified duration and content in an instructional detachment of the regiment or other unit.[138] Although these were not demanding requirements, relatively few Cossacks were in fact promoted to uriadnik. The table of organization of a Don cavalry regiment called for 50 uriadniks and 750 ordinary Cossacks in peacetime, and the promotion seems to have been a matter of considerable prestige in the militarized society of the Cossacks. In addition to these non-career noncoms there were supposed to be a mere six career noncoms called 'starshyi vakhmistr' (literally 'senior watch-master') per cavalry regiment.[139]

The War Ministry lacked the funds to train enough officers, to train them well and to pay them adequately, problems that applied with particular severity to the Cossack officers, whose training and sustenance were supposed to rest as much as possible on Cossack financial resources. At the opening of the reign of Alexander II there were no military schools in the Cossack territories although the Novocherkassk gymnazium included a modicum of military training in its curriculum. The best that was offered to train Cossack officers of noble birth (and no others) was a system whereby the voisko paid various cadet corps and one artillery school for the privilege of sending their candidates to study and gain a commission. In all there were only 144 such positions, a modest number considering that it was a seven-year course, which only about 20 per year could finish at best. In the period 1857–62 only about one Cossack officer in 95 had the benefit of this kind of formal training. Of the other 94, a few were transfers from the regulars, but this was not popular. The result was that in Cossack units most officers were promoted from the enlisted ranks, on the basis of seniority and the passing of a modest exam. Under this system, members of the nobility had to serve only four years in the ranks (two in the Don and Zabaikal voiskos), while ordinary Cossacks could be commissioned only after 12 years.[140]

The situation was not a great deal better among the regulars. If only one Cossack officer in 95 had finished a formal school for officers, one regular officer in 49 had this distinction. War Minister Miliutin addressed himself to this problem among his other reforms, and in the 1860s replaced the old system, which rested on the cadet corps, with a network of military gymnaziums, military schools (voennaia uchilish-cha) and junker schools (iunkerskaia uchilishcha). The gymnazium was a reformed version of the cadet corps, with a seven-year programme, offering general education along with some military instruction. Its graduates, and some from civilian schools, could enter the two-year professional course in one of four (by 1864) military schools, which produced commissioned officers. The junker school was less lofty. It took its students from army enlisted personnel (largely members of the nobility who had enlisted with the goal of becoming officers) and at the end of a two-year programme (three after 1902) submitted them to an exam. Those who passed on a certain level were commissioned and those who passed with less distinction were given the rank of 'portupei-iunker' (literally 'shoulder-belt cadet') and could be promoted to officer by the commander of the unit they had come from and to which they now returned.[141]

The Cossacks, as part of their integration into the regular army, were included in this programme. A total of 90 places were reserved for them (mainly the Dontsy, with 65 at their disposal) in the military schools, at voisko expense. As with the regular army, however, the great majority of officers were to be trained in the junker schools. In Warsaw, Vilno and Elizavetgrad junker schools there were three special 'Cossack sections' with a total of 120 places. Four predominantly Cossack junker schools were established: Orenburg (1867), serving the Orenburg, Ural, Siberian and Semirechenskoe voiskos; Novocherkassk (1869), for the Don and Astrakhan voiskos; Stavropol (1870), for the Kuban and Terek; and Irkutsk for the Zabaikal and Amur (1872). In 1881 these institutions had places for 655, all of whom were to be uriadniks who volunteered. Before a new regulation in 1876, they had to be nobles.[142] But there was trouble in fulfilling this potential supply of officers because of the low educational level of the Cossacks, evidently lower than the applicants to the non-Cossack junker schools. This was a kind of distinction, considering that one contemporary observer of the examinations for completion of the programme at a regular army junker school wrote that some candidates, despite a course in geography, could not find Russia on the map. To deal with this problem a special preparatory year (making three years altogether) was introduced in the Cossack junker schools in 1876, and the total number of places in the schools was decreased.[143]

The reformed system of training definitely improved the professional background of Cossack officers. In contrast with the negligible proportion that had formal military education previously, 9 per cent had finished military schools and 30 per cent junker schools in the years 1871–80. But 28 per cent still gained their promotions by exam, after serving in the ranks, and for a time, in the war of 1877–8, even the exam was waived, providing that some kind of schooling had been completed.[144] It was clear to the War Ministry that additional military educational facilities were needed for Cossack officers. In 1881 (perhaps trying to take advantage of the advent of Alexander III and a more pro-Cossack administration), the War Ministry advanced a proposal to open a military gymnazium of 400 places (and an additional 200 external or correspondence places) in Novocherkassk and three military pro-gymnaziums elsewhere in the Don territory. Blocked once by the State Council, the idea went to a committee representing the War Ministry, Ministry of Finance, Ministry of State Control and the Don voisko, from which it emerged with the tsar's approval in 1882. But in 1883 the State Council determined that the proposed budget of 500 000 rubles for the institution in Novocherkassk was too much for the treasury 'in its present state'. The project languished, and in 1888 the War Ministry was still trying to arouse interest in building a military gymnazium, noting that the programme to place Cossacks in military schools outside the voisko often led to the departure of the Cossacks from the estate, after repaying the stipend that they had received.[145]

The same poverty that constrained the improvement of officer training was painfully evident in the pay of Cossack officers. The situation was chronically bad among the regular officers, whose remuneration was scarcely raised between 1859 and the end of the century.[146] But for the Cossack officers, the situation was worse. In 1841 their pay was set at two-thirds of the regulars on the assumption that, unlike the regulars, they had the benefit of land grants from the voisko. Although such land grants did exist, and there were some aristocrats who had acquired substantial holdings, the lower Cossack officers were actually in a state of penury.[147] The situation was, however, somewhat better for regimental commanders, their deputies and sotnia commanders, who received, while on active duty, the standard mess allowance for their rank, which was more than their base pay.[148] In 1858–61, the state at least raised the pay scale of officers of the Don, Orenburg, Ural, Kuban, Terek and Siberian voiskos to the level of the regulars, passing this cost on to the voiskos as a 'temporary' measure, which lasted until 1884 in some voiskos and 1902 in others.[149]

Upon receiving his commission, the Cossack officer typically began a long-term career. In most cases he served only in Cossack units, and only in the voisko of his birth. Transfer to the regulars or other voiskos was legally possible, but it never became a sufficient drain on the supply of officers to be considered a problem in official reports. As a decorative vestige of Cossack peculiarity, the officers were permitted to retain the traditional names for ranks below colonel (polkovnik). An officer started as a khorunzhyi, then might be promoted to sotnik, pod'esaul, esaul and voiskovoi starshina.[150]

Unlike the ordinary Cossack, the duration of the officer's service was not governed by any regulation that stated the length of this obligation, nor was it divided into definite active-duty and off-duty periods. True, the law of 1869 gave him the right to resign at any time, but not many younger officers seem to have availed themselves of this option. Few had alternative careers before them, and it required time in service to win a land allotment and more time to gain sufficient promotion to have a good-sized allotment.[151] In the Don, Orenburg and Ural voiskos, the life of the typical Cossack officer alternated between three or four years on active service in the first turn and roughly the same period in off-duty status. In guards units and the other voiskos, all officers were on active service throughout their careers.[152] The obvious consequence of this system was that the Cossacks did not have enough officers to man the second and third turns in case of mobilization. True, most units in peacetime maintained a larger officer complement than was required by the wartime table of organization, so some officers would be transferred from the first turn to the second or third turns in time of need.[153] And in the Don, Orenburg and Ural voiskos, the officers on off-duty status would be called up, even though there were about half as many of them as there were vacancies in the table of organization. In 1895 the War Minister noted the shortage of officers in case of mobilization and expressed the hope that in 10 or 12 years they could afford to have enough officers on off-duty status to cope with the problem. But for the present, he acknowledged, the financial plight of the officers on off-duty status was sufficiently bad that one could not think of adding to their number. One would simply have to muddle through, filling many of the gaps with temporary promotions of noncoms to the rank of 'zauriad-praporshchik' (noncom-subaltern), a system inaugurated in 1894.[154]

The half of his career cycle in which the Don, Orenburg or Ural Cossack officer was on off-duty status was indeed not a very profitable time for the army or himself. He had to appear for a month's training camp, for which he was paid, with the second- and third-turn Cossacks, twice in the interval between tours of active duty (two out of four years in many cases). But it was agreed by contemporary commentators that his professional skills were allowed to decline.

Certainly his economic position declined, unless he was fortunate enough to be a member of the Cossack landed aristocracy. Until 1884 he received only the portion of his full salary that the voisko normally covered, one-third, which was only 138 rubles per year for the lowest rank (at a time when a Cossack horse cost about 80 rubles). In that year the officers of the Don, Ural and Orenburg voiskos who were on off-duty status began to receive full pay, but various writers continued to maintain that the Cossack officer on off-duty status could not support himself on his pay. One expressed dismay that impoverished officers became debtors of ordinary Cossacks when both were off active duty. Another, writing in 1911, by which time the economy of the country had advanced considerably, said that they tended to go to the cities and work in all manner of office jobs – a better picture for the personal finance of the officer but not helpful to his military readiness.[155]

For the War Ministry, the ultimate measure of the effectiveness of all these efforts was the ability of the Cossacks to mobilize all three turns in time of war. It was all very well to maintain some 50 000 Cossacks on active service in peacetime, but the main point of maintaining the martial estate was to provide the substantially larger force that would be required in a major emergency. The only full test of this ability in the nineteenth century came in the Russo-Turkish War of 1877–8, when the new service regulations were still a novelty on the Don and had not yet been applied to the Kuban and Terek voiskos. In the case of the Orenburg Cossacks, the new system had just come into effect, and there had not been time to convert some infantry units to cavalry, as called for in the new plan. But on balance, the new system worked well enough to please the War Ministry. The contemporary official history maintained that 'the mobilization of the Cossack units that were called up generally was executed speedily and fully justified the advance calculations ...'[156] The secret report of the War Minister was only moderately less satisfied, concluding that the experience of the war showed that the Don and Orenburg voiskos could mobilize the second and third turns with equipment on schedule, but the same could not be said for the Kuban and Terek. The Kuban could not raise the third turn; the Terek could, but in such poor condition that it was impossible to send these forces to the war zone. But these shortcomings reflected the absence of the Don model regulations on service, said the report, with some justice. The original expectation when the new Don regulation on service obligations was introduced had been that the third turn would be weak with respect to men and horses, so any successful mobilization on that level came as a pleasant surprise.[157]

Statistically, the Cossack performance was impressive. Before mobilization in 1876 there were 1872 Cossack officers and 51 489 enlisted men on duty; at the peak of mobilization, in July 1878, when war with the Western powers was feared, there were 3672 officers and 140 882 enlisted men in the active ranks. The Cossacks, when mobilized, constituted 70 per cent of the tsar's cavalry, roughly 120 000 Cossacks and 50 000 regulars. True, only about 11 000 Cossacks were present in the Balkan theatre of operations, but this was explained by the need for the Astrakhan, Kuban and Terek voiskos in the Caucasian zone and the general difficulty in transport and logistics in the Russian Empire.[158]

The War Ministry had to make various practical concessions in the course of mobilization. It permitted the Don to deliver 10 rather than the requested 20 regiments of third-turn cavalry and allowed both the Kuban and Orenburg voiskos to substitute some infantry units for the cavalry that was wanted. Indeed, there was a general shortage of horses, or suitable horses, in the third turn, and in the Don the ministry waived its usual requirements concerning the size of the horse. It was also expedient to accept substandard uniforms. In the mobilization on the Don, only one set rather than two was deemed acceptable, and the Kuban troops of the second turn were permitted to wear their own clothes. This means that they all wore the cherkeska, though not of uniform design. Officers were in particularly short supply in the Kuban, Terek and Orenburg voiskos; regular army officers had to be used to obtain the minimum needed in the Kuban. The formation of supply trains was improvised and shaky. In their former status as irregulars the Cossacks had rarely had a wagon-train for logistical support. Now they were ordered to have eight-days' dry provisions, and wagons were needed, although nothing had been prepared. Various emergency expedients were tried, such as buying wagons from German colonists, but the problem was never solved systematically. Speed of mobilization varied widely, depending to a considerable degree on the existence of telegraph and rail links. Don units of the second and third turns were able to board trains for transport towards the Balkans from two to four weeks after call-up. In the Orenburg and Ural voiskos, however, there were serious difficulties, particularly when regimental commanders were late in appearing, which occurred in Orenburg. Finally, there were many Cossacks who simply could not afford to report for service and had to receive subsidies from the voisko or stanitsa. This most often involved the purchase of a horse despite the theory that they maintained their horse throughout their reserve duty in the second turn. This could be a serious problem even among the Dontsy, who on the whole performed well. The southern part of the voisko territory, around Novocherkassk, was extremely short of horses and its Cossacks required an average of 75 rubles each in aid. About half a million rubles were dispensed throughout the Don and 100 000 among the Orenburg Cossacks (less elsewhere), a substantial drain on the assets of the voisko.[159]

The difficulties were serious, but few mass mobilizations ever go smoothly, and the War Ministry was justified in thinking that the Cossacks had done relatively well. The Don aristocrat, N. Krasnov, conveyed this in his recollection of his own experience in taking command of two Don regiments:

> Before they were organized into sotnias and regiments, along with the Cossacks who had been designated for service, sat their fathers, mothers, wives, and children; around the service mounts, nibbling on hay that had been carried from their homes, stood wagons, loaded with food supplies ... Looking into their animated faces and considering their morale, talking with elders and young Cossacks who had been called to service, we noted with satisfaction that the majority of Cossacks on off-duty status came very willingly to service, without regret abandoning their farms, especially so considering that the Khoper [region] Cossacks had suffered serious losses in farming in the previous years.[160]

But Krasnov acknowledged that there had been a certain 'roughness' in the mobilization of the Cossacks generally. To attempt to smooth this out and introduce a higher degree of regularization was a major goal of the War Ministry, which devoted special efforts to this task in the late 1880s and early 1890s. In 1888 a new section of the Main Administration of Cossack Forces was established to deal with mobilization, and later in the same year it ordered that all Cossack voiskos should establish 'atamans of the military otdels' to take responsibility on a regional scale within the voisko for the induction of conscripts and mobilization of the second and third turns in time of need.[161]

In 1889 the presence of the new office dealing with mobilization was evident in the trial mobilization of four Don cavalry regiments and two artillery batteries of the second turn. The results were deemed fairly satisfactory, although the quality of the horses was not what it should have been, and 4 per cent of the troops turned up with no horse at all. As a result of this experience, the War Ministry conducted a series of trial mobilizations, including units from all the voiskos of European Russia. Most ambitiously, in 1895 two Don, one Kuban and one Orenburg regiments of the second turn were sent to Smolensk to join large-scale manoeuvres as a 'Composite Cossack Division'.[162] There was also a new concern for logistics; for example, a plan was drawn up in 1894 to provide 36 cartridges per trooper and a supply of spare horseshoes.[163]

The two most important innovations to emerge from this concern with smooth mobilization came in 1892. Both of these schemes were involved in the 'link' (zveno), consisting of three regiments (or separate sotnias), one from the first turn, one from the second and one from the third. Since 1888 these triads had been formed on a regional basis; for example, in the Cherassk otdel the 7th Don regiment was on permanent active service, the 22nd formed the second turn and the 37th regiment the third.[164] In a more populous district there might be more than one of these triads, but in all cases they had a distinct territorial basis.

On 26 April 1892 the War Ministry established in the voiskos of European Russia a system to provide replacements for casualties in time of a war serious enough to bring about at least the partial mobilization of the second turn. This was possible because the number of Cossacks eligible for service, even after deducting those who were excused for some reason, exceeded the requirements of the units raised in European Russia.[165] The new regulation provided that for every mobilized cavalry regiment or infantry battalion (including those in the first turn), there should be one reserve sotnia to replace losses. This reserve unit should be formed from four categories of personnel: (1) young Cossacks just coming due for active service; (2) Cossacks of the second turn who previously had been excused from active duty; (3) Cossacks of the second turn who were not enrolled in the table of organization of any unit as a result of the general surplus of eligible men; (4) members of the third turn.[166]

In case of partial mobilization of the second turn, no men from that source were to be used in reserve, to prevent the breaking-up of supposedly ready units. To complete the considerable complexity of this concept, the reserve sotnia was to be formed within the same link as the regiments or battalions that they were to back up. Because of its complexity, it is not surprising that there were difficulties in implementing the scheme in practice during the Russo-Japanese War and the revolution of 1905, when there was a full Cossack mobilization. Official figures for the beginning of 1906 show only eight reserve hundreds of cavalry and infantry, when in theory there should have been 124.[167]

The second major innovation in dealing with mobilization which was introduced in 1892 attempted to use some of the officers of the Don who were on off-duty status to assist in mobilization planning and management. This system, like the plan for reserve hundreds, was also based on the link of three regiments. Each first-turn regiment was to include in its command two senior and two junior deputy commanders (with the rank of voiskovoi starshina). However, only one senior and one junior deputy commander would be with the regiment; the other pair would be on active service in the home territory of the link, serving full-time (paid by the voisko, not the state treasury) as 'staffing supervisors' (zaveduiushchii ukomplektovaniia), under the aegis of the okrug ataman. This latter official would, as before, have ultimate responsibility for administering mobilization arrangements. But in the new system, unlike the old, he would have trained full-time specialists to deal with the maintenance of lists, inspection of troops at annual assembly and a multitude of other details in peacetime. The deputy commanders would rotate on a four-year basis from their duty on the Don and with the regiment in, let us say, Odessa, remaining part of the same link at all times. In case of mobilization, all four deputy commanders would be concentrated on the Don, two of them becoming regimental commanders of activated second- and third-turn regiments in the link, the other two their deputies. The first-turn regiment would still have a deputy commander because there was a fifth deputy commander in the first-turn regiment who did not participate in the new rotation. In the entire Don oblast there were 34 of these new officers who were responsible for mobilization. In addition, each of the 17 links would contribute two lower-rank officers (sotniks) from among those on off-duty status to assist the 'staffing supervisors'. The system was intended not only to provide much more effective management of mobilization arrangements, but also to join the officer staff of each link into a more tightly-knit group, in which the senior officers, and some of the junior, had worked together both on active service and in the home district. Such an improvement was not cheap, but the War Ministry once again succeeded in passing most of the cost to the voisko. The state paid the salary of the two additional officers (deputy commanders) who would be on active duty with the first-turn regiment – on paper, a total of 34 officers at a given moment. The voisko paid the salary of about 85 officers who would be serving in the home area to improve mobilization management. The total wartime complement of officers for the entire Don was raised by only 11, from 1444 to 1455.[168] This system would have done much to improve the prospects for successful mobilization in other voiskos, and in 1894 the War Minister reported that he hoped that this would be done in the voiskos of European Russia in the course of 10 or 12 years.[169] But in fact it never was, most probably for fiscal reasons. This was surely the reason why an accompanying goal, stated in the same report, was not met: to create outside the Don a pool of officers on off-duty status equal to about 40 per cent of the wartime table of organization.[170]

The War Ministry also sought to improve the utilization of Cossacks over the age-limit of the third turn (32) in case of mobilization. In 1896 the goal of the planners in St Petersburg was ambitious. The Cossacks of the reserve category (aged 32–7) should be formed into regiments of a 'fourth turn', and members of the general levy (to the age of 43) should also be formed into shadow regiments. Apparently the authorities had second thoughts about the wisdom of increasing the Cossack military obligation to this extent, and when a law actually emerged in 1902 it merely required that the men of the reserve keep their uniforms and equipment (not horses) in readiness.[171]

Still another problem concerning mobilization was the provision of horses to Cossacks of the third turn, who were not obliged to maintain mounts in peacetime. After taking a census of the equine population of the Don, Kuban and Terek voiskos in the early 1890s, the ministry concluded that something should be done and in 1896 considered a proposal to impose a special tax on members of the third turn in order to pay for new horse-breeding facilities. But the next year it retreated from such an increase in the burden of military service and issued a law that did nothing in peacetime and would partially transfer to the voisko the cost of providing horses to the third turn in case of mobilization of the Don, Kuban and Terek forces. According to this law, the horses for the third turn would come 'mainly' from 'the Cossack population', a formulation that neither produced usable animals nor imposed any specific obligation on the Cossacks of the third turn. The law implicitly recognized this weakness, for it went on to state that if the Cossacks could not provide enough horses, the state would requisition them from non-Cossacks living in the Don, Kuban and Terek voiskos, the state compensating their former owners and the voisko reimbursing the state. A horse shortage, actual or ostensible, was therefore in the interest of the Cossack of the third turn, who could avoid this major purchase if state requisitions were required.[172] Attempting to deal with the actual supply of horses in these voiskos, the ministry in 1901 supposedly obliged each Kuban and Terek stanitsa to establish a breeding facility, and in 1905 issued an extremely detailed law on this matter for the Don.[173]

Even to oblige the Cossacks of the second turn to maintain suitable horses while on off-duty status was a struggle for the War Ministry and the lower authorities. The Cossacks who were finishing their active service in the first turn, if they owned a horse that could pass inspection, were tempted to sell it, replacing it not at all or with an inferior specimen, or swapping it, along with a cash consideration, for the inferior horse of a Cossack who had to go on active service. A law of 1890 attempted to forbid such practices among the Dontsy, and the following year the press reported that a Cossack named Danilov had been sentenced to three years of additional service because he sold his horse and did not replace it when he finished the first turn. The culprit Lobachev, who sold his horse when starting the second turn, was given another because he could not afford to buy one and proceeded to sell that horse as well. He was sentenced to four years of additional active duty. The uriadnik Leonov sold his horse when entering the second turn and gave an 'impudent explanation' to the ataman of the stanitsa when the latter confronted him. He was merely demoted to Cossack, and it is not clear that he ever did buy a new horse. The authorities in the stanitsa of Romovskaia became convinced that such difficulties were the result of vodka and billiards and decreed that no Cossack of the second or third turn who lacked the obligatory equipment and mount could enter a tavern or billiards hall.[174]

These were the trivial signs of a major problem: the efforts of the War Ministry to regularize the Cossacks had passed the point of diminishing returns. The burden of military service under modern conditions was beyond the means of the pre-modern Cossack economy, and the state would be in danger of undermining the usefulness of the martial estate if it continued to press the kind of demands that it had imposed on the Cossacks in the last quarter of the nineteenth century.

MOBILIZATION AND IMMOBILITY

Throughout the 1890s the annual reports of the War Ministry, published and secret, gave no indication that the Cossack system of military service faced any serious problem. Year after year the inspection of the new class joining the first turn revealed satisfaction with the contribution of almost every voisko.[175] The beginning of a recognition that there was indeed a problem came in 1898 with the appointment of a new War Minister, Gen. A. N. Kuropatkin, and his response to a report from the assembly of the Don nobility.[176] Kuropatkin quickly appointed the Don Cossack General N. A. Maslakovets to lead a commission to investigate the economic threat to the fulfilment by the Dontsy of their military obligations. Starting work in January 1899, this commission filed its report to the War Minister the following August, and convinced him that there was indeed a serious problem: changes in the military obligation would be necessary to overcome the economic difficulties. The main recommendations of the commission concerning ameliorations in the system of service were reduction of the active-duty force, reduction of the obligations of the preparatory category and the second and third turns, payment of 100 rubles to each Cossack starting active duty to assist him in purchasing a horse and a 12-year loan at 4 per cent to assist him in paying for his equipment.[177]

Before taking action on these proposals, Kuropatkin decided to inspect the Don in person and did so for about a month in the spring of 1900. Without commenting on the human side of the poverty that he encountered, Kuropatkin concluded that 'if measures are not taken, the Don Cossacks soon will be unable to fulfil their military obligation ... The situation is undoubtedly alarming.'[178]

He then established another commission, chaired by the ataman of the Astrakhan Cossacks, to consider ways of reducing the burden of military service for the Dontsy. This cautious body recommended only one change, which was enacted in 1901 on a temporary five-year basis: Cossacks of European Russia in the second turn need attend only one summer training camp in four years instead of three, and in the third turn none at all.[179] The War Minister himself was willing to go further and in the same year enacted another, probably more important change: each Don Cossack should receive 100 rubles upon starting the first turn to enable him to buy a horse, the cost of which was generally estimated to be not much over this figure at the time.[180] In 1904 this was extended to the Kuban, Terek and Orenburg voiskos, although the Orenburgtsy received only half as much.[181] Only one other amelioration of Cossack military service appeared in the first four years of the century. It had no major economic impact, but was a fitting symbol of the retreat of the War Ministry from its former goal of making the Cossacks virtually indistinguishable from regulars. In 1903 a law ruled that Cossacks were permitted to serve with uniforms and equipment that did not match. For example, the law explained, one might wear a greatcoat and hood of different colours, or various other items might depart from the prescribed forms, providing that they served their purpose.[182]

The Japanese attack on Russian forces in Manchuria in February 1904 sorely tested the very weaknesses in the Cossack system with which the authorities had been concerned. The location of the fighting, remote from the populous parts of the Empire, posed the same problem for the Cossack forces as it did for the army as a whole. The voiskos of Russian Asia were relatively small, hardly able to contribute much of what was needed to deal with a large and modern Japanese army, but the second and third turns and even part of the reserve category of the Amur, Ussuri, Zabaikal and Siberian voiskos were mobilized in February 1904.[183] For these units, it was the second mobilization in four years. They, along with the second- and third-turn units of the Semirechenskoe voisko, had been mobilized from the summer of 1900 until the following summer in connection with Russia's participation in the European campaign against the Boxer Rebellion in China.[184] In April 1904 four Orenburg and two Ural second-turn regiments were mobilized, but it was only after the Japanese victory at Mukden in February 1905 that the regime called up any second-turn units of the more westerly voiskos.[185] In March 1905 a total of 14 regiments from the Don, Kuban and Astrakhan voiskos were mobilized, as well as five additional Orenburg and Ural regiments, which meant that there were on active service by the spring of 1905 25 regiments of the second turns from the voiskos to the west of Ural'tsy.[186] Of these, the equivalent of about 15 reached the general area of the war by the end of the conflict or shortly thereafter, not all of them serving in regimental order. The most noteworthy Cossack force in the war was a Don Cossack cavalry division of four regiments, which served as a separate command under the supreme command in the war zone. Also present in the area of the Japanese war were the equivalent of five or six infantry battalions and a few artillery units from voiskos west of the Ural'tsy.[187]

The war with Japan ended in August 1905, but by this time the rebellious people of the Russian Empire were superseding the Japanese as the main enemy of the tsarist regime, which continued to mobilize second-turn and even some third-turn units of the European voiskos. There was one major call-up in July–August of at least nine Don, Kuban and Terek regiments and another in November 1905–January 1906, involving at least nine Orenburg and Astrakhan regiments, along with six Kuban infantry battalions and six separate Don sotnias.[188] In the chaos of the time, the War Ministry seems to have missed making a permanent record of some of its orders, so the count is not wholly reliable. In any case, the War Minister subsequently reported to the tsar that as of the opening of 1906, all of the second-turn regiments of the Don, Kuban, Terek, Astrakhan, Orenburg and Ural voiskos were on active duty, along with 12 third-turn regiments and all of the Kuban infantry. The call-up was so large that there were not enough Cossack officers to command it, and 48 regular army officers had to be assigned temporarily to Cossack units.[189]

Beginning in January 1906, the second- and third-turn units of the Siberian and Amur voiskos started demobilization, and by May all of the mobilized units from the Ural voisko and those to the east had returned to off-duty status, excepting two Ural regiments and three Zabaikal sotnias.[190] But in the first half of 1906 none of the second- or third-turn units of the Don, Kuban, Terek or Astrakhan voiskos was demobilized, even if they had been in the Japanese war, and six more Don and Orenburg third-turn regiments were called up in January 1906.[191] Having gained the upper hand domestically at the end of 1905 with the suppression of the Moscow uprising, the regime wanted to keep a large Cossack force available in European Russia until the threat of revolution receded to a low level. Consequently the first demobilization of Don, Kuban and Terek second- or third-turn units did not occur until July 1906 when the Kuban infantry went home.[192] In the autumn of that year eight third-turn regiments of the Don, Astrakhan and Orenburg voiskos returned to off-duty status, but at the opening of 1907 there were still 37 second-turn regiments and six separate sotnias on active duty.[193] The War Ministry was unhappy about keeping these men on protracted service and wanted to replace about 12 000 of them, who normally should have graduated into the third turn by 1907, with about 6000 Cossacks of the preparatory category, paying each of the latter a bonus of 100 rubles. It also proposed the demobilization of a quarter of the activated forces each month, which apparently implied a return to total demobilization by about the end of 1907.[194] In general the military leadership was unhappy about the mobilization of reserves or the assignments of any troops, Cossack or non-Cossack, for internal security assignment. It considered that this seriously interfered with the primary task of providing external defence and frequently protested along these lines.[195] But the tsar and his civilian ministers saw the survival of the government as the first priority and were not very obliging to the military. In 1907 only 14 mobilized Cossack regiments of the second or third turns were demobilized, leaving 23 regiments on active duty at the opening of 1908.[196] A year later there were still 11 Kuban second-turn regiments on active duty, and two of these were not demobilized until 1910. Incompleteness in the published orders of mobilization and demobilization make it impossible to present a full picture of the length of the active service imposed on each second- and third-turn unit. It is clear, however, that at least six unlucky Kuban and Terek regiments of the second turn served about four years, from the summer of 1905 until the summer of 1909.[197] On the low end of the scale, four Orenburg regiments and one Astrakhan of the third turn served only about eight to nine months, going home in August or September 1906.[198] Between these extreme cases most units, and particularly the second-turn Don cavalry regiments, had about 2½ years of mobilization.[199]

With the addition of these second- and third-turn troops, the total number of Cossacks on active duty rose from 53 563 enlisted men in January 1904, on the eve of the Japanese attack, to a peak of well over 120 000 at the beginning of 1906. Just how much over was unknown to the War Ministry owing to the absence of reliable figures from the Priamur military okrug. By the opening of 1908 the total number on active service receded to 65 816 as demobilization brought the active-duty force back to peacetime levels.[200]

Where did these reinforcements serve after the end of the war in the Far East? Among the nine military okrugs west of the Urals, the largest increase, comparing 1 January 1904 and 1906, was in the Caucasian okrug, which gained over 11 000 men, or 34 per cent.[201] The violence of the insurrection among the mountaineers required this even though the Caucasian military okrug had the largest number of Cossacks on duty of all the okrugs before the turmoil started. The next two largest reinforcements were in the Kazan and Moscow okrugs: over 8000 men each. Because these okrugs lay in the interior of Russia they did not play an important role in plans for the defence of the frontiers and therefore had under 1000 Cossacks each before the revolution of 1905. The reinforcement, reflecting both worker and peasant insurrection, was therefore a vastly larger percentage increase than the one in the Caucasus, on the order of tenfold. The Don oblast, itself a military okrug, was the next largest gainer between January 1904 and January 1906. Although it was the home of the largest concentration of Cossacks in the Empire, it was not an area in which very many of them performed their military service in normal times. But it was also home to a substantial number of miners and factory workers, who were making this period a most abnormal time; hence this reinforcement. Four of the other five military okrugs of European Russia gained about 2000 Cossacks each, the Odessa okrug somewhat more: 3200.[202]

The War Ministry referred to the activities of these Cossack troops in this period not as 'counterrevolution' but as 'service within the Empire'. It is well known and generally agreed that the Cossacks played a major role in the suppression of the revolution of 1905, but it is remarkably difficult to document this systematically. One reason for this is the reticence of tsarist officialdom to write anything that would enlarge the image of the revolution, which so embarrassingly revealed the hostility to the regime of so much of the populace. While there is a 16-volume official history of the Russo-Japanese War, there is not even a small published study under the auspices of the War Ministry about the more successful overlapping campaign against the revolution. As for the Cossacks themselves, they were divided in their attitude to the revolution, but generally unanimous in their embarrassment about the amount of blood they had shed within the Russian fatherland. While Cossack voiskos and regiments often sponsored official histories glorifying their exploits in various wars, there was no disposition to produce such literature concerning their 'service within the Empire'. Nor were the victims of this action and their heirs, the large Soviet historical establishment, more inclined to write about Cossack repression of the revolutionaries. The reason for this reticence seems to be the embarrassment of the revolutionaries concerning the effectiveness of even small numbers of Cossacks against much larger numbers of revolutionaries. There is a large body of Soviet publications providing eyewitness accounts of revolutionary events from 1905–7, but it is hard to find in it even brief allusions to the clashes between Cossacks and workers or peasants.

One minor episode that illustrates the fear that the Cossacks inspired in revolutionaries appears in the memoirs of a participant in the public funeral procession of the Bolshevik N. E. Bauman in Moscow in October 1905. Some reactionaries sought to break up the proceedings merely by shouting 'Cossacks! Cossacks!' but on this occasion 'a calm voice' frustrated the attempt by calling out, 'Comrades, keep calm! This is a provocation. You are protected by a combat team!' But the memoirist leaves the clear impression that the reactionaries were right in believing that the mere name 'Cossack' might have been enough to scatter the funeral procession.[203]

There were enough cases in which the Cossacks really did appear, for example, in the Odessa okrug, where a force of only 33 Cossacks commanded by an uriadnik easily dispersed a crowd of 300 peasants who were armed with pitchforks, clubs and revolvers, or the 100 Astrakhan Cossacks who needed only their nagaikas to disperse a demonstration estimated at 1000 in the city of Astrakhan.[204]

It is not only the embarrassment of War Ministry, Cossacks and revolutionaries concerning the events of 1905–7 that inhibits research on Cossack military action in this period. The operations were scattered and often fragmented into small units, sometimes combining Cossack forces with police or soldiery. For example, in December 1905 a particular sotnia of Astrakhantsy was divided into two commands, one of which deployed 25 men on one estate belonging to the Naryshkins, 15 on another of their estates, 5 in the hamlet of Dubovo, 45 in the town of Gusevsk and 5 on the Chikhaev estate. The other command posted 7 in the village of Gregorevka, 29 in Mikhailovsk and 8 on the Satin estate.[205]

Such small details, sometimes called 'flying squads', frequently moved around to deal with fresh outbreaks. The 3rd Don Ermak Timofeevich Regiment, for example, was not together in one place for three and a half years. In 1905–6 its first sotnia moved from Riga to Mogilev and vicinity, the second and sixth to Vilno and various points in Kovno guberniia, the third all over Kurland guberniia, the fourth to Smorgon and Vitebsk and the fifth to Gomel and several nearby places.[206]

It was not really a military campaign but a series of brawls between Cossacks who were usually mounted and better armed than their adversaries. Whether they were better organized and led was sometimes questionable. Because there were not enough officers to command all of the small units that were sent here and there, and because of a traditional penchant for looting, the conduct of the Cossacks was sometimes as riotous as that of the perpetrators of the 'disorders'. In Kazan, for example, Cossacks with nagaikas charged a meeting at the university. After a bomb was hurled at them from the seminary, Cossacks and regular army infantry began to fire at the crowd, killing 6 and wounding 36. Some workers replied with pistol shots. The Cossacks were drunk, they shot randomly, especially at the windows of the university, the seminary and 'the old passage'. There were no officers in sight, and the Cossacks looted a watch store and liquor store, committing much 'petty hooliganism'.[207]

If no systematic description of the Cossack campaign against the revolution is possible, perhaps the following recollection by a worker of Odessa will have to suffice to summarize hundreds if not thousands of similar encounters over a huge part of the Russian Empire in 1905–7. The memoirist was a worker in the 'Gena Factory' in Odessa, one Anton Subda, the date 13 June 1905.

In the distance a Cossack unit appeared, in front of which rode a police officer and a Cossack officer ... who proceeded through the factory gate and stopped about 20 paces away. They were quickly surrounded by the crowd. The police officer drew his revolver and threatened to shoot, but his horse was pulled down by the crowd. The Cossack officer nimbly escaped. The workers then threw rocks and the Cossacks retreated. Whistles, hoots, a thunderous roar, the cries of women and the tramp of horseshoes blended in general chaos. And we did not stand still but pursued the Cossacks ... We went as far as Shapiro's mill, the Cossacks were far ahead. Satisfied with our victory, we returned to the factory ... The Cossacks, going as far as the sugar mill, stopped and regrouped. After several minutes they appeared and, riding at a gentle trot, stopped where they had been before. A trumpeter sounded his horn, the Cossacks came forward. It seemed somehow terrifying ...
'Fire!', commanded the officer.
'Tra-ta-ta-ta-ta!', spoke the Cossack rifles.
'Comrades, brothers, don't shoot!'
'Tra-tra-ta-ta-ta-ta!', came the reply.
'Save yourselves!'
Everyone scattered in flight. Ten paces ahead of me Comrade Fedor Kirpichnik was running. He stumbled. 'Get up! The Cossacks are catching up!', I shouted to him. But in vain. A bullet had passed through his back had come out through the other side. He died instantly ... There were other corpses lying in the gate of the Liutov Factory.[208]

It was not only Cossacks in active duty units who participated in counterrevolutionary actions. The War Ministry sanctioned the formation in the Don, Kuban and Terek voiskos of 'self-defence units' on a local basis to defend Cossack settlements against insurrectionaries who in the Kuban and Terek were peasants and mountaineers and in the Don mainly peasants, for the industrial workers were the concern of units on active duty. Just how substantial this operation became is difficult to say, since it was left to local authorities and not reported to the ministry. It seems to have been a serious effort in the Don at least, because the ministry donated 60 machine-guns to the Don voisko for self-defence units, authorized the establishment of a school in the use of these new weapons and issued rifles to Cossacks who were still living at home, a departure from standard practice for a generation past.[209] An indeterminate number of Cossacks from the more westerly voiskos also served as mercenary guards for estates and factories. In at least one case, the employment was arranged by the zemstvo of Tula guberniia, making it a semi-official affair. An official historian of the Astrakhan voisko complained that the number of second- and third-turn Cossacks who had gone off for this kind of employment depleted the ranks of the mobilized units, but the authorities were satisfied that the guards existed and allowed them to stay where they were when the call-ups came. Some may have been over-age in any case and not part of second- or third-turn units.[210]

The victories that the Cossacks won against revolutionary adversaries were not free of cost. Accurate casualty figures are hard to determine, but at the end of 1907, when the serious revolutionary violence was past, the War Minister reported that a total of 3115 Cossack losses had been replaced in accord with the tsar's order of 27 October 1905, that is, well after the Japanese war.[211] Presumably this included not only the dead but also the seriously wounded, and it may have included victims of illness as well. Combat dead seem to have been few in number among the Cossacks. A ceremony in 1912 honoured 20 Don officers and men who died in Finland, presumably in connection with fighting, but commonplace action against poorly-armed crowds produced only scattered Cossack losses, such as the trooper who was killed by stones while dealing with a crowd at night in 'a Jewish district' of Odessa.[212]

Judging by Cossack complaints, casualties were not nearly as serious a problem as the mobilization of labourers in the second and third turns. In the Duma and elsewhere there was a great outcry against this hardship, even when there does not seem to have been any particular objection to counterrevolution as such.[213] Finally there was the imponderable matter of the opprobrium that the Cossacks earned among the multitude who at least sympathized with the revolution. Even a monarchist writer in the official newspaper felt obliged to deny that the Cossacks are 'evil and cruel by nature', and another conservative acknowledged that in Astrakhan city off-duty Cossacks were called 'the tsar's dogs', 'parasites', 'hired skins' (goons) and 'yellow bitches'.[214] Many Cossack spokesmen, especially in the Duma, were sensitive to such hatred, which was something new. Granted, the Cossacks had been engaged in police action before, but never on such a scale and with such widespread public recrimination.

At times Cossack dissatisfaction with counterrevolutionary assignments led to some form of mutiny. A Soviet historian counts a dozen such cases among Don Cossacks, and an American scholar has found about two dozen cases among all the voiskos.[215] Most of the units involved were members of the second and third turns, who were in general distressed to find themselves mobilized in peacetime.[216] The four most serious cases involved units of the Kuban voisko, three of them infantry, one, the most threatening of all, the Kuban Second Urupskii Cavalry Regiment. This unit expelled its officers, elected replacements, with a former uriadnik as commander, and for 54 days in December 1905–February 1906 marched unopposed around the territory of the voisko. They issued various radical proclamations and tried to make contact with other Cossack units and workers, particularly in the oil centre of Maikop, but, in the words of a Soviet historian, 'maintained a passive, temporizing position, and did not utilize a series of favourable moments to win over the pro-revolutionary masses'. A punitive force cornered the rebels, and after a four-hour artillery bombardment, they surrendered without a fight.[217]

There were a few occasions on which off-duty Cossacks not only objected to call-ups but even carried out demonstrations that might be considered pre-induction mutiny. The most famous case occurred in 1906, involving the Don stanitsa of Ust-Medveditsa, which voted against mobilization for police service, and the Cossack officer F. K. Mironov. When he was arrested, after delivering to the Duma the resolution against mobilization, 2000 Cossacks arrested a regional commander and obliged the release of Mironov.[218] The regime punished the leaders of the Cossack mutinies, but with relative lenience, considering the nature of the infractions and the number of executions that were meted out to various non-Cossack rebels in this period. The main leader of the mutineers of the Second Urupskii, their elected commander, one Kurganov, was sentenced to 20 years at hard labour and Mironov was merely deprived of his rank and dismissed from the Don voisko. There were no capital sentences among any of the Cossack revolutionaries, which suggests that the regime was loath to antagonize the martial estate, on which it depended so heavily.[219]

Prudently attempting to maintain the loyalty of the Cossacks, the regime presented them with various favours during and somewhat after the revolutionary crisis. Some of these were merely honorific. All but one of the voiskos received charters in 1906–7, thanking them for their services. The atamans of the voiskos received nasekas (ceremonial maces) and numerous banners were issued to various regiments and voiskos.[220] In 1906 a new 'composite' guards regiment was created, involving personnel from eight voiskos that, with the exception of the Ural, had not previously had a role in the guards or household convoy.[221] Individual Cossacks received decorations, too numerous to count. The men of the Ermak Timofeevich Regiment, for example, received for their counterrevolutionary actions in the Baltic 16 orders of St Anna, 29 medals 'For Bravery' and 55 'For Zealous Service'.[222]

The regime also dispensed more tangible rewards, not as much as the Cossacks wanted but more than was customary. In 1905 mobilized Cossacks of the second turn received a bonus of 100 rubles, the third turn 200, and all who had been on active duty for more than six months received a new uniform, along with a separate grant of free underclothes and sheets. Another grant went for equipment and uniforms for first-turn troops who were 'protecting order', but it represented an average of only about 8 rubles per trooper. The following year Cossacks of the first turn received a sum of similar size, but the second and third turns did much better, with a grant representing an average of about 30 rubles per capita. The families of the latter two categories also received a flat grant of 75 rubles that year, and the families of all Cossacks who had served over four years (including first-turners who had not been released on time) were promised an indemnity of 250 rubles in case of the death of their man.[223] Since 1897 a law had provided for the indemnification for the loss of horses, which was probably a greater risk than the death of the rider.[224] On one occasion, which probably was not unique, the indemnification offered by the central government was supplemented by the city government, which was hoping to inspire the morale of the counterrevolutionary forces. The Samara city officials volunteered a sliding scale of payments, from 1.15 rubles for a horse wounded in action against a mob to 75 rubles for an officer slain. In the same spirit the Vilno city authorities offered a Cossack force there gift packages containing tobacco and similar soldiers' needs, and Vitebsk guberniia, with more sense of symbolism than practicality, gave a sotnia an icon of the Saviour.[225] In addition to all this, the Cossacks were included in various morale-building ameliorations that the regime granted to the army as a whole, such as an increase in the per diem for soldiers' food.[226]

The War Ministry also sought to appease Cossack opinion by resuming its reconsideration of the terms of military obligation, a process that continued in dilatory fashion into the years just after the revolution of 1905. In that year one of the proposals of the Maslakovets Commission that had not been accepted previously received action: the term of the preparatory category was cut from three years to two, raising the age of induction from 18 to 19. In 1909 this term was cut still another year, making it merely a one-year stint starting at age 20.[227] This reduction in the total service obligation of the Cossack by two years presumably gratified the martial estate, but it was a cheap concession because it did not cut the number of active-duty Cossacks and eliminated only local-level training, which the War Ministry had in any case written off as almost worthless.[228] Another cheap concession earned the ministry no gratitude. During the period of large-scale mobilizations, there had been no summer training assemblies for the second turn, and in 1910 this exercise was cut back to three weeks for the Don and Kuban. Coming so soon after the strenuous exertions of the counterrevolutionary campaigns, this led the Cossacks in the camp to mutiny. At least 224 were jailed and then pardoned in 1912.[229] Otherwise there were only trivial concessions in the last years before the war, such as a new law on compensation for equipment and horses lost in the line of duty, reduction in the training obligation of Cossacks who were not needed to make up the first turn, provision to return to the heirs of Cossacks dead in the line of duty their horse and equipment.[230] The War Ministry considered a more serious change: reduction in the length of the first turn from four years to three, following a similar reduction in 1906 of the term of most non-Cossack draftees.[231] But nothing was decided.

This might be the epitaph for the last years before the war with respect to Imperial policy on Cossack military service. On the one hand, they had evidence that the burden of this service had to be reduced if the system were to survive. On the other hand, the revolution of 1905 had demonstrated that the regime could ill afford to diminish the Cossack force. Drawn in these opposite directions, the tsar's government was immobilized.

3   Bureaucratic-Military Governance

Казачьи области-это огромныя
казармы, с казарменным распо-
рядком, с солдатской зависимостью
от всякаго начальства обязан-
ностью строжайшаго чинопочитания,
неразсуждения и безусловнаго
подчинения.

The Cossack regions are vas
racks with barracks routine
diers' obedience to every au
ity, the duty of strictly obse
rank, unreasoning and unc
tional subordination.

F. Kriukov, 1907[1]

In understanding the governance of the Cossacks in the reigns of the last three tsars, the romantic image of the wild horseman, brandishing pike or whip, is much less apposite than the figure of the dreary bureaucrat, plying his pen at a desk in St Petersburg and never laying eyes on a rank-and-file Cossack unless he should chance to see one of the guards regiments in the street. In this era only faint vestiges of Cossack self-rule remained, as bureaucratic institutions in the centre and the separate voiskos increasingly took charge, supervising closely whatever remained of local self-rule. Although this administrative system bore some resemblance, and deliberately so, to the civil institutions of the Russian Empire as a whole, the Cossacks were the only estate to have its own governmental chain of command, which was under the War Ministry and not the Ministry of Internal Affairs, the latter being the principal authority for the non-Cossack populace. As Kriukov lamented, the Cossacks, including men, women and children, lived under a special military bureaucracy, quite apart from the military command to which Cossacks were subjected if they were on active service.

THE COSSACK AND THE LAW

The segregation of the Cossack administrative order from the one that

84

applied to the rest of the Empire is especially striking with respect to law. This is not to say that the Cossack population was subject only to martial law. An enactment of 1870 in fact placed the Cossacks under civil law, except when they were on active duty or if they violated the laws concerning their military obligation when not on active duty.[2] But the process of legislation for the Cossacks differed substantially from the pattern that applied to laws concerning other portions of the population. Even before the reforms of 1905–6, most legislation of the Empire was passed by the State Council before the tsar enacted it as law.[3] A draft law usually went first to one of several departments of the Council for review by legal experts, then to its full session. Some of the more important enactments concerning the Cossacks did follow this route, but to a large extent legislation on the martial estate was submitted not to the State Council but the Military Council. This was an assemblage of generals, mainly retired, appointed by the tsar. In 1905 they numbered 52. They were supposed to promulgate law concerning the armed forces and in general watch over the army and War Ministry. Legislation passed by the Military Council was supposed to find reflection in the *Code of Military Laws,* prepared by a codification section, which was the only bureaucratic office subordinate to the Council.[4] The comparative weight of the State Council and the Military Council in dealing with the affairs of the Cossacks is suggested by the number of laws that each produced in a reasonably representative period, the first half of 1882: 140 for the Military Council and 19 for the State Council.[5]

This peculiarity of the legislative process for the Cossacks was at least the result of conscious policy, but it was quite unintentional that the Cossacks were virtually placed outside the codified law of the Russian Empire from 1865 until the turn of the century. This was not only a unique situation among the estates of the Empire, but a serious handicap to the orderly administration of the Cossacks. M. M. Speransky's great achievement, the *Code of Laws of the Russian Empire,* which came into force in 1835, was basic to the rational administration of the country. It not only provided legal norms on a vast variety of questions, it also served as an index to the particular laws from which the code was digested. The articles of the topically-arranged code referred to the numbered, chronologically-arranged laws in the *Full Collection of Laws of the Russian Empire,* also compiled by Speransky and continued thereafter, on which any given article in the code was based. The civil code was the bible of the dutiful Russian public administrator and, by virtue of its comparative simplicity, a great boon in a country that lacked an adequate supply of well-trained bureaucrats. Parallel with the *Code of Laws*, but less comprehensive in its impact, was the *Code of Military Laws*, the first edition of which appeared in 1838.[6] This work, like the *Code of Laws*, served as both digest and index, and covered a wide range of military legal-administrative matters but not military field regulations. The governance of the Cossacks, as a martial estate, depended on both the *Code of Laws* and *Code of Military Laws*. In theory the flow of civil and military laws concerning the Cossacks should have been reflected in periodic revisions of the two codes. Responsibility for updating the *Code of Laws* was assigned to a special office of the State Council which had difficulty enough in keeping abreast of the unceasing enactment of particular laws. After 1857 no complete, official revision was ever published at one time, although various 'incomplete editions' were published officially and from the end of the nineteenth century various unofficial, complete editions were produced by entrepreneurs.[7]

Thus the bureaucrats who governed the non-Cossack bulk of the Russian Imperial population at least could rely with some assurance on the *Code of Laws* and, in military affairs, on the *Code of Military Laws*. But through administrative inadvertance the Cossacks were left outside these codes for three decades beginning in 1868. It will be recalled that in 1856 the ataman of the Don had requested a revision of the Don statute of 1835, and that the War Ministry established five regional committees to draft a modernized Cossack law for all the voiskos, a task that was transferred in 1865 to a single 'Temporary Committee for the Review of Cossack Statutes', sitting in St Petersburg.[8] In 1868 the War Ministry submitted to the Second Section of His Majesty's Own Chancellery, which routinely reviewed proposed legislation before it was submitted to the State Council, a draft of a new statute of the Astrakhan Cossack voisko. The legal section of His Majesty's Own Chancellery noted in reply that the draft did not include any indication of the changes that it would require in the *Code of Laws*. This led to an exchange of opinions between the heads of the Main Administration of Irregular Forces of the War Ministry and the Second Section of His Majesty's Own Chancellery. In December 1868 these authorities decided to suspend the inclusion in the *Code of Laws* of enactments pertaining to the Cossacks, owing to the complexity of the ongoing general review of Cossack law and the assumption that the completion of this task would enable the legal specialists to make a comprehensive codification of their work. On 5 June 1869 the tsar approved this, retroactive to 1 January 1868, no doubt with the understanding by all concerned that War Minister Miliutin would soon achieve his goal of producing modernized and comprehensive statutes for the various Cossack voiskos.[9] But matters did not work out this way. Although the Temporary Committee for the Review of Cossack Statutes produced a variety of new laws on military and civil matters, these were piecemeal. The authorities never produced a comprehensive, modernized statute for each voisko, following the precedent of the Don statute of 1835. Years passed, and the practice of omitting Cossack law from updated editions of the *Code of Laws* became an accepted norm. Moreover, the suspension of codification of civil law made it difficult to proceed with codification of military law, if only because of the problem of continually defining the distinction between the two categories. Thus, following a revised edition in 1869, the Cossack sections of the *Code of Military Laws* were omitted from that work.[10]

From an early date this was a highly inconvenient situation. In the words of the official history of the War Ministry, which was not given to hyperbolic self-criticism, 'in one section of the Administration of Irregular Forces they did not know what legal enactments had been drawn up in another'. Among the various voiskos it is fair to guess that ignorance of the pertinent legislation was even more endemic. To attempt to resist this encroaching administrative chaos (an unintended result of an attempt to rationalize administration), the head of the Main Administration of Irregular Forces ordered the publication of an annual, chronological list of all laws and quasi-laws concerning Cossacks, which could be used by administrators both in St Petersburg and the far-flung voiskos. This substantial publication, *Collection of Government Decrees on the Cossack Voiskos,* was merely a compendium of laws and quasi-laws, not a codification. Seeking to fill the evident need for a simpler synopsis of the legal picture, the Main Administration of Irregular Forces in 1878 attempted to publish its own, unofficial code in three volumes. But the job was not done very effectively, perhaps because the functionaries in the Main Administration were accustomed to leaving the work of codification to the appropriate department of the State Council, and the effort was not repeated.[11] The administrators who dealt with Cossacks perforce learned to rely on the annual collection of government decrees on the Cossacks, and its publication continued until the end of the monarchy, years after Cossack law had been reintegrated into the *Code of Laws.*

By the 1890s it seems that few remembered that the omission of Cossack law from the civil and military codes was intended to be only temporary. In any case, it was not initially a desire to wind up this business that motivated the new head of the Main Administration of Cossack Forces (as it was now called), one General Bunakov, to start the process that led to the end of the anomaly. Bunakov simply noticed that his staff was abnormally slow in getting through their work, and he appointed an internal commission to investigate. The result was a report blaming the slowness on the absence of Cossack law from the military code and the lack of any index to the annual volumes of *Collection of Government Decrees on the Cossack Voiskos,* which now constituted 45 volumes, some bound in two actual books because of their size. Some employees of the Main Administration, who no doubt had been there longer than their chief, at this point informed him that one of his predecessors, General Prince Shakhovskoi, had ordered the preparation of a subject index of the contents of the annual collection. One might expect that this job, if done well, would have satisfied the need for an index, but it seems that Shakhovskoi regarded this work as his personal property and had taken it with him when he left the office. A member of a wealthy clan, he probably paid for this index with his own funds.[12]

In any case, Bunakov took effective measures to deal with the problem. A new commission was established in 1896 to arrange the resumption of the codification of Cossack law, chaired by a general from the chancellery of the War Ministry and including representatives of the Main Administration of Cossack Forces and the Codification Department of the Military Council. As a result of their report, the Shakhovskoi index was purchased from its owner for the substantial sum of 8500 rubles and in 1896 was published in five meticulously organized volumes. With this aid, work was undertaken to provide the codified material on the Cossacks. This was no small task, partly because of the difficulty in deciding which laws should be considered civil and which military. The first fruit of this effort was the publication in 1897 of the portion of the 'Statute on Military Obligation' covered in volume four of the *Code of Laws.* This was a relatively simple task because it relied heavily on the Don model of 1875. The *Code of Military Laws,* volumes ix and x, which covered the Cossacks, proved more difficult and were finished only in 1908. Thus it was that the Cossacks were restored to full recognition in the system of laws of the Russian Empire only a few years before its demise.[13]

THE CENTRAL ADMINISTRATION

Despite the absence of codified law for many years, the authorities who ruled the Cossacks were able to issue an ample stream of individual laws, creating a centralized system of civil administration over the voiskos. This was largely the work of a relatively small number of officials, very few of them Cossacks, many of them civilian career bureaucrats, in the office of the War Ministry that specialized in Cossack affairs.

Prior to the formation of this office, responsibility for Cossack administration at the centre was entrusted to Department of Military Settlements, a body which was primarily concerned with the visionary scheme that Alexander I had started. In it there was no particular sub-office that specialized in Cossack problems, so it was hardly likely that the tsar's bureaucracy would succeed in establishing effective centralized control over the voiskos. But with the coming of Alexander II the military settlements, which had become a symbol of repression, fell into disfavour, and in 1856 the tsar decided to disband them. In August 1857 the Department of Military Settlements was reorganized as the Administration of Irregular Forces. On 8 January 1858 this body was formally inaugurated at a ceremony attended by Alexander II, his heir apparent, who was the August Ataman of All Cossack Voiskos and the younger son of the tsar, the future Alexander III. Such monarchial attention surely was not lavished on just any office that appeared in the Imperial bureaucracy. The Don ataman also attended, along with some ordinary Cossacks from the guards regiments, the only actual members of the martial estate to witness this bureaucratic celebration.[14]

In the following decades this office remained essentially the same in basic function, although its name and size altered. In 1867 Miliutin established 'main administrations' in the War Ministry, as the basic division of labour at the centre, and the Administration of Irregular Forces became one of them.[15] Then, as we have seen, the trend to regularization of the Cossacks led to the replacement of the word 'irregular' with 'Cossacks'.[16] The institution remained the 'Main Administration of Cossack Forces' until 1910, when a general reorganization of the War Ministry transformed the body into the 'Cossack Section of the General Staff'.[17] Names aside, this office of the War Ministry was the supreme authority over both civil and military Cossack affairs. By 'military' one does not mean the command of active-duty troops, but the administration of conscription, training outside extended active duty and the provision of uniforms and equipment. This was formally stated in a law of 1869, but the principle was already well established.[18]

· The body of personnel in the Main Administration grew approximately with the size of its subject, from 90 in 1867 to 199 in 1907. Then the dissolution of the Main Administration in favour of a section of the General Staff led to a reduction (mainly of clerks) to 117. This administrative body at all times had a 'commander', a general. From 1857 to 1889 he was assisted by a single deputy (colonel or major-general), then from 1889 to 1897 two deputies (the second a civil servant) and then three deputies (one a civilian). But only one of these survived the reorganization of 1910. Assisted by a small secretariat, this command directed an array of sections, which grew in number from three in 1857 to ten in 1902, then receding to six in 1910. The sections were in turn divided into 'tables' (24 in 1897). The area assigned to each section was in some cases military and others civilian, and the section chiefs were correspondingly military officers or civil servants until 1910, when the military took over entirely (a colonel and six lower officers in each section). In the military sector the general nature of the responsibilities was not, to repeat, the command of troops. Cossack units on active service reported to line commanders, such as the commander of a cavalry division, and not to the Main Administration in St Petersburg.[19]

In the civilian sector, the relatively modest number of bureaucrats exercised sweeping authority over Cossack life. The frailties of the actual administrative system on the lower levels should rule out the word 'totalitarian' in describing this power, but the annual volumes of collected laws, quasi-laws and more or less judicial rulings suggests the characterization 'bureaucratic omnipotence'. As a well-informed and dispassionate anonymous Russian writer put it in 1875, 'not one department [of the Russian state] actually has such full authority in decisions on daily life and questions of property as has the Department of Military Settlements or the Administration of Irregular Forces that was formed from it'.[20] The bureaucrats in St Petersburg not only dealt with such weighty matters as the legislation regulating the workings of the local stanitsa, they also attempted to deal with a wide variety of much lesser matters, for example: approval of the decision of the Rostov-na-Donu city duma regulation which established the price for slaughtering one piglet in the municipal abattoir at 25 kopeks; the establishment of one stipend for Cossacks at the St Petersburg Conservatory; the termination of the department of eastern languages at the Novocherkassk Gymnasium; the appointment of the Kalmyk translator to a court of the first Don okrug; the admission of non-Cossacks to the Novocherkassk insane asylum; the charter of the 'Vladivostok Association of Bicycle Sport'.[21] Granted, many of these matters were not initiated in St Petersburg, but they all had to pass through the hands of the small crew of bureaucratic employees, who carried on their unglamorous work at vast distances from the people whose lives they attempted to regulate. As a non-Cossack Russian writer put it in 1875, 'in nine out of ten cases, if not more, the opinions and decisions of the local authorities that dealt with questions of the [Cossack] estate, were approved at the highest level in St Petersburg'.[22]

This degree of centralization inevitably generated a torrent of paperwork for the Main Administration. In 1870 it received 11 169 cases requiring action, and by 1898 the number had risen to 20 671.[23] Although the administration of the Russian Empire was accustomed to centralization, the caseload of the Main Administration of Cossack Forces was regarded as excessive. Even the official history of the War Ministry speaks of the need for 'more normal' relations between the centre and the regions. On the instigation of the War Ministry, the tsar commanded in 1898 some degree of decentralization, which resulted in a flurry of (central) bureaucratic activity but little else. The Main Administration reported that decentralization could be applied only to civil matters of minor import, and a special commission claimed to show that such delegation of authority would reduce the caseload by only 84 cases per year. They also advanced an ingenious legal pretext for not doing better: some voiskos were in a limited sense administered by governors who were appointed by the Ministry of Internal Affairs. Surely these officials could not be given more authority over Cossacks than they had over other subjects? The Military Council rejected this and told the Main Administration to try again. Finally, in 1901 a new law identified 13 kinds of questions that the voisko administrations could settle on their own, for example, the fixing of funeral expenses for non-Cossacks who died in Cossack hospitals.[24] This had no significant affect on the rising tide of paper. By 1904 the caseload of the Main Administration was almost half as great again as it had been in 1898.[25]

Until 1897 there was at least some element of Cossack representation in the work of the central administration. Neither the commander of the operation nor his staff were members of the martial estate.[26] But there did exist two bodies that offered the Cossacks some chance to express their interests in the legislative activities in St Petersburg. One of these was envisaged as a permanent part of the central administration, in 1857 called the 'General Office' (Obshchee prisutstvie), renamed the 'Consultative Committee of the Main Administration of Irregular Forces' in 1867, dropping the word 'consultative' in 1869. The basic membership of this body was the head of the Main Administration, his deputy and five representatives of the voiskos. These representatives were to be selected by the (non-Cossack) ataman of their voisko, with the approval of the commander of the Main Administration, and were to serve for a three-year, renewable term. In addition, the commander of the central administration after 1869 had the right to invite an unrestricted number of other experts to join the deliberations of the committee, with voting rights. This sometimes meant the invitation of Cossacks who were supposed to be experts on some particular issue. The regular representatives of the voiskos on the committee were not considered fully-fledged state officials, receiving no remuneration from the state treasury, although the voiskos presumably supported them. They were supposed to consider every piece of proposed legislation, bringing to bear their knowledge of local conditions. This required a considerable level of activity. For example, the committee met 46 times in 1890. Originally they were explicitly deprived of any power to take decisions, but in 1882 they received the right to settle various technical questions, largely economic (e.g. the rental rates for voisko land).[27]

The other body that was integrally connected with the central administrative apparatus was the 'Temporary Committee for the Review of Cossack Statutes'. Chaired by the commander of the central administration of Cossack troops, and including a flexible number of appointees from his staff, this committee contained ten Cossack representatives: three from the Don, one each from the Kuban, Terek, Astrakhan, Ural, Orenburg and Siberian voiskos, and one from the two more easterly voiskos.[28] To assist the assumedly vast legislative work of the committee, it was given its own chancellery, consisting of personnel from the central administration. In practice, their work was the same as that of the legislative section of the Main Administration, with which this chancellery was merged in 1872.[29] As we have seen, the Don delegates on this committee actually used it as a forum in which to express their opposition to the plans of the War Ministry, the one recorded occasion when the central administration of the Cossacks encountered open resistance within its own structure.[30] The Temporary Committee ceased to meet as a separate body after its chancellery was disbanded in 1872 and was formally abolished in 1888, but three of its members, representing the Don, Astrakhan and Ural voiskos, sat in on meetings of the Committee of the Main Administration after 1872.[31]

In 1898 the War Ministry dispensed altogether with Cossack representation in the legislative process, disbanding the Committee of the Main Administration. There does not seem to have been any particular political conflict behind this move. In its internal memorandum recommending the change, a staff official of the Main Administration argued that the agency now had much greater familiarity with the voiskos than at the time of the founding of the committee, that rail transport made it possible to make direct contact with the voiskos (it took 'only' two weeks to reach the Ussuri), and that some of the delegates did not always know about all aspects of their voisko. In case of need it was possible to call for a specialist on a particular problem. This is plausible, but the fact remains that the central authorities had eliminated the one form of participation in the legislative process concerning their lives that Cossacks had previously enjoyed.[32]

THE VOISKO

The establishment of a strong central administration of Cossack civil affairs within the War Ministry reinforced the segregation of the martial estate from the rest of the population, as did the retention of special Cossack military obligations. Against this was a long-standing trend of the tsars' government to homogenize Cossack civil administration with that of the rest of the Empire. As early as 1802 the State Council opined that 'the forms of government in relation to their [the Cossack voiskos] administration have always and should always incline towards bringing them closer to the general pattern of the other guberniias'.[33] Alexander II reemphasized this point when he addressed the Temporary Committee for the Review of Cossack Statutes in 1868.[34]

If the central authorities and the ordinary Cossacks were to benefit from the assimilation of Cossack governance with that of the rest of the Empire, this could occur neither on the ministerial level nor on the local, stanitsa, level. At both the top and bottom separate Cossack civil institutions appeared necessary if the special military service were to continue. Hence, homogenization had to focus on the intermediate level, the voisko. Although the requirement of special military service also restrained homogenization on this level, various steps were possible that did not risk the merging of Cossack military command into the general state administration. Moreover, it was on the level of the voisko that the regime had the most to fear concerning Cossack particularism. It was the consciousness of being a Don or Ural Cossack, for example, that had led and could lead again to difficulties for the tsars, so it was particularly the voisko institutions that needed to be homogenized with the rest of the imperial state. But if this was the main trend in legislation on the civil affairs of the voisko, it was by no means thoroughgoing. Apart from the need to maintain the peculiarities related to military obligation, the authorities retained some residual respect for the political sensitivities of certain voiskos (notably the Don and Ural) and also found the task of drafting uniform legislation simply too difficult. The War Ministry succeeded to some degree in assimilating the administration of the voiskos to the ordinary norms of the Russian Empire, but in so doing produced a variety of inconsistencies among the eleven voiskos that existed by the end of the nineteenth century.

Before the homogenizing reforms of Alexander II, Cossack civil administration on the level of the voisko was based on the model of the Don statute of 1835. The ataman of the voisko reported only to the War Ministry, and his primary responsibility was the administration of Cossack affairs. For this purpose he had a small staff, divided into several departments, which existed to deal specifically with Cossack affairs, and there was a special Cossack court. The jurisdiction of the ataman of the voisko did not extend beyond its boundaries, and the voisko was not regarded as a subordinate part of any other subdivision of the Empire.

The key point in the homogenizing reform was the attempt to transfer to the Ministry of Internal Affairs the 'general' administration of the Cossacks (including the police and courts), leaving to the War Ministry only the management of the Cossack finances on the voisko level and military administration.[35] To expedite the working of this dual subordination it was convenient to give the same official two titles.[36] As civil governor of a territory, including both non-Cossack and Cossack inhabitants, he reported to the Ministry of Internal Affairs, but, as nakaznyi ataman of the Cossacks in the territory, the same person reported to the War Ministry on Cossack economic and military matters.

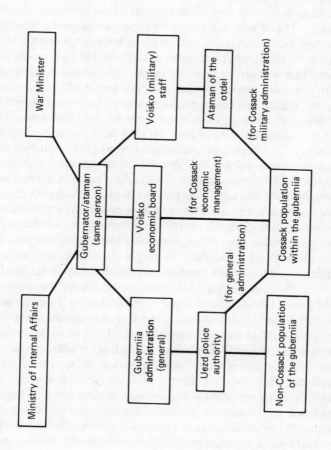

CHART I: *Voisko administration: the Orenburg model of 1865*

This basic shift in administrative principle was never applied to the Don and Astrakhan voiskos, but in 1865 the model for the new arrangement appeared in a law on the reorganization of Orenburg guberniia.[37] (See Chart I.) The title of nakaznyi ataman of the Orenburg voisko was now joined to that of the governor of Orenburg guberniia. The official occupying these posts reported primarily to the Ministry of Internal Affairs, and exclusively so on 'general' administrative matters, which was his primary obligation. He was responsible for a territory that was larger than the voisko land within it and included a majority of non-Cossacks. Moreover, the specifically Cossack apparatus on the voisko level all but disappeared. The former chancellery of the ataman, the civil and executive 'expeditions' (the archaic Cossack term for an administrative office), the medical department, the office of the procuror and the construction and survey offices vanished and their tasks were assumed by the general administrative offices of the guberniia, which conformed to the standard pattern of the Empire.[38] Police authority, the basic control that the tsars exercised through the office of governor-general or governor, over the entire guberniia was on the standard lines. It made no special provisions for Cossacks, relying on the same police apparatus, under the Minister of Internal Affairs, that dealt with the populace at large. This consisted of a police superintendent (ispravnik) and his staff on the level of the uezd, which was a subdivision of the guberniia. In addition, the new judicial institutions of 1864 replaced former Cossack courts. Like the peasants, who retained special volost courts, the Cossacks continued to maintain their own courts on the corresponding level, the stanitsa.[39] Had it not been for the special military obligations of the Cossacks, the new form of voisko administration would have included no specifically Cossack institutions. But the task of maintaining service rosters, holding summer training assemblies and managing arsenals was beyond the competence of the normal guberniia bureaucracy, as was the task of managing the financial affairs of the voisko, which held land and other assets and had to pay various bills.[40] Consequently there remained in the administration of the Orenburg guberniia a 'voisko economic board' to tend the special economic affairs of the Cossacks and a 'voisko staff' for the military responsibilities. In the Orenburg voisko the staff directed three regional subdivisions called the otdel, each headed by an 'ataman of the otdel'.[41]

This model indeed went a considerable distance towards the assimilation of Cossack governance into that of the normal guberniia. In the reign of Alexander II the authorities tried to apply the Orenburg model to most other voiskos, and in general succeeded, despite many inconsistencies in detail. For example, when the Kuban and Terek voiskos appeared in 1860, the result of a rearrangement of the former Black Sea and Caucasian Line voiskos, the new voisko territories were not parts of a larger guberniia or oblast, as the Orenburg voisko was a part of Orenburg guberniia. In fact, part of the Kuban voisko was outside the new Kuban oblast in the adjacent Black Sea oblast. The same person held the office of oblast commander and nakaznyi ataman of the voisko, but it was impossible to say which office was an appendage of the other.[42] And the judicial institutions varied among the voiskos because the reformed courts were not installed in their fullness simultaneously throughout the Empire.[43]

Then there were small anomalies concerning the structure of what little remained of the exclusively Cossack administration. In the Siberian and Zabaikal examples there was no military staff, its functions transferred to the staff of the military okrugs in which the voiskos were located.[44] In the Semirechenskoe and Amur voiskos there were no subordinate military otdels within the voiskos. In the Amur voisko the tiny economic board was saddled with police authority, no doubt because there was little alternative police apparatus in this remote and unpopulous area.[45] The economic boards were not quite identical in structure, and in the case of the Ural voisko there was after 1874 a major anomalous institution, an implied tribute to potential rebelliousness of the Ural'tsy. This was, as a supplement to the economic board, a 'general congress of delegates', consisting of 62 representatives from stanitsa assemblies of household heads, one delegate from the clergy and one from the non-Cossack populace of the voisko.[46] Although the general congress could only advise the economic board, it was specifically empowered to consider a wide range of important issues in the life of the voisko, including fisheries, land use and the peculiar Ural practice of 'hiring' Cossacks for active service. Moreover, the congress elected from its midst three 'deputies' to serve on the economic board, and every three years it joined with the officers and civil servants of the voisko (numbering 60 to 70) to elect three other members of the economic board (two councillors and the treasurer). This meant that all the members of the board except its chairman, whom the ataman appointed, were elected with the participation of delegates of the ordinary Cossacks, a privilege found nowhere else.[47] This substantial degree of representative self-government did not last long. As we have seen, the Ural Cossacks, troubled by the new military obligations, boycotted the elections to the general assembly when it came into being in 1874.[48] The authorities chose not to wait indefinitely to see if the dissatisfied Ural'tsy would change their tactics and use the congress to pack the economic board with dissidents. In 1880 a new law provided that the ataman himself should chair the board and appoint a majority of its members.[49] The general congress, with its three deputies to the economic board, survived, but the leadership seems to have been retained by the members of the starshina or in any case higher officers. By 1898 only one of the 27 chairmen of the congress had been an ordinary Cossack and all the others were men of considerable rank. Nevertheless this assembly remained to some extent an authentic organ of self-government, in which minorities periodically proposed such heretical ideas as the reduction of the military obligation, and many practical matters concerning fisheries were settled.[50]

Why was the Orenburg model of homogenization not applied to the Don voisko? The sensitivities of the Dontsy probably had something to do with this, although in truth their traditions were little respected as matters worked out. Most likely the key point was that the War Ministry was reluctant to yield civil control of so important a territory. True, a superficial change in names paid tribute to the concept of homogenization. The old label 'Land of the Don Voisko' (Zemlia Voiska Donskago), with its implications of autonomy if not nationhood, yielded in 1870 to 'Oblast of the Don Voisko' (Oblast' Voiska Donskago) 'to conform to the terms generally used in the Empire'.[51] But this was not a voisko that happened to coincide territorially with a normal civil oblast, as in the Kuban and Terek, much less a voisko that was but a portion of some larger, non-Cossack territory, as with Orenburg. The 'voiskovoi nakaznyi ataman' of the Don (as he was called from 1865, restoring the honorific 'voiskovoi', which had been dropped in 1836) did not hold this title concurrently with some non-Cossack administrative label, as did all the other voisko heads except Astrakhan. However, he continued to have the rights of a governor-general and was the commander of the Don military okrug.[52]

Unlike the other voiskos, excepting Astrakhan, the Don ataman reported only to the War Ministry. This applied not only to the military affairs of the voisko (handled by the 'voisko staff', headed by the 'chief of staff for the Don voisko') but also to general civic administration, including police and economic matters.[53] (See Chart II.) This was in the hands of a relatively substantial voisko bureaucracy (in 1875, 72 rank-holding civil servants), which had as its primary responsibility the

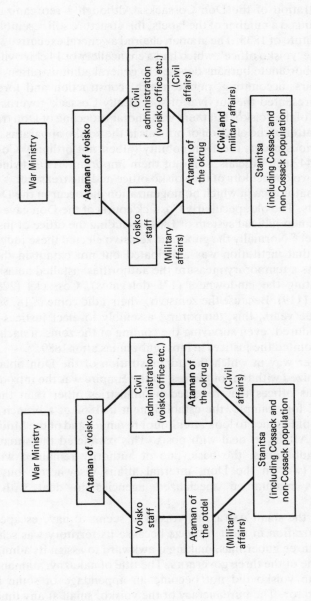

CHART III: *Don voisko after 1885* (Kuban and Terek after 1888)

CHART II: *Don voisko before 1885*

administration of the Don Cossacks. Although a reorganization in 1870 changed a number of the labels, this structure still resembled that of the statute of 1835. The ataman chaired a general executive council, called the 'voisko office', which had a chancellery of 14 chinovniks and seven subordinate bureaus devoted to general administration, economic affairs, accounting, public health, construction and forestry.[54] This represented the survival of specifically Cossack governance on the level of the voisko, but there was a notable decline of Don tradition in the matter of the election of officials in the voisko apparatus. Under the previous order, the Don nobility (albeit not ordinary Cossacks) elected 44 such officials, some of them important. This dwindled in 1870 to two councillors of the voisko office and the treasurer.[55]

One major area in which homogenization did occur in the Don was the courts. The old, peculiarly Cossack courts of the Don gave way to the reformed judicial system of 1864, including the office of justice of the peace.[56] Normally the guberniia zemstvo elected these judges, but in 1870 that institution was anticipated but not extant in the Don oblast. As a temporary measure the authorities installed an assembly representing the landowners (175 delegates), Cossacks (228) and peasants (119). Because the zemstvo, when it did come in 1875, lasted only three years, this 'temporary' assembly to elect justices of the peace endured, even surviving the coming of the zemskii nachal'nik, who appointed the justices in most guberniias after 1889.[57]

Another way in which the administration of the Don oblast was homogenized with that of the rest of the Empire was the introduction of various offices that reported to ministries other than the War Ministry, for example, the establishment in 1862 of a branch of the Ministry of Finance to look after liquor revenues and of the Ministry of Internal Affairs to deal with posts. This paralleled the situation in normal guberniias: the basic line of authority remained with the ministry (war in the Don, internal affairs elsewhere), but other ministries maintained specialized agencies to deal with their interests.[58]

As for the small Astrakhan voisko, it seems to have escaped civil homogenization in most respects because its territory was scattered through three guberniias, making it awkward to assign its administration to one of the three governors. The title of nakaznyi ataman of the Astrakhan voisko did not become an appendage of some higher administrator. The bureaucracy of the voisko, small at any time, was not deprived of an 'executive section' along with an economic one, meaning that it still held responsibility for general administration. The normal police apparatus under the Ministry of Internal Affairs did not take over in the voisko, which maintained two districts (otdel), each headed by a commander who exercised police, economic and military control. The judicial affairs of the voisko were, however, brought into line with the reformed imperial system.[59]

The sum of the efforts of the War Ministry to obey Alexander II and homogenize the civil administration of the Cossacks with the normal pattern of the Empire thus produced a substantial, if uneven, result. In the reign of Alexander III, the same authorities set about undoing much of their former labours, and in this also achieved a substantial, still less uniform result. The initiative for this change appears to have come from the War Ministry and the Cossack administrators reporting to it. In the annual report for 1884, the War Minister noted that the aim of legislation in the previous 15 years had been to end the isolation of the Cossacks. 'Experience, however, showed that the issuance of these [reforms] in many cases did not suit the tasks of the military department and the requirements of the Cossack population as an estate, the main obligation of which is military service.'[60] He went on to report that the commander of the Caucasus military okrug had requested that the Kuban and Terek voiskos be placed under the sole administration of the War Ministry. As in the Don, this authority rather than the Ministry of Internal Affairs should supervise civil administration, acting through the commander of the military okrug, who would assume the title 'voiskovoi nakaznyi ataman'. The tsar approved the establishment of a commission, meeting in Tiflis, starting in December 1884, which in only three months produced a draft law on such a change. There were various legal complexities, particularly the administration of the Cossack Moslem mountaineers, but in 1888 the new system came into force. Henceforth, the civil governance, including police authority, of the Don, Kuban, Terek and Astrakhan voiskos, embodying about 70 per cent of the total Cossack population, was fundamentally under the War Ministry. The non-Cossacks resident in these voiskos, constituting in 1890 about 60 per cent of the total population there, also lived under the general administrative and police authority of the War Ministry.[61]

In the Don and Caucasian voiskos there was an additional form of militarization of police authority over Cossacks, but not the rest of the population. This was adopted in the Don in 1885 and the Kuban and Terek as part of the reorganization of 1888. (See Chart III.) In principle this militarization of police administration had already existed in the Astrakhan voisko. Previously in the Don the entire mainstream of administration had reported to the War Ministry, but within this structure there were separate military and civil authorities on the level under the voisko. The military authority, responsible for rosters, training, arsenals, was called the ataman of the otdel (the military subdivision of the voisko) and the civil authority (corresponding to the uezd ispravnik) was called the ataman of the okrug. The former reported to the military staff of the voisko, the latter to the civil administration. This failed to satisfy the military authorities in the Don, and in 1885 the War Minister reported that the Don ataman found that the civilian character of the okrug (police) administration was undermining the martial character of the Dontsy.[62] Hence the reorganization that took effect in 1885 and was applied in the Kuban and Terek in 1888.[63] The ataman of the otdel (the former military office) disappeared, his function transferred to the ataman of the okrug. This officer now took charge of both military and police administration. The otdel was an important level of responsibility in the whole system because it was the lowest one on which professional, appointed career personnel represented the central authorities. In the Don a major-general or colonel held the job, assisted by a staff officer and two lower officers to run the military side and five civil servants to handle civil affairs. Certainly this succeeded in joining military and civil authority under military control, but it may have burdened the ataman of the okrug with more than he could handle. According to an officer who had served in this post, he had to cope personally with 50 000 paper actions a year and so could not do an effective job.[64] There also was the question of the competence of the military to deal with routine civilian business. Even in the Don, the authorities implicitly acknowledged that this was a potential problem, for in the two okrugs where non-Cossacks outnumbered Cossacks the new system did not apply. In 1885 the War Minister expressed interest in establishing the okrug ataman as a military–civil authority in the Orenburg voisko, but nothing came of this.[65] In 1891, however, a new law on the administration of the stanitsa gave the military administrator on the level of the okrug, as it was called in the Don, or otdel as it was called in the other voiskos, a modest (but arbitrary) degree of authority over the elected officials of the stanitsa. Such enhanced civil authority for the ataman of the okrug/otdel applied not only in the Don, Kuban, Terek and Astrakhan voiskos, where police authority lay with the military, but also in the Orenburg, Ural, Siberian and Zabaikal, where most civil and police authority was under the Ministry of Internal Affairs.[66]

A final point on which the policies of Alexander II were reversed under his heir concerned the right of most voisko atamans to report directly to the tsar. The absence of this right supposedly prevented the tsar from learning directly, not just through the War Minister, about the needs of his Cossacks. So in 1896 the tsar 'commanded' that all voisko atamans submit an annual report to him, a gesture that does not seem to have changed the character of the actual reports nor to have gained any real concessions to Cossack interest.[67]

By the 1890s, then, the system of administration of the civil affairs of the Cossacks on the level of the voisko had been subjected first to attempts to civilianize and thus homogenize the system, then to militarize it, making it less akin to the normal system of governance in the Empire. Neither tendency triumphed completely in its time and there was a continuing tendency to make varying arrangements to accommodate local conditions. The result was a confusing tangle and a degree of military control of civil life that many Cossacks found distressing.

THE ABORTIVE ESTABLISHMENT OF THE DON ZEMSTVO

One of the most important reforms of Alexander II was the zemstvo, which was introduced to 34 guberniias of European Russia in 1864–75. This institution provided a limited form of representative government on the level of the guberniia and its subdivision, the uezd. The guberniia zemstvo assembly was elected from among the deputies to the uezd assembly, which in turn was elected by assemblies of rural landowners, town property-owners and peasants elected by volost assemblies of delegates from communes. The first category, which approximated the land nobility, was heavily overrepresented, but the peasants were guaranteed a share in the representation. The zemstvo was entitled to levy taxes to support its work, which included roads, schools, public health and agronomy.[68] To introduce this institution to the Don oblast would be to underscore the assimilation of the civil governance of that area to the normal pattern of the guberniia, for only these units (and not borderland or Siberian administrative entities) had zemstvos. If this was negative from the point of view of Cossack particularism, this might be offset by the practical benefits that the zemstvos were expected to bring, and often did.

The record of the efforts of the government to establish the zemstvo in the Don is complex but exceptionally revealing, for it is the only substantial case in the nineteenth century when Cossack public opinion surfaced in an elected assembly. At the opening of the episode, the tsar and his chief advisers strongly favoured the zemstvo in general, were hopeful that it could be widely disseminated in the Empire, and in particular wished to see the Don adopt it. Unlike various border areas, whose doubtful loyalty made self-government a risk, the authorities regarded the Don as completely reliable. If the Don did not receive its zemstvo shortly after the basic law of 1864, it was because of legal complexities and not authoritarian ill-will. In 1865 the War Ministry asked the Don voisko committee, which was supposed to draft a new statute, to include in its work the establishment of the zemstvo, but before the end of the year War Minister Miliutin had closed this committee in order to obtain better control over the legal drafting process as a whole.[69]

In 1866 the Don ataman petitioned the War Ministry for the right to establish a special commission in Novocherkassk to take up the zemstvo question, and in January of 1867 this body began its work, chaired by the ataman. This was a gathering of 28 delegates, representing in unequal proportions all the main interests of the area: nobles with estates, nobles without estates, Cossack merchants, ordinary Cossacks, peasants and Kalmyks.[70] In the long run these interests proved deeply divided on the zemstvo question, but in 1867 they were able to agree quickly on a plan. This was forwarded to the War Ministry in October 1867 and the committee disbanded.[71] At this point the project bogged down. The central Cossack administration was working on the new system of civil governance for the voisko and wanted to see the result before passing on any particular plan for zemstvo institutions. Indeed, the new law on the civil governance of the Don, coming into force in 1870, did not mesh with the proposed law on the zemstvo, so the War Ministry asked the Don to revise it.[72] This did not represent deliberate obstructionism by the War Ministry. On the contrary, in his secret report for 1870 the minister not only affirmed his intention to introduce the zemstvo to the Don and Orenburg initially, but to all the voiskos subsequently.[73] In Novocherkassk a new commission began work in February 1871 and, like its predecessor, was able to reach agreement on a plan in short order, the draft reaching the War Ministry in 1872.[74] At this level another delay ensued, because the War Ministry and the Ministry of Internal Affairs both wanted the zemstvo to report to them. The former argued that the Cossacks were a military estate and that only the War Ministry had the necessary background to deal with them, while others argued that the Ministry of Internal Affairs, which supervised the zemstvo in all the guberniias, was the only competent authority in this matter. The issue sharply divided the Committee of the Main Administration of Irregular Forces, pitting the military officers against the civil servants. The former held a majority and at length settled the draft law in favour of subordination of the Don zemstvo to the War Ministry.[75]

In this form the law passed the State Council, which, however, failed to clear a parallel law for the Orenburg voisko, owing to technical problems concerning the handling of voisko financial assets.[76] The zemstvo of the Don oblast differed from the normal zemstvo in both the subordination to the War Ministry and its electoral system. In place of the conventional three curiae of electors for the uezd zemstvo assembly, there were four: landowners, merchants, Cossacks and peasants. In five of the seven okrug assemblies (parallel to the uezd assembly), the ordinary Cossacks held a majority. Only in the Miusskii okrug did the heavy preponderance of peasants win them the upper hand, while the landowners exceeded the Cossacks by 15 to 11 in the Cherkassk okrug. The peasants were the heavy losers in the voting arrangements, receiving only 40 okrug assembly members out of a total of 302. Except for 14 merchants' representatives, the whole affair was dominated by the Cossacks (127 representatives) and landowners (121), except in the Miusskii okrug.[77]

Another peculiarity of the Don zemstvo was the withholding from the zemstvo of the previously existing medical facilities of the oblast. These few institutions (a hospital, a pharmacy and six quarantine stations) were the property of the voiskos, for the use of Cossacks only, and interpreted by the authorities as part of the tsars' inalienable grant to the Cossack estate. The normal zemstvo took over whatever provincial medical facilities existed, but in the Don a special law of 1876 declared these to be military hospitals in perpetuity.[78] This at once faced the zemstvo with an enlarged task of building up its own medical services and ensured that the Cossacks would not see any particular need for rudimentary medical services that duplicated what they already had.

By this time some of the officers in the Main Administration had come to doubt the desirability of zemstvo institutions in the Don. Later the War Ministry was to claim that from the start it doubted the success of the new institutions and considered it prudent not to transfer these medical institutions to the zemstvo.[79] Such doubts contributed to the failure of the enterprise, but this cannot be blamed entirely on the military hierarchy. From the beginning, many ordinary Cossacks and also the nobility rejected the zemstvo plan of 1875.

At the base of this problem lay the real attachment of a great many Don Cossacks to their estate and the conviction that the tsars had granted them privileges that could not be diminished. The coincidence of the establishment of the zemstvo and the large mobilization for the Russo-Turkish War of 1877–8 no doubt reinforced this belief. A local newspaper wrote that 'the Cossacks in the past war have gained the conviction that their heroic service on the field of battle will be sufficiently rewarded by the abolition of the zemstvo on the Don'.[80] According to this line of reasoning, the Cossacks had strained their resources to provide traditional military service. In return, they should be assured their traditional separation from the 'taxed estates'.[81] But the new zemstvo imposed new taxes on all the estates. An anti-zemstvo song summed up the grievance:

Who is it, brothers, who despoils,
Loots and ravages our voisko?
Who is it, brothers, who imposes
Taxes on our land?[82]

From various localities Cossack spokesmen asserted the popular attachment to the traditional privileges of the estate: 'stanitsa assemblies see in the zemstvo tax the first move in the conversion of the Cossacks into a taxed estate'; '... the deputies from the stanitsa assemblies say that once the Cossacks have agreed to pay the zemstvo tax they would at once become a taxed estate'; '... the Cossacks considered the zemstvo tax in cash to be the soul of the capitation tax.'[83]

In reality the impact of the zemstvo on the taxation of the Don Cossacks was not so simple. Before the introduction of the new institution, the Cossacks had born the obligation known as 'zemskie povinnosti', which also applied to non-Cossack areas.[84] This included the maintenance of roads, ferries, posts, jails, storehouses for grain reserves and churches. Traditionally this was a tax rendered in labour and materials, but even before the advent of the zemstvo it was to some extent becoming a cash obligation. When the zemstvo appeared, it took over the public services supported by the 'zemskie povinnosti', and it required taxes in cash to do the job. Thus the Cossack perception that the zemstvo tax was wholly new was partly an illusion, one that was temporarily enhanced when a form of state subsidy that had been paid to assist the Cossack 'zemskie povinnosti' was suspended in 1875. The subsidy was reinstated two years later, but not before many Cossacks had formed the opinion that the zemstvo was costly to them and that it was part of a trend to diminish their privileges.[85]

The willingness of ordinary Cossacks to turn against the zemstvo was encouraged by the administration of the voisko, and especially the deputy ataman for civil affairs, General Maslakovets. Friction quickly developed between the administration and the zemstvo, for example, concerning a peremptory order to the zemstvo to deliver a specified amount of fuel for the jail.[86] Soon the official newspaper of the voisko, which was received by every stanitsa administration, was finding fault with the zemstvo and asserting that the old administration served the true interests of the Cossacks.[87]

The zemstvo leadership vainly tried to deal with the charge that the institution cost too much by urging that the state contribute more to the upkeep of the voisko. Zemstvo advocates also tried to educate ordinary Cossacks concerning the benefits of the zemstvo, with scant success. A zemstvo leader carefully explained to the assembly of the stanitsa of Novocherkassk that formerly the ferry alone had cost them 9000 rubles per year, while now they paid only 2000 and had schools, veterinarians, doctors, and so forth. 'All that is so', the Cossacks responded, 'but just the same we don't need the zemstvo!'[88]

By 1877 the zemstvo faced a Cossack tax boycott. Some 68 of the 112 stanitsas refused to pay the tax, and many sent the authorities statements such as one that requested 'the establishment of our former rights and abolition of the zemstvo, or the arrangement of things so that they never demand money from us for our land and also do not take over our land'. In 1879 the boycott spread to the election of zemstvo representatives, 34 stanitsas refusing to send delegates to the okrug-level assembly and the Khoper okrug refusing to send representatives to the oblast assembly. The zemstvo office of this okrug ruefully summed up the situation: 'the Cossacks do not recognize the legality of the taxes and consequently do not recognize the legality of the zemstvo itself ...' The authorities treated this 'mutiny' with unaccustomed lenience, arresting a few of the boycotters from the Khoper okrug, then acquitting them.[89]

The Cossacks' rejection of this form of self-rule attracted the attention of the War Ministry, which still professed to favour the adaptation of the zemstvo to the Don.[90] It encouraged the formation of a 'Special Commission for the Review of Problems concerning the Practical Application to the Oblast of the Don Voisko of the Law on Zemskii Institutions'. Chaired by General Maslakovets, this body opened in November 1879 in Novocherkassk. The three representa-

tives from the zemstvo on this commission were outvoted by the four
critics of the institution, who concluded in a report in May 1880 that:
'in the Don the zemstvo does not enjoy the sympathy of the majority of
the population ... There is no reason to count on a change for the
better in zemstvo affairs in the present conditions.'[91] Maslakovets then
attempted to undermine or destroy the zemstvo. He wrote and
published a lengthy tract to this end and prepared a petition, signed by
250, which he took to St Petersburg. His proposed 'reform' was to
abolish the zemstvo on the okrug level and to subordinate the
oblast-level assembly to the voisko authorities. The zemstvo assembly,
for its part, requested that they have direct representation on any
deliberations on their fate.[92]

The War Minister at this point was willing to accept the abolition of
the zemstvo but still hoped to find a way of adapting it to the Don. He
proposed to the Don ataman that they abolish the existing zemstvo,
wait 18 months for tempers to cool, then have a new commission
consider the problem. The ataman wanted a commission right away,
and obtained permission to arrange the election of a body that came to
be known as 'the Commission of 106'. Meeting for ten days beginning
20 November 1881, it consisted of three groups that met in mutual
isolation, one representing the peasants and merchants, one the
landowners, mine-owners, horse-ranch proprietors and the voisko
administration, and one the ordinary Cossacks.[93] The latter were
elected in the assemblies of the stanitsa, in which the Cossacks
expressed renewed hostility towards the zemstvo and fear that the
commission would somehow infringe their traditional privileges. In
several cases the assemblies at first declined to elect any deputies, and
in one the election took place only after they were reassured of their
rights by a reading of the charter issued to the Don by Alexander II in
1863.[94]

The authorities informed the Commission of 106 that it could not
recommend the reduction of the Cossack military obligation, nor the
award of any new subsidy from the state. They were, however, asked
to state what kind of executive organ the oblast should have, and this
led to an unpleasant surprise for the authorities. The Cossack group
criticized both the pre-zemstvo regime and the zemstvo for 'useless
expenditures' on such services as midwives, doctors and veterinarians,
and they went on to state that it would be

desirable if in Novocherkassk there were established an elected
economic civil administration. Along with this institution a voisko

krug [assembly] should be elected annually, consisting of one representative from each stanitsa, which should consider and decide all matters of self-government and should present our needs to the state ... It is desirable that all civil officials be elected representatives from the populace of the region.[95]

This 'considered opinion', stated the Cossack deputies, should be presented to the person of 'His Imperial Highness, the All-Merciful Lord'. To emphasize their desire to revive the myth of the free Cossack, the deputies asked for the return to the krug of 'all the regalia and all the charters by which the tsars had guaranteed Cossack rights'.[96]

A similar request emerged from the group that represented landowners. After starting with sharply divided opinion for and against the zemstvo, the speeches of the zemstvo activists persuaded a majority that to correct the former 'arbitrariness' of the Don administration some form of elected self-government was needed, and this could replace the present zemstvo. As for the peasants and merchants, they unanimously favoured retention of the zemstvo. If opponents of the zemstvo achieved a majority of two groups against one within the Commission of 106, they had unwittingly tapped the reservoirs of Don Cossack self-consciousness, antagonism towards the militarized bureaucracy and zeal for self-government. Judging by the annual secret report, the War Minister did not inform the tsar of this, nor the petition of the Cossacks, but simply concluded that they opposed continuation of the zemstvo, which was 'temporarily' suspended by a decree of 24 March 1882.[97] The voisko administration appointed new 'committees for the management of local taxes [zemskie povinnosti]' on the level of the oblast and the okrug, because somebody had to carry on the maintenance of roads, ferries, etc. These committees were minimal bodies, which were really run by a single 'permanent member' and a few clerks, quite incapable of undertaking any significant programme in the public interest.[98]

The 'temporary' suspension of the zemstvo in the Don proved eternal, but this does not mean that the War Ministry had set itself absolutely against the institution by 1882. In that year the ministry created a new commission on the question, which in 1885 recommended a body that would merely represent the voisko administration and would be consultative.[99] Nothing came of this. In 1890 a new law on the zemstvos already extant in the normal guberniias strengthened the authority of the governor at the expense of the zemstvo, and in 1894 the Ministry of Finance suggested that this model might be suitable for the Don.[100] Thus in 1896 a new commission met in Novocherkassk and produced a draft that was a slightly modified version of the 1890-model zemstvo. On receiving this proposal, the Main Administration of Cossack Forces added the idea that the voisko administration, not the local communities, pay the cost of roads, ferries, etc. While this no doubt would have appealed to the Cossacks, it threatened the solvency of the voisko, which probably explains why nothing came of it. The draft was submitted to yet a new commission in 1903, which met in St Petersburg and was quickly disbanded. By that time it appears that the opinion of most War Ministry officials was swinging against the idea of a zemstvo for Cossacks.[101]

THE CITIES

In both official ideal and practical reality, the Cossacks were not city folk. If not holding sparsely-settled border areas, they were intended to live in a setting where they could develop and maintain their skills as cavalrymen, and they were sustained in this by land grants. Nevertheless, pockets of urban development appeared within the territory of Cossack voiskos, owing to the presence of natural resources, such as coal and oil, or the growth of commerce and light industry associated with developing agriculture.

The largest concentration of urban population on Cossack territory after 1887 lay around the delta of the River Don, including Rostov-na-Donu, its close neighbour Nakhichevan (so named by Armenians who migrated from the Crimea) and Taganrog. Increasing prosperity attracted a diverse assortment of ethnic groups and legal social estates, but very few Don Cossacks. Even though the latter were close at hand, their traditions and military obligations up to the age of 38 inhibited their movement even to nearby cities. In 1900 the districts that included the cities around the mouth of the Don reported a population of over 850 000, of which only about 21 000 was Cossack. Even these people lived mainly in the rural areas outside the cities themselves.[102] If the territory of this partly urban area did not attract many Cossacks, it did engage the interest of the War Ministry, most probably because of its potential as a source of revenue. The territorial-administrative situation of this area was anomalous, an annoyance to bureaucrats in and out of the War Ministry. A roughly U-shaped strip of land surrounding the Don delta belonged until 1887 to Ekaterinoslav guberniia, which lay to the west of the Don Cossack oblast, separated from the enclave at the mouth of the Don by a strip of Don oblast territory that ran to the shores of the Sea of Azov, the Miusskii okrug. There was also an enclave within the enclave, for the actual delta of the Don (lying in the hollow of the U) belonged to the Don oblast and played an important role in the fishing rights of the Don Cossacks.

Beginning in 1838, various representatives of the Ministry of Internal Affairs proposed to eliminate the anomalous enclaves by the creation of a new guberniia, which would include the area around the delta and Miusskii okrug.[103] The War Ministry resisted this diminution of Cossack territory and in 1886 proposed instead that the Don voisko absorb this part of Ekaterinoslav guberniia. It was now the turn of the Ministry of Internal Affairs to defend its territory, arguing that the non-Cossacks in the cities should not be subject to Cossack administration. The problem went to a special conference of the ministers of war, finance, state domains and justice and the Don ataman, chaired by Alexander III. In its single meeting, on 28 May 1886, the tsar simply and arbitrarily decided the matter in favour of the War Ministry. To work out the legal details, the tsar appointed a committee to meet in the Don capital, Novocherkassk, chaired by the presumably neutral governor of Kursk guberniia.

When this committee had completed its work and a draft was forwarded to the Department of Law and the State Economy of the Council of State, new civilian resistance surfaced. K. P. Pobedonostsev, the Procurator of the Holy Synod (also the former tutor of the tsar and one of his influential advisers, a lawyer by training), drafted the case against complete territorial absorption of the enclave by the Don oblast. He argued that the Cossacks were not subject to ordinary civil administration because of their special military role, and, correspondingly, a non-Cossack populace should not be subject to the military administration that applied to the Don oblast. Instead, the enclave should be placed under the personal administration of the Don ataman, acting as a governor-general. Otherwise, the enclave would retain its non-Cossack civilian administration. This compromise formulation had the support of 18 members of the pertinent department of the State Council, against a minority of one – the War Minister, General P. S. Vannovskii. In a rebuttal to Pobedonostsev he argued that the proposed annexation of non-Cossacks was not particularly novel. The Don oblast already included about 700 000 peasants. The oblast administration governed on the basis of the laws applicable to the Empire as a whole. Military officers often were appointed to administrative responsibilities under the Ministry of Internal Affairs. Civilian ministries already operated local agencies on Don Cossack territory. The nobility of the enclave could merge with the Don nobility. In conclusion, the War Minister asked why the administration of the Don oblast should be considered abnormal and why it should be feared that the population of the enclave would be subject to a purely Cossack rule. This convinced Alexander III, who on 12 April 1887 gave his assent to the annexation of the enclave on the terms desired by the War Ministry.[104]

The law consummating the annexation of Rostov-na-Donu and Taganrog to the oblast of the Don voisko was adopted on 19 May 1887. Various adjustments were necessary to accommodate the new situation. Each of the two cities became the centre of an administrative okrug with the Don oblast, each with its own police administration. Rostov, Nakhichevan, Taganrog and Azov all retained the system of urban self-government that had been introduced to the Empire in 1870.[105] But the zemstvo institutions that had existed in the rural part of the former enclave were abolished. Jews were no longer permitted to settle in the annexed area, for they were excluded from the Don oblast, but those Jews who were already there could remain. Cossacks, who were entitled to carry on trade without being taxed elsewhere in the oblast, could not do so in the annexed territory. To deal with its new urban responsibilities the administration of the Don voisko added a new office, chaired by the ataman and including representatives of the urban self-governing bodies. Various budgetary adjustments placed certain funds at the disposal of the War Ministry rather than the Ministry of Internal Affairs, but the obligations of the War Ministry also increased.[106] If the War Ministry hoped that the Don voisko would experience some sort of bonanza as a result of its expansion, it was disappointed.[107]

During all the bureaucratic skirmishing over this territory, little was said about the impact of the annexation of this non-Cossack population on the Cossacks as an estate. The zeal for expansion emanated from the War Ministry in St Petersburg, not from the Don Cossacks themselves. It was never explained how the expansion would benefit them, and it is curious that the opponents of the annexation did not argue that the survival of the Cossacks as an estate would be threatened if they were numerically overwhelmed in the Don, the largest and basic voisko. Apparently it was not clear in 1887 that there would be such a boom in the population of the cities, approaching a million in the early twentieth century. Certainly the War Ministry became aware of the increasing size of the responsibility that it had assumed. The main administration of Cossack voiskos was expanded in 1889 to take on the paperwork related to the newly-acquired urban centres, but the backlog of unsettled business concerning this area was so great by 1897 that a special commission was established to investigate the problem. It recommended an expansion of the staff of the Main Administration, which was done in 1898.[108] Soon the War Ministry realized that the Main Administration of Cossack Forces was not capable of dealing with the burgeoning urban population of non-Cossacks within various voiskos. The War Minister became aware that he was faced with a mass of papers that had no relation to the military or even the civil life of the Cossacks and that it was continually necessary to apply to the Ministry of Internal Affairs for guidance concerning its norms for urban administration. In 1901 the War Ministry implicitly admitted that their appetite in 1887 exceeded their digestive capacity a decade later, and 15 cities, all of which enjoyed the institutions of urban self-government, were transferred from the administration of the War Ministry to Internal Affairs. These were: Rostov-na-Donu, Taganrog, Nakhichevan, Grushevsk-Aleksandrovsk, Azov, Ekaterinodar, Eisk, Maikop, Temriuk, Anapa, Vladikavkaz, Piatigorsk, Mozdok, Kizliar, Georgievsk and Groznyi. Technically these cities still remained on voisko territory, but they were in effect removed from voisko and War Ministry control.[109]

The one city that contained a substantial Cossack population was Novocherkassk, the administrative centre of the Don oblast. Yet this city did not receive the normal institutions of self-government until 1912. The territory on which the city stood was part of a Cossack stanitsa, which meant that land ownership there was not unqualified and not taxable in the manner of private property in other cities. The expenses of the city were in any case paid by the voisko and not the local authority, which consisted of a committee appointed by the ataman. In 1871 that authority took a feeble step towards establishing urban self-government in its capital, authorizing the election of some local residents to the existing committee, which would then consider ways of adapting the urban law of 1870 to Novocherkassk. But they soon decided that this was impractical, and the ataman proposed to the State Council that they go back to the old system, dispensing with any elected element in the governing committee of the city. This was too much for the Council, which insisted that at least a token elected representation be retained: one Cossack and one non-Cossack resident on a committee of ten, chaired by the deputy ataman for civil affairs. A new commission appointed by the War Ministry produced an unacceptable draft in 1872, and in 1881 the tsar established still another commission, which examined the suitability for Novocherkassk of the normal system of urban government – and decided in 1884 that it was not suitable. Three years later this led the War Ministry to solve the problem by making permanent the temporary system that had been in place since 1872: a committee of ten with one elected Cossack and one elected non-Cossack.[110]

But the same pressures that impelled the War Ministry to retreat from the full responsibility of running Rostov-na-Donu finally led it to conclude that even the most Cossack of cities needed more civilian self-government. A law of 1912, effective the following year, transferred responsibility for Novocherkassk to the Ministry of Internal Affairs and applied the normal system of urban self-government. The growing Kuban and Terek cities of Armavir and Kislovodsk joined the list of 'Cossack' cities under the system in 1913 and 1914. However unwillingly, the War Ministry was obliged implicitly to acknowledge that cities were alien enclaves within the Cossack territory which it could not administer by military means.[111]

THE STANITSA

Elected self-government of and by the Cossacks survived principally in the stanitsa and its subdivisions, which were variously called the poselok, vyselok, khutor and zaimok. As a physical entity, the stanitsa might vary a good deal over the vast territories of the voiskos. In about 1880 they ranged in population from under 400 males and females to over 22 000, constituting a single nucleus of dwellings in some cases or as many as 50 widely-dispersed settlements in others. In the Don, for example, stanitsas were large areas that embraced many settlements, which meant that the population of some of them was about the same as the entire Astrakhan, Semirechenskoe or Amur voiskos around 1880. In contrast, almost every settlement in the Kuban and Terek was classified as a stanitsa, with the result that the Kuban, with not much over half the population of the Don at this time, had almost twice as many stanitsas – 202 against 110. At this time it is reasonably clear that there were in all 590 stanitsas in the Empire, but it was only in the 1890s that the central authorities began to establish an authoritative list of all stanitsas and their subdivisions. Notwithstanding their diversity, all stanitsas reflected the important legal fact that they were the only administrative unit in which the ordinary Cossack populace exercised predominance over other social estates and some measure of autonomy with respect to the War Ministry–voisko hierarchy.[112]

The Don statute of 1835, which served as the basis for local government in most other voiskos, did not attempt to regulate the stanitsa in great detail and did not recognize the existence of any smaller divisions.[113] In large measure it left the governance of the stanitsa to the entire 'obshchestvo', that is, the assembly of all adult, male Cossacks. They elected an ataman and two judges for three years, assisted by two clerks. Most of the important decisions, including the allotment of land and the imposition of judicial sentences, were left in the hands of the whole assembly. Along with vestiges of primitive democracy, there were marks of cultural backwardness. According to an old-timer on the Don who was interviewed in 1892, illiteracy, corruption and arbitrariness reigned in the 1860s. Every 1 January one of the clerks would travel to Novocherkassk with a report, but more importantly a load of gifts for various officials, for example a hen or a fox skin, which each local household had donated. The ataman of the voisko would appear on inspection and give orders, which evidently bore some weight. In the stanitsa only the clerks were likely to be literate, the judges signing their papers with a seal.[114]

The Temporary Committee for the Review of Cossack Statutes, wishing to bring the governance of the Cossacks closer to that of civilian estates, tried to approach the reform of stanitsa administration on the basis of the law of serf emancipation. This act of 19 February 1861 established two levels of peasant self-government, the primary 'rural community' (sel'skoe obshchestvo) and the higher level, called the 'volost'. The very idea of applying the peasant model, even after emancipation, to the Cossacks was not flattering to their pretensions of traditional independence. The length and detail of the new law on the stanitsa, promulgated on 13 May 1870, also implied a diminution of autonomy, for it was about three times as long as the comparable section of the Don statute of 1835, spelling out in more detail what the stanitsa could and could not do.[115] While the powers of the stanitsa assembly were ill defined and implicitly broad in the statute of 1835, the powers of the 'skhod', as the assembly was renamed in 1870, were tightly defined in 21 points. Participation in the skhod was restricted to heads of households, while formerly any Cossack over serving age could join in. Non-Cossack heads of household who resided in the stanitsa now received the right to participate, except on matters pertaining only to Cossacks. The new law also saddled the stanitsa and its skhod with responsibility for financing the equipment of Cossacks who were starting active service if they could not cover this themselves. In most non-military matters the powers of the skhod resembled that of the peasant assembly, including the right to allocate land allotments and to exile undesirables, both important decisions that required a two-thirds vote.

A major innovation in the stanitsa law of 1870 was the introduction of a subordinate level of administration, the poselok, vyselok, khutor or zaimok. The aim was to provide each nuclear settlement of 20 households or more (fewer upon special request) with its own self-government. To this extent it extended the scope of self-government, especially considering the difficulty that residents of outlying settlements might have in attending meetings in the principal town of the stanitsa. On the other hand, the new level tended to replace direct participation with representation, for the skhod of the poselok was entitled to send a representative delegation (not less than three) to the stanitsa skhod when it was inconvenient for each head of household to attend.

Considerable responsibility rested on the ataman of the stanitsa, whom the skhod elected except in the mistrusted Ural voisko. Here the ataman of the voisko appointed this local official. In all voiskos he served as presiding officer of the skhod, which he convened, and was head of the standing administration. This consisted of assistants (an optional office at the pleasure of the skhod), the treasurer, and at least three 'representatives' (doverennye), all elected by the skhod. The skhod could delegate much of its routine business to the administration, which was served by clerks who were either elected or hired and who had the reputation for carrying on much of the real work of the stanitsa government.[116] The ataman of the stanitsa also exercised modest police and judicial authority, including the imposition of a fine up to one ruble or obligatory labour service or imprisonment without trial. Cossack or other unprivileged persons residing in the stanitsa needed the permission of the ataman to leave it, and he had the power to grant this to Cossacks of the combatant category for as much as three months and to others as much as a year. Because of the Cossacks' military role, the ataman of the stanitsa automatically received the assimilated rank of 'khorunzhyi' (the lowest commissioned rank), if he did not hold this or higher rank.

Although he was not a troop commander in any sense, the ataman of the stanitsa was responsible for executing the orders of the Cossack military command with respect to the muster of Cossacks for active duty, bearing whatever equipment was required. As a vital official in the mobilization machinery, the ataman of the stanitsa was exempt from active service. If he completed two terms of three years in office, he was exempt for life; after three terms he could also choose one son to be exempt. As for financial rewards, the ataman was not necessarily well off. The law merely stated that he should receive a minimum salary of 150 rubles; anything additional was up to the skhod, which also set other salaries for officials. The powers of the ataman of the poselok were far more modest. He had no military responsibility and his vaguely defined police responsibility was not reinforced by any authority to impose punishments. Nor was any minimum remuneration specified for this official.

Cossack tradition endowed the stanitsa assembly with judicial powers, but the law of 1870 followed the peasant model of setting up separate courts, consisting of 4 to 11 judges elected by the skhod. These courts could deal only with cases involving Cossacks or members of the taxed estates. They could impose only relatively modest penalties, for example a maximum of seven days in jail, and, unlike the peasant courts, they could not inflict corporal punishment.

In the early 1880s, while the 1870 model of stanitsa government was in force, the pioneer ethnographer Mikhail Kharuzin studied the Don Cossacks at first hand, leaving an account that comes closer to real life than the laws and official documents.[117] The stanitsa skhod, he tells us, met rather rarely. It was convened by a crier who walked the streets of the main town of the stanitsa, usually on the eve of the meeting, calling, 'Sirs, honorable community [obshchestvo]! Tomorrow there will be a stanitsa sbor [skhod]. Neither ride nor walk away!' In the outlying hamlets, the khutors, it was up to the local ataman to go from door to door with the announcement.

Starting the actual meeting could be a problem, because a quorum of half the eligible participants was hard to find, not surprising considering that some of the outlying hamlets were a day's journey from the main town of the stanitsa. Sometimes householders would make such a journey, only to find that there was no quorum and the meeting was rescheduled for the following week. The presence of a quorum was usually a boisterous and chaotic scene. A resident of Luganskaia stanitsa who had attended many such meetings wrote that they could not be compared to the peasant assemblies, which were smaller and far less noisy. A person who has been to a Don Cossack stanitsa assembly, he claimed, would have a headache for a week after as a result of the crush and shouting. 'Picture to yourself more than one thousand people, impossibly jammed together and shouting with all their strength. If the ataman gives a report on something of interest to the residents of the stanitsa, they raise a roar and shout ... [so that] only those next to the orator understand the question or report.' Many of the worst offenders, he claimed, did not even have a vote (evidently Cossacks who were not household heads). Kharuzin writes that the meetings in moderate weather were usually held outdoors in the maidan (square in front of the stanitsa izba or cottage, the administrative building), and in winter inside the izba. The writer from Luganskaia reported a meeting in very cold weather in January which took place in the maidan because there was no room indoors and lasted from after the noon meal until evening – and the press of people was so great that 'one's ribs suffered'.

Kharuzin himself observed only somewhat less riotous meetings. After a general discussion, in which 'all talked at once', creating a 'terrible hubbub', the ataman would decide that an issue had been sufficiently debated and his aide, the 'esaul'tsa', would ring a bell and silence would descend 'not rapidly' with cries of 'quiet down, that's enough'.[118] In cases requiring a majority of two-thirds, the vote was taken by division into groups for or against. After the outcome was settled, the Cossacks would say 'V dobryi chas' (good luck).

The rough character of stanitsa democracy was particularly evident in the election of the ataman. The law did not specify the compensation for this official, and practice varied among stanitsas. Some actually paid money, others voted to do so and did not, still others awarded an extra share of hayfields and sometimes payment was with the labour of some of the Cossacks who were eligible for communal labour. But the main compensation seems to have been the opportunity for graft. 'Everyone will accept bribes and entertainment for such is the custom on the Don' and 'Without entertainment there's nothing doing on the Don' were among the sayings that Kharuzin often heard. With this incentive there was usually competition for the post of ataman, and with this temper of public life a good deal of corruption in the electoral process. The tavern was the principal institution of election campaigning in the stanitsa, the wealthy candidates entertaining the impoverished with vodka and such delicacies as a whole roast ram. In one stanitsa he found six candidates for ataman, each holding forth at a different tavern. The law required that votes for ataman be cast by dropping balls in urns, a new and confusing procedure for Cossacks who sometimes placed balls in more than one urn, or dropped in a handful. Kharuzin and many of the Cossacks he talked to found the atamans thus elected to be a rather unsatisfactory lot, occasionally including illiterates.

The picture of the stanitsa courts was no more edifying. Kharuzin often heard it said that 'Without vodka there will be no judgement.' 'When you bring a petition to court, you must entertain it; to consider the case, again entertain; and on completion of the case entertain again.' Sometimes the court would accept entertainment from both sides and decide in favour of the most generous host. In some places the business of the court was conducted in taverns, although vodka was not the only form of bribery.

Despite the opportunity for bribe-taking, service as a judge was unpopular and avoided by the wealthier Cossacks. In some stanitsas all Cossacks served by rotation, excepting those rich enough to purchase their exemption. Where the skhod chose them there was sometimes a real election and sometimes merely a call for volunteers acceptable to the meeting. The exact size of the court varied, and in some stanitsas they chose to provide three shifts, each of which served for four months of a year. The law did not specify their compensation, and practices varied considerably. Some stanitsas paid the members of its court nothing, while others offered an extra share of meadow and some paid a modest sum in cash – 20 to 50 rubles a year from local funds or a fee of perhaps 25 kopeks from each plaintiff (more rarely the defendant as well).

The courts were unpopular not only because of their venality but also because most Cossacks felt that they did not control crime as well as the traditional justice of the assembly, which had often meted out harsh corporal punishment. Kharuzin found that the stanitsa courts were reluctant to deal with criminal cases for fear of exceeding their authority. Cossacks told him that the malfactors among them had no fear of the punishments at the disposal of the stanitsa courts: a short jail sentence or small fine but no flogging. As a result, there was a certain amount of vigilante justice (samosud), a practice that predated the law of 1870. Kharuzin reports an instance in which two thieves were killed by persons unknown, one surviving for a few days with head-wounds inflicted by a sharp weapon. In another case a thief was found lying by the banks of a river, his face so badly mutilated that his parents could identify him only by his clothing. In still another case a suspected horsethief (a non-Cossack) was overtaken in the steppe and given such a beating with fists and clubs that he 'was ill for a long time, and to this day can only walk with crutches'.

The intention of the stanitsa law of 1870 was to form a Cossack system of local self-government that would be fairly compliant with the wishes of the higher levels of administration. Various means to this end were written into the law. The ataman of the stanitsa had to be confirmed in office, following his election, by the head of the okrug or uezd. That authority had the arbitrary power to punish all stanitsa officials with fines of up to five rubles and arrest up to five days. The decisions of the stanitsa court could be changed by a justice of the peace or, if the court had 'obviously exceeded its authority', by the okrug or uezd administration.[119] But in practice a good deal of latitude remained to the ordinary Cossacks in the stanitsa, and their exercise of it distressed the higher authorities before the decade of the 1870s was over. The voisko administration became aware that it had not received any specific authority to issue instructions to the stanitsa, nor to conduct inspections of their activities. This was rectified in a law of 1878 which, however, stipulated that any instructions from above should not violate the law of 1870 nor infringe the powers of the stanitsa.[120] Because of these restrictions it appears that the right of instruction had little impact, but the inspections by various government officials that followed soon after the law was issued led to considerable change.

The inspectors reported a disastrous state of affairs in the self-government of the stanitsa. The official view, sustained by at least a few unofficial observers, was that the skhod was a disorderly shambles, in which corrupt, self-serving members of the body dominated. The War Ministry report for 1883 maintained that soon after the law of 1870 was enacted it became apparent that it was impossible to convene a representative skhod in large stanitsas, and it was often impossible to obtain a quorum of half the eligibles. When the skhod could act, the resulting decisions were often subject to the influence of 'kulaks' (rich Cossacks) and horse-breeders, wealthy interests which were able to assert their own interests over those of the majority. Official opinion also held that the courts were slow and partisan. The disarray of the system

led to a decline of the economic welfare of the stanitsa and to the development among the population, and especially the youth, of inclinations alien to the Cossack estate, for example, the absence in the family and home of honour and esteem for elders, in the service

of the destruction of discipline and insufficient zeal and punctuality
with respect to induction into obligatory service, which in the past
was unknown or encountered rarely ...

A special cause for concern was the decline of the communal fiscal
resources, which were needed to pay for the equipment of Cossacks
who were due to go on active duty but could not afford the necessary
equipment. The War Ministry maintained that many stanitsas were
bankrupt, the result of the unscrupulous dealings of 'kulaks and
various kinds of exploiters', who were able to gain control of the
stanitsa administration in the absence of sufficient numbers of
responsible Cossacks.[121]

Some unofficial commentators, no doubt people whose sympathies
lay with the establishment, agreed. The author of a substantial essay
on the Orenburg Cossacks even used the same term, kulaks, to
describe the element that had come to dominate the stanitsas in that
voisko. He also called them 'miroedy' (literally peasant commune-
eaters), echoing a common charge concerning the system of peasant
administration on which the stanitsa law of 1870 was based. These
connivers, he maintained, bought the votes of 'idlers, drunkards', who
would sell communal resources if the 'opchestvo' (an illiterate
pronunciation of obshchestvo, the old term for the assembly of the
stanitsa) 'was entertained with vodka'. In the Orenburg voisko, this
writer claimed, a particular loss was the sale of timber from stanitsa
woodlots, even to the point of causing serious soil erosion. He agreed
with the War Ministry that there had been a decline in Cossack
self-esteem. For example, the Orenburg Cossacks formerly had worn
their uniforms most of the time. Now they generally preferred the
'townsman's coat'.[122] Official concern about the situation in the
stanitsas was probably well founded, although it might have been more
apt to attribute the problem to the Cossack tradition of local
self-government, or to a basic, long-term decline in Cossack commitment to the system of service that had been imposed on them. After
all, the unregulated stanitsa self-government before the Don statute of
1835, and even that system between 1835 and 1870, had offered the
Cossacks just as much opportunity for democracy and its abuses. What
the War Ministry wanted was not so much tradition as control from
above.

In 1882 and 1884 the War Ministry enacted two measures towards
this end on the recommendation of the ataman of the Don. The first
was a supposedly temporary decree which for five years gave the

atamans of the Don, Kuban, Terek, Astrakhan, Orenburg, Semire-chenskoe and Siberian voiskos the right to assign a Cossack as much as four years of extra military service. Such a punishment was to be applied on recommendation of a Cossack's family, his stanitsa or higher officials, but no specific infraction had to be proven to incur this harsh penalty. At the end of the first five-year period the decree was renewed for another five.[123] The second measure, which applied only to the Don, reduced the size of the skhod by making it a representative body (one 'tenth-man' for every ten households) rather than an assembly of all household heads.[124]

The request of the ataman of the Don to change this feature of the stanitsa governance inspired the War Ministry to authorize a commission in Novocherkassk to undertake a broader reform. At the end of 1884 this body produced a draft, which reached the ministry in 1885. It found favour, and the ministry circulated the draft to the other voisko administrations for their consideration. By the opening of 1886 all the voiskos except for the Ural, Zabaikal and Amur had returned their own drafts, which were fairly close to the one prepared in the Don. The War Minister now formed a committee, chaired by the head of the Main Administration on Cossack Forces and consisting of the delegates to the Committee of the Main Administration from the Don, Kuban, Astrakhan, Orenburg, Siberian and Semirechenskoe voiskos and a special delegate from the Terek, which lacked a regular seat on this standing committee.[125] Because of the exceptional importance that the ministry attached to this problem, it went about the preparation of the new legislation with unusually elaborate proce-dures. To assist its labours the committee was provided with a printed book in which the Don draft appeared in parallel with the proposals of the other voiskos in order to highlight alternative opinions.[126] The draft law that resulted from this study was resubmitted to the administrations of the various voiskos for review and then returned to the committee at the Main Administration, reinforced with some additional representatives from the Don. At this final stage of review the committee reversed itself on one significant point: it deleted the right of the stanitsa court to impose corporal punishment (up to 20 lashes) for 'minor misdemeanours', a degradation that would have paralleled the existing law on peasant administration.[127]

The tsar signed the new law on 3 June 1891 for adoption at the start of the next year in the Don, Astrakhan, Orenburg, Terek, Kuban, Siberian and Semirechenskoe voiskos. The Military Council was to prepare adaptations of it to the other voiskos, which was accomplished by the end of the century in all cases except the Ural.[128] In publishing the new law, the War Ministry issued a public relations statement in the form of an 'order', which called attention to the defects of the old system and affirmed that the new law would bring better order to the stanitsa assembly and the court, would entrust responsible positions to 'worthy persons', and would secure the punctual induction onto active duty of Cossacks and payment of their debts to the government. 'Beyond this the new statute gives the voisko command the right of control and leadership in the activities of all the organs of communal administration.'[129]

The institutions established in 1870 remained: on the stanitsa and lower levels an assembly, an ataman administration and stanitsa court.[130] But within this framework there was indeed a marked shift in favour of authority, a change more substantial than the law of 1890 on the zemskii nachal'nik brought to peasant affairs.[131] The authorities aimed at improving, from their point of view, the quality of the personnel involved in stanitsa self-government. The ataman was no longer simply elected by the assembly in four major voiskos. In the Don and Orenburg voiskos the stanitsa assembly elected three nominees and in the Kuban and Terek two, from whom the voisko administration would choose the ataman. A critic of the system later claimed that in some cases the administration did not care for any of the nominees and simply made its own appointment.[132] The voting was to be by secret ballot in the presence of an official from the voisko administration. The stanitsa ataman and the judges had to be at least 33 years old, and the ataman had to take a loyalty oath in the presence of the head of the military otdel in which the stanitsa was located. No longer was the remuneration of the ataman fixed by his neighbours. He was now paid according to a scale ranging from 150 rubles per year in a stanitsa of 150 households or less to 1500 rubles in one with over 4000 households. This latter sum was considerable, approaching the salary of a colonel. The ataman was also eligible to receive cash bonuses and medals.[133]

There were important changes in the assembly of the stanitsa, called the skhod in the law of 1870, renamed the 'sbor' in 1891. In place of representation by one man from every ten households, there was a sliding scale, ranging from one representative per household in communities with 30 or fewer households to one per ten households in communities with 301–1000 households. In larger stanitsas, and in the Don almost all were larger, the administration would fix the norm. To facilitate this representation, the law provided for voting districts, and the authorities had to arrange the system so that the number of non-Cossack members of the sbor would in no case outnumber the Cossack members. This would be no small task in some areas, owing to the numbers of peasants relative to the Cossacks. Along with non-Cossacks, the young Cossacks were mistrusted and excluded up to the age of 26, but all the elected officials of the stanitsa or the khutor sat in its sbor. Having assumedly collected a suitable membership in the sbor, the government wanted to ensure that they actually participated. The quorum was raised from half to two-thirds of the members, and any member failing to attend the sbor without an excuse was to be fined. Apart from selectivity, the law attempted to employ exhortation to achieve the desired conduct. It enjoined the sbor to see that the punishments at its disposal served as 'a strong defence and affirmation of ancient customs, of good morals in the community and family, piety, respect for rank and honour to the elders'.

The authorities were not content to rely on the new forms of selectivity to provide loyal and effective administration in the stanitsa. They also strengthened the controls over Cossack self-government. The immediate authority over the stanitsa was placed in the hands of the ataman of the otdel, the military officer who was responsible for mobilization and training of Cossacks in an area containing a number of stanitsas.[134] The choice of a military line of control rather than the civil was understandable because of the emphasis that the new law placed on fulfilment of military obligations. Broadly speaking, the ataman of the otdel became the counterpart of the zemskii nachal'nik in the counterreform law on peasant self-government. He was obliged to inspect each stanitsa annually. In addition to the right of imposing minor punishments on wayward officials, which the law of 1870 had established, the ataman of the otdel could remove from office all stanitsa and khutor officials. In the case of the ataman of the stanitsa and the 'honorary judges' (members of a new appeals court for several stanitsas), this could only be a temporary suspension, pending the decision of the voisko administration. But the voisko could not only remove the ataman from office, it could also suspend completely stanitsa self-government, appointing its own ataman, who could govern without a sbor if the authorities believed the circumstances warranted this.

To attempt to provide the ataman of the otdel with the practical means of supervising the work of the stanitsa institutions, an array of new bureaucratic requirements appeared. The sbor of the stanitsa had to submit a budget to the higher authorities and stick to it. The agenda of the sbor had to be submitted in advance of meetings to the ataman of the otdel. The stanitsa administration had to keep 14 kinds of non-fiscal record books and balance the accounts every month.

Most important of all, the law held the stanitsa as a whole responsible for the proper fulfilment of the military duties of its members and for all fiscal or labour obligations. To enable the stanitsa to impose these exactions, it received imposing and arbitrary powers that it had not possessed previously. The sbor, which was responsible for paying whatever was needed to equip impoverished Cossacks who were called to active duty, received the means to squeeze the last kopek out of those who relied on communal help. The sbor could now expropriate any income (such as rent) from property; it could hire out the laggards as labourers and take their pay; it could assign a trustee to take over their affairs; it could sell their property and keep the proceeds; and it could deprive them of their land allotment for a specified period. Any one of these measures could be ruinous to a Cossack household.

But the War Ministry would not approve the recommendation of the drafters of this law that the sbor have the power to require extra military service. Evidently the authorities were uneasy about equating this 'sacred duty to the tsar' with punishment. The ataman of the voiskos, it will be recalled, had this power on the basis of temporary decree, which expired in 1892. These authorities, familiar with the practical problems of coercing Cossacks to impoverish themselves in order to buy equipment for military service, wanted the decree extended. The ministry, following a one-year extension of the old decree, obliged the atamans with a new decree without definite term, issued on 8 February 1894. Now, however, the power to order additional military service was less arbitrary. The voisko ataman could apply it only for such definite infractions as failure to obtain the proper equipment for active service, or the intentional loss of a horse while on active duty.[135] In practice this meant that the stanitsa could not impose the penalty but merely had to persuade the voisko authorities to send a particular Cossack on extra duty because he lacked a suitable horse or had otherwise offended.

Having dwelled on the efforts of the drafters of the new law to enhance authority at the level of the stanitsa, it is fair to add that they made some gestures in the direction of improving the material welfare of the community. At least the stanitsa was empowered to seek ways of improving agriculture or to establish a local bank, not that any money from the Imperial treasury was offered. On balance it was a tough law, and it is a measure of the docility of the Cossacks that it was accepted without noticeable outcry. On the contrary, the main unofficial Cossack newspaper of the day, *Donskaia rech'*, greeted the law with the folksaying, 'God is not without mercy – the Cossack is not without happiness!'[136] Newspaper reports concerning its introduction were generally favourable: there seems to have been considerable agreement that the law of 1870 really had been a failure.

It is doubtful, however, that the new system solved the problem of quality in Cossack self-government. Newspaper reports from various localities in the Don concur in lamenting the suitability of candidates for the ataman. It was hard to find candidates who were not drunkards or bribe-takers, wrote one local correspondent. Another reported that a former ataman offered to devote part of his salary to the local school, if elected, 'which evoked laughter and caustic remarks'. Elsewhere a stanitsa succeeded in electing two supposedly good men as ataman, one following the other, but they resigned in six months and other suitable candidates declined to run. In another locality, when an okrug official (required by law to attend the election) nominated a friend, the Cossacks rejected him by acclamation because he was not sociable enough, shouting 'Ne nado [no way]! He's a smart-ass! He reads the newspaper! Is friendly with the justice of the peace ... Ne n-a-a-ado!' Elsewhere a writer complained that the members of the sbor rented 1000 desiatinas of communal land to themselves at modest cost. An editorial writer of the newspaper said that the general opinion was that the office of ataman was filled with people of low moral character, that barely literate men were asked to supervise communities of 2000 to 3000 people, which tended to make them 'blind tools in the hands of the clerks'.[137]

Despite these criticisms, the elections in the Don, at least, should have gratified the authorities' hopes of obtaining atamans of stanitsas who would respect the establishment. Nearly complete results show that only 4 ordinary Cossacks were elected compared with 55 uriadniks and 38 officers, 10 civil servants and 1 Cossack nobleman who was in neither the military nor civil service. Such an assortment may have included venal and poorly educated men, but it is clear that they were overwhelmingly men with some status in the Cossack system and stake in the regime.

CONFLICT IN THE DUMA

With the law of 1891 on stanitsa administration, the bureaucratic modernization of Cossack governance reached its apogee. Thereafter problems grew and solutions stalled. There was, however, one major addition to the political side of the Cossack question: the establishment of the State Duma. This representative institution, a response to the revolution of 1905, brought very little actual change to the administration of the voiskos. The Duma was legally incapable of pushing through measures that the tsar and his ministers opposed, and with repect to the Cossacks, most Duma deputies were not strongly committed to reform. Nevertheless, the very existence of the Duma was a significant innovation in the political life of the Cossacks, because it gave voice to the martial estate as an interest group and demonstrated that on the whole the Cossack population was deeply dissatisfied with the existing system of governance.

The electoral system of the new Duma was improvised by the regime with a view to its own survival.[138] The authorities started with the assumption that the rule of one-man-one-vote would be a disaster for their interest, but the very nature of the authoritarian tradition made it difficult to estimate voting behaviour. Without experience it was hard to determine the best means of rigging the electoral system in order to achieve a satisfactory result. Working hastily under the threat of revolution in 1905–6, the officials of the Ministry of Internal Affairs who drafted the electoral scheme evidently had little time or even inclination to study the Cossacks as a constituency. At the Peterhof conferences, chaired by the tsar, at which senior civil servants and some invited outsiders discussed and modified the draft, the Cossacks were not even mentioned.[139] The conferences were preoccupied with larger issues, including the basic questions of whether or not to use the existing estates as the curiae in the new electoral system. On this a mixed policy emerged: the peasants and the Cossacks each formed an electoral curia, while the rest of the populace formed curiae according to their wealth or occupation, not membership in one of the legal estates. The regime thereby decided to treat the Cossacks as peasants, albeit a privileged species of peasant. It did not choose to give the Cossacks special representation in the new upper chamber, the reformed State Council.[140]

The notoriously complex electoral system for the Duma is particularly intricate with respect to the Cossacks, owing to the division of the estate into 11 voiskos. The Don, Astrakhan and Orenburg Cossacks were treated in the basic electoral law that covered the guberniias of European Russia. In each of these cases, the Cossack pattern paralleled that of the peasants in normal guberniias, but with the numbers weighted in favour of the Cossacks. Each stanitsa chose two delegates per uezd (in the Don, okrug) assembly of Cossack electors, which chose two delegates to the guberniia assembly that elected the actual Duma deputies. Here the Cossack electors joined colleagues from the other electoral curiae. One Duma deputy from each guberniia had to be a peasant, chosen by the peasant electors only, and the Don, Astrakhan and Orenburg Cossacks each enjoyed the same privilege.[141] The other voiskos participated in the Duma elections according to four separate laws that the state issued as an afterthought to the main body of the new fundamental laws. The stanitsas of these voiskos sent representatives to purely Cossack electoral assemblies, one assembly in each voisko, excepting the Amur and Ussuri, which had a single, joint assembly. The Kuban assembly elected three deputies to the Duma and the other assemblies one each.[142]

The result of this legislation was a guarantee of at least 13 Cossack Duma deputies. This was hardly a large number in a parliament of over 500, but it was the only representation guaranteed to an estate as such, excepting the peasantry. A more impressive measure of the regime's hopes for the Cossacks lay in the way the assembly of electors in the Don oblast was rigged. A total of 177 electors sent 11 deputies to the Duma. The peasants constituted a majority in the oblast but received only 14 electors, compared to 79 from the Cossack stanitsas and another 47 from the landowners, who were mainly Cossack nobles. The residents of the smaller cities of the oblast sent the remaining 37 electors. The result was that, except for the mandatory peasant deputy, the Don electoral assembly sent only Cossacks to the Duma.[143]

There was among the Cossacks a keen sense of economic grievance, which was a major element in the political awakening of the martial estate. The first important organized form of this movement was an ephemeral 'Cossack Union', formed by a few educated Don Cossacks in Novocherkassk in September 1905. One of its founders, S. Ia. Arefin, drafted a programme entitled 'Cossack Needs', which not only revived the myth of bygone Cossack love of freedom and equality but also compared the Russian tsars with the Tatar khans and the Poles as historic enemies of the free Cossack. Denying that the Cossacks had outlived their time, the programme concluded that they would play 'a more glorious and honourable role, specifically in the struggle for a better form of government, against autocracy and arbitrariness, in the struggle for freedom and rights not only for themselves but also for all the oppressed'. This programme called for the revival of the krug as the basis of self-government, the distribution to Cossacks of voisko reserve land and landlords' estates, with compensation to the latter. A 'standing army of militia' should replace the existing form of Cossack military service.[144] The Cossack Union to some extent modelled itself on the All-Russian Union of Peasants, and sought to inspire the ordinary Cossacks in their stanitsas to emulate the peasants in drawing up 'instructions' to express their will. To this end Arefin and some associates visited four Don stanitsas in the autumn of 1905, and in this period of freedom they even succeeded in arranging special convocations of the local assemblies to hear them. Arefin recalls that in Starocherkassk the proposed instruction, incorporating 'Cossack Needs', was adopted 'unanimously' and in Kagal'nitskaia almost so. But in Khomutovskaia stanitsa there were reservations, not concerning political freedom, but on the proposal of a militia of all estates. 'And won't this turn us into muzhiks [peasants]?', asked the Cossacks, sensing the implied contradiction between equality and Cossack privilege. The propaganda of the democratic Cossack intelligentsia reached only a small portion of the Don, let alone the other voiskos, and the authorities confiscated most publications in this vein.[145] But Cossack voting behaviour in the Duma elections shows that a large part of the Cossack populace, and not only the Dontsy, approved of the general drift of the democratic programme.

Not all the Cossack Duma deputies provided for in the electoral law appeared in the Tauride Palace during the short life of the First Duma, 27 April–8 July 1906. The elections in most of Siberia did not occur in time for those deputies to take their places in St Petersburg, but the Don sent ten Cossack deputies, the Kuban three, Orenburg three and the Ural and Terek one each – a total of 18. Of this total, 11 were members of a party or Duma group that was repugnant to the regime: seven Kadets (Constitutional Democrats), three Trudoviki and one member of the 'Party of Democratic Reform'. Two more deputies listed themselves as non-party but demonstrated their adherence to the liberal wing by supporting the major anti-government interpellation sponsored by the Cossack liberals.[146]

Some idea of the way in which this came about emerges from a good-humoured memoir of one of the Don deputies to the First Duma, the writer F. D. Kriukov. A Cossack by birth, and secondary school teacher by profession, he was living in Nizhnii Novgorod when he learned in early March 1906 that Glazunovskaia stanitsa had elected him to the Cossack electoral assembly in Ust-Medvedinskii okrug. Proceeding with great difficulty through spring floods and mud, he joined a gathering of 36 electors, representing 18 stanitsas. Two, he learned, had been chosen illegally by voice vote (not secret ballot) in their stanitsas. Five or six he classified as intelligentsia (mainly teachers), the rest mainly atamans of their stanitsas or uriadniks, ostensibly a conservative lot. But this was not actually the case. With one exception, Kriukov recalled, nobody really knew what party he belonged to. A clergyman-elector said that as far as he was concerned they might elect anyone except a 'sotsial-demokrant' [sic]. There was one exception, a former marshal of the nobility and member of an eminent Don clan, N. V. Efremov, who spoke on behalf of something called the 'Monarchist–Constitutionalist Party'. But he failed to mention specifically Cossack interests and so was not very appealing. Kriukov did address himself to these matters in a speech and found support on all sides. He (and not Efremov) was among the 13 electors who went on to Novocherkassk to elect the actual Duma deputies. Here the real business seems to have been settled in advance of the formal assembly of electors in a meeting in the home of the marshal of the nobility of the oblast, V. I. Denisov. Although there was still little formal party affiliation, there was a clear division between those who leaned towards the Kadets and those who favoured the 'right'. The latter advanced various candidates, but when these were asked 'and how much land do you have?' their popularity collapsed. One potential rightist deputy, a merchant, lost his credibility when somebody asked him about his religious affiliation: he was a member of the Molokane ('Milk-drinkers' religious sect). As it turned out, all the known rightists were defeated in the actual election, but five Don Duma deputies who had held their peace in the debates proved to be fairly conservative. Four were in close touch with the Don administration, which rewarded them later with promotion from uriadnik to khorunzhyi, the lowest commissioned rank. Kriukov maintains that one of these took orders and cash from the ataman of the Khoper okrug, who even drafted a fictitious 'instruction' from his constituency.[147]

The election to the Duma of a preponderance of liberal deputies from the Cossack voiskos reflected the formation of an intelligentsia within the martial estate. These deputies were educated men who were as critical of the autocratic tradition as their non-Cossack counterparts in the Russian Empire. Among them were three teachers, one lawyer, one priest, one journalist/land surveyor, a city administrative employee, a landowner–aristocrat and a scientist, as well as an ordinary Cossack and a stanitsa ataman. Five had had higher education. Notable among them were I. N. Efremov, wealthy landowner and descendant of Don atamans, V. A. Kharlamov, landowner and teacher in the Novocherkassk gymnasium; N. A. Borodin, a corresponding member of the Academy of Sciences who listed himself as a zoologist and was the author of a massive scholarly work on his ancestral Ural Cossacks; and Kriukov. In a meeting of electors in Novocherkassk, prior to their formal assembly, the conservative nobleman A. P. Leonov attempted to persuade the ordinary Cossacks to disown such denatured Cossacks. 'I am a Cossack! I am a native-born Cossack ... an old uriadnik! Not a masquerade-Cossack, like all these teachers, lawyers, justices of the peace, but a true Cossack.'[148] But in the main this kind of argument did not prevent the Cossack electors from identifying their interests with the small liberal intelligentsia that had evolved within the estate.

Against 13 more or less liberal Cossack deputies, the regime could count only five avowedly conservative Cossack deputies, all from the Don, four stanitsa atamans and a landowner, and all members of the 'Party of Peaceful Renewal'.[149]

Not only did the Cossacks use their favoured position in the electoral system to increase the numbers of liberals in the First Duma, the Cossack deputies also openly attacked the conservative myth of tsar and Cossack, proposing in its place the myth of a bygone era of Cossack liberty and democracy. Their main vehicle was an interpellation of the War Minister concerning the mobilization of second- and third-turn Cossacks for counterrevolutionary service. This antagonistic inquiry was proposed on 2 June 1906, signed by 48 deputies, including nine Cossacks representing four voiskos (Don, Orenburg, Ural, Terek). At this time the interpellation was proposed to the Duma as an item requiring special priority in the agenda, but it failed to gain approval on this basis and so appeared again in the regular order of business on 13 June, having been rewritten in the interval.[150]

This interpellation appealed to the principle that the regime should not violate its own laws. Thus the authors of the interpellation on Cossack mobilization were obliged to show that the regime had violated its own laws in calling up the second- and third-turn Cossacks for internal security duty. This was not easy, considering that the tsar legally enjoyed complete military command over the Cossacks of serving age, a continual complaint of Cossack advocates who protested the burdensomeness of military obligation.[151] The interpellation attempted to deal with this problem by raising the technical legal objection that the order for mobilization was not promulgated through the Senate, as required by the 'Code of Fundamental Laws', which had been published only on 23 April 1906. The first version of the interpellation disingenuously suggested that the tsar himself perhaps was not responsible for the mobilization, that it was really the work of the War Minister or Minister of Internal Affairs. The former, it was alleged, 'placed the mobilized Cossack regiments completely at the disposal of the Ministry of Internal Affairs, which made of them a cadre of armed police servitors'.[152] This was the political crux of the matter. The backers of the interpellation could not argue that the use of Cossacks for counterrevolutionary purposes was actually illegal, providing the correct forms were observed in issuing commands, but they could use a legal technicality to ventilate their objection to the use of the Cossacks as security troops and to the whole military-bureaucratic system of governance on which it rested. Beyond this there was the possibility of bringing pressure to bear to demobilize the second- and third-turn Cossacks, a measure that would at once alleviate the economic difficulties of the Cossacks and limit the capacity of the regime to suppress revolutionary disturbances. In the original version of the interpellation, presented on 2 June, there was no explicit call for demobilization, which, Kharlamov explained in his speech, was not within the legal rights of the Duma. But there was considerable popular Cossack pressure to bring about demobilization. Deputy Bardizh reported that the Kuban Cossacks had given their deputies an instruction that they 'do not request but demand the rapid disbandment of the Cossacks of the second and third turns', and Kharlamov himself read similar communications from the 41st Don regiment and an unnamed Don stanitsa, as did Sedel'nikov. The second and final form of the interpellation therefore ended with the question: 'What measures will the War Minister adopt and when to disband the incorrectly mobilized Cossack regiments of the second and third turns?'[153] While this unfriendly query was added, the revised version dropped the implication that the tsar was perhaps not responsible for the mobilization. One may guess that this touch had been included as a gesture to the myth of tsar and Cossack, but was deleted when the sponsors of the interpellation decided that it was far too credulous and generous concerning Nicholas II.

In the debate, seven Cossack deputies supported the interpellation, while three opposed it. Kharlamov summarized the main thrust of the liberal Cossack position on the interpellation:

> such police service [as the Cossacks had been called on to perform in 1905–6] is incompatible with the title of Cossack, as a warrior and defender of the fatherland. Among the local Cossack populace there awakens that old Cossack spirit of freedom which created the Cossacks, which lived in them and which in the course of centuries our Russian autocratic bureaucratic government destroyed in the Cossacks.

This argument was pressed with passion and at times openly revolutionary sentiment. Kharlamov quoted an instruction from a stanitsa which stated that a government that does not fulfil the peasants' and workers' demand for land and freedom cannot be regarded as a people's government; 'this government serves only the interest of the rich and the propertied classes ... It is self-evident that our honour and conscience does not permit us to remain longer in the service of such a government.' The Cossack deputy Arakantsev ended his address: 'Let us join together for the common struggle against the common foe!' Another, Sveshnikov, also alluded to revolution and mutiny:

> Every day I receive letters from all the regiments, not only from our own Orenburgtsy but even from the Don Cossacks, which, sending their deputies, ask them to take counsel with the revolutionaries ... I know the mood of many regiments and say that if the Cossacks are not released [i.e. if the second and third turns are not demobilized], then they will ride off on their own.

The Don Cossack priest Afanas'ev attacked the patriotism on which Cossack service to the tsar was based: 'I, as a resident of the Don, know which clique created this patriotism, instilling it in the ignorant Cossack ... but I can bear witness that this is not the patriotism of the peaceful people.' Vydrin from the Orenburg voisko warned: 'The government should remember that it is impossible to exploit the Cossacks endlessly, that their patience can be exhausted ... They do not wish to fight with the Russian civilians and do not wish to ruin them and themselves.' Borodin read a letter from the 7th Ural regiment, which, after avowing loyalty to tsar and fatherland, protested that the mistreatment of 'innocent peasants' was contrary to their conscience and ended with the appeal: 'Deliver us from this shameful and reproachable service. It is not service but damnation! It is harmful to our fatherland.' Kriukov stressed the unbearable burden that the state placed on the Cossacks, the arbitrariness of the military administration of the stanitsa:

> What is a zemskii nachal'nik compared with our military adminis-
> trator, for whom the law is written neither in letters nor syllables,
> with an administrator whose breath fills the stanitsa with three-
> storey words when he comes to visit, turning his attention to the
> Cossack who has not yet performed his military obligation as well as
> to the old man, his father.

(He evidently refers to the commander of the okrug.) Sedel'nikov quoted a letter from a stanitsa of the Don which tried to dispose of the argument that the Cossacks had a vested interest in the inequitable distribution of land: 'Our grandfathers and great-grandfathers were all equal among one another, and we don't know whence there began in our midst the parasite-landlords [darmoedy-pomeshchiki] whom the Cossacks now defend.'[154]

Obviously the debate was wandering from the question of the legal forms by which the second- and third-turn Cossacks were mobilized. The conservative Cossacks resisted the proposed interpellation, claiming that the anti-regime stance of its adherents did not reflect the opinion of most Cossacks. In the Don the authorities attempted, not very successfully, to mount a campaign in support of the conservative deputies. A mere seven stanitsas of the oblast were induced to send 'instructions' attacking the interpellators. Two of these asserted that more Cossacks should be called up to strengthen those who were already on duty 'for the defence of our dear Russia and the reigning house, which is so close to our hearts'.[155] None of this had much impact in the Duma with its liberal majority, which heckled the conservative Cossacks when they attempted to defend the official position. In the end the Duma adopted the interpellation 'unani-mously', which suggests that even the conservative Cossacks lacked the hardihood to turn out and vote against it.[156] But nothing specific came of this parliamentary manoeuvre, for the tsar dissolved the First Duma on 8 July 1906, certainly not as a result of the interpellation but very much in response to the liberal opposition with which it was associated.

Elections to the Second Duma began in January 1907. Although the government stayed with its original electoral law, which had failed to produce a conservative legislature, it made some effort to improve its performance in the Cossack constituency. The demobilization of the second- and third-turn units had started before the election, and the state increased its economic aid to the Cossacks, although not necessarily as a deliberate election manoeuvre.[157] More specifically, the government sought to punish or harass some of the undesirable deputies to the First Duma. Four of the liberal Cossacks (Afanas'ev, Kriukov, Sedel'nikov and Borodin) signed the Vyborg Manifesto, a protest against the dissolution of the First Duma, which called for various kinds of non-violent resistance to the government, including abstention from military service. For this they were deprived of their political rights, meaning that they could not be re-elected, and were sentenced to three months in jail. Kriukov and Kharlamov lost their jobs in educational institutions, and the latter was obliged to leave Novocherkassk, while Arakantsev was fired from his job with the office of the procurator. But the most persecuted of all was the priest Afanas'ev, who was unfrocked and ordered to a monastery. Upon his refusal to go he was jailed.[158]

Despite these efforts, the Cossack deputies to the Second Duma were even more disagreeable to the regime than those in the First. All the voiskos except the Amur and Ussuri sent deputies to the capital, a total of 20, 13 of whom were Kadets, 2 Trudoviki and 1 for each of the Party of Democratic Reform, the Popular Socialists and the moderate right. One deputy was independent and the party loyalty of another was uncertain.[159] Many of the deputies, especially from the Don, received communications from their constituents, urging them to press for various reforms, although the local authorities succeeded in preventing all but two stanitsas on the Don from sending any formal instructions to their deputies.[160]

The most striking new development among the Cossack deputies to the Second Duma was an attempt to form a caucus to represent their interests, regardless of party affiliation. The idea had occurred to some deputies before the opening of the Duma, and on 20 February 1907, 17 Cossack deputies met in the Catherine Hall of the Tauride Palace and agreed to form a group. The initial suggestion was to call it 'The General-Cossack Fraction of the Duma Opposition', but on second thoughts they agreed to water down the partisan sound of this and simply call it the 'Duma Cossack Fraction'. In practice, 'Cossack Group' seems to have become the most common usage.[161] With visible enthusiasm for the idea, the group met twice on 21 February and elected as their chairman the Kuban Cossack F. A. Shcherbina, a corresponding member of the Academy of Sciences and author of weighty studies on the history and economy of his native voisko.[162] The same meeting adopted a four-point explanation of the motives for the formation of the group: to raise Cossack political consciousness, to add authority to the speeches of individual Cossack deputies, to 'cleanse the reputation of the Cossacks' following the 'sad role of the Cossacks in the liberation movement', to link the Cossack populace and the deputies.[163] Proceeding in this spirit, Shcherbina proposed a programme aimed at self-government, reduced military service and land reform and a drafting commission of three (Arakantsev, A. I. Petrovskii and Kakliugin) set to work on the document. By 27 March they had held 12 meetings, but well before that date a schism had opened within the group. To some extent this was a matter of right and left. From the first the Astrakhan deputy, Poliakov, nominally a member of the moderate right and a former deputy to an okrug commander, had been an anomaly in the predominantly liberal Cossack group. That he attended its meetings at all seems to have been testimony to the potential appeal of Cossack self-interest across the usual lines of right and left – unless he considered it his duty to attend the meetings so as to inform the authorities about their nature. When the Second Duma was dissolved Poliakov supposedly told Arakantsev 'Now you are in my hands ... I will report ... all your mutinous speeches in the sessions of the group.'[164] He and three other members of the group objected to the draft of the programme presented by the commission, because it included a preliminary section that took a liberal stand on a variety of issues that had no special connection with the Cossacks. The most divisive of these issues was a demand for a political amnesty, the abolition of the death penalty and the need for closer ties with the people. Poliakov certainly disagreed in principle on these points, but he was alone, and the effective resistance came from deputies whose objection to the liberal programme was not so simple. These were Karaulov (Terek), Zaplatin and Vopilov (both Oren-burg). The latter two were, respectively, Trudovik and Kadet, the former somewhat uncertain in party affiliation but sufficiently objectionable to the government that it took judicial steps to prevent his re-election to the Third Duma. According to an unfriendly witness, they did not oppose the disputed points on principle, but did not want to see them included in a declaration of Cossack aims. Linked to this matter of tactics was an uncomfortable one of procedure, which was inherent in the division of the Cossacks into 11 voiskos. The Don Cossack (and lawyer) Petrovskii, as secretary of the group, proposed statutes, according to which a simple majority of its members could determine joint policy. The effect of this was to give the Don Cossacks control of the group if they voted as a bloc.[165] Karaulov emerged as the leader of the dissenters. As depicted by his opponent Petrovskii, he was a rather erratic and devious character, who at one point said that he had been asleep at the meeting at which the disputed programmatic points were first read, and had therefore failed to make timely objection. Petrovskii also asserts that Karaulov, without informing the other deputies, published on 5 March in the conservative *Terskie Oblastnie Vedemosti* an article attacking the Don deputies for being too far left, for wanting to merge the Cossacks with the peasants, for being soft on Jews and for wanting to dominate the other Cossacks. This last point came to the fore on 14 March when Poliakov, Karaulov, Zaplatin and Vopilov, joined by the Kuban deputy Bardizh (who was not a dissenter in other respects), opposed simple majority rule within the group and instead asked for the rule of unanimity.

There was no agreement on this point, but on 27 March a compromise appeared to be reached on the programmatic differences. The three disputed points (amnesty, death penalty and links with the people) were dropped and each member was permitted to take his own stance on points not specifically covered in the programme. But in mid-April the Don deputies thought better of this compromise and withdrew from the Cossack group, which for the remaining few weeks of the Second Duma consisted of the ten non-Don Cossacks, minus Poliakov, who had in practice quit the group.

This shambles probably owed much to simple lack of political experience among the Cossack deputies to the Second Duma. Certainly there is no evidence of any substantial disagreement on the matter that had first brought them together: the common interest of the martial estate. It was probably a basic tactical error to try to link this concern with general issues of Russian politics and to ignore the traditional division of this common cause into the separate interests of the several voiskos, the smaller of which did not wish to be dominated by the largest. The portion of the programme of the group that caused dissension was not the part that stated Cossack goals, nor was the chief dissenter, Karaulov, wanting in enthusiasm for Cossack interests. On the contrary, his enemy Petrovskii, who is inclined to exaggerate Karaulov's leanings to the right, characterizes him as 'dominated by a mania for the most non-stop and uncultured "Kazakomania" '.[166]

The Second Duma lasted only from 20 February to 3 June. It did not become substantially involved in the affairs of the Cossacks, although the interest of the chamber was focused on them for a moment in the debate on Stolypin's field court martials. The Don deputy, Petrovskii, threatened the regime with Cossack mutiny: 'They set the Cossacks against the liberation movement. But this may be only for the present. I say to you: soon will come the time, and it is growing closer, when not one Cossack will raise a nagaika, and will not unsheath ...' Before he could say 'sabre' Petrovskii was interrupted by a storm of protest. Purishkevich, a right-wing leader, shouted: 'A lie, not true! ... Get out!' The Astrakhan Cossack deputy Poliakov interjected that Petrovskii was a Cossack in title only, a reference no doubt to his occupation as a lawyer. The chairman restored order with some difficulty.[167]

When Stolypin dissolved the obstreperous Second Duma on 3 June 1907, the regime issued a revised version of the electoral laws. The object was to obtain a legislature that would be comparatively compatible with the government, and to a considerable extent it succeeded.[168] The more conservative sectors of the population were given an even greater degree of overrepresentation than they had enjoyed in the previous system. As for the Cossacks, their representation was reduced in size and somewhat deliberalized in character. The former change came about by simply dropping all representation from the Semirechenskoe and Siberian voiskos, by reducing the Kuban delegation from three to one, and by cutting down the number of Cossack electors in the Don oblast assembly of electors. Formerly there had been 70 Cossack electors out of 177 in the Don oblast, now there were only 20 out of 142.[169] The deliberalization of the Cossack Duma contingent was accomplished partly by the device used in the country at large: the further inflation of the numbers of landowners and wealthy urban residents in the guberniia-level electoral assemblies. As a practical matter, this applied only in the case of the Don, for the only Cossacks who had a chance of election elsewhere were the ones who filled the mandatory Cossack seat in this or that guberniia or oblast. In the Don, where most of the members of the landowners' curia were Cossack nobles, it was still possible to return more than the one mandatory Cossack, although this would probably include noble Cossacks. In addition, the local authorities tried to prevent, legally or otherwise, the election of undesirable individuals. The Terek deputy Karaulov complained that the regional court issued a decree excluding him from the elections to the Third Duma because of 'his relations with the workers'. He succeeded in having this overturned by the Senate after the election was over. The same procedure was used, to exclude a Don (Kadet) deputy Ushakov, and the only Social Democrat ever returned by the Cossacks, the Zabaikal Cossack I. V. Voiloshnikov from the Third Duma. These cases stood out because the victim was a former Duma deputy, but there was also an undetermined number of instances in which less eminent persons who had been chosen as electors on the guberniia/oblast level lost their civil rights. This meant that they could neither be candidates for the Duma, nor influence the election of others.[170]

Unlike the First and Second Dumas, the last two Dumas at least completed the election process throughout the vast Empire, in the autumn of 1907 and 1912, respectively. Both included eight mandated Cossack deputies (Don, Kuban, Terek, Astrakhan, Orenburg, Ural, Zabaikal and Amur/Ussuri), and the Don sent to the Third Duma seven additional deputies who appear to have been Cossacks and to the Fourth six additional apparent Cossacks.[171] If the anti-liberal efforts of the government were not entirely in vain, nor were they strikingly successful. In the Third Duma there was one social Democratic Cossack deputy, five Kadets, two Progressivists, three Octobrists, three moderate rightists and one rightist.[172] In other words, more than half stood to the left of the Octobrists, who were themselves a species of liberal, albeit cautious and willing to cooperate with the government. In the last of the four Dumas the situation among the Cossack deputies decidedly worsened from the viewpoint of the government. Of 14 presumed Cossacks in the chamber, nine were Kadets, four Progressivists and one non-party.[173] In sum, the repeated efforts of the regime to manipulate Cossack elections of Duma deputies could not produce results that were compatible with the myth of tsar and Cossack. Exactly what the voting behaviour of the Cossacks reveals concerning the aspirations of the estate is hard to say, but it certainly seems to suggest a desire for some kind of liberalization of the system of military–bureaucratic governance.

This is what the Cossack deputies attempted to bring about, with scant success, in the Third and Fourth Dumas. Their overriding grievance was the rule of the War Ministry. Kharlamov was the most eloquent and persistent orator on this theme. On two occasions he equated the civil administration of the Cossacks with the military settlements of Arakcheev, a name despised by all Russian liberals and a system infamous for its harshness and rigidity.[174] The War Ministry, he charged, lacked the competence to deal with the civil administration of the Cossacks: 'neither the main Administration of Cossack Forces nor the War Ministry can have such organs, forces, information and materials as the Ministry of Internal Affairs possesses'. To some degree the War Ministry acknowledged this state of affairs by entrusting to other ministries, such as education and finance, some of the tasks that it could not handle. To take on itself the total civil administration of the Cossacks would require the War Ministry to establish 'in miniature' the entire state bureaucracy, which would be 'absurd'. Apart from its doubtful competence, the War Ministry was insensitive to the human needs of the Cossack population. It saw only the Cossacks 'caracoling in Petersburg and performing riding tricks in the Mikhailovskii Manège'; it forgot 'the needs of their families, their children, their wives, mothers, the old Cossacks ... and it does not trouble itself about them'.

Kharlamov rebutted the argument of the War Ministry that the separation of the military and civil authority over the Cossacks would result in 'the lowering of the fighting qualities of the Cossacks', and that this had been demonstrated by the experience of the Kuban and Terek voiskos in 1878. He maintained that the fighting qualities of the Don voisko under the statute of 1835 had been demonstrated in the prolonged war with the mountaineers 'in which the bones of the Don and other Cossacks lay in vast quantities on the fields of Georgia and the Caucasus Mountains'.[175]

Not only did the War Ministry cling to its legal authority over the Cossacks, it violated the Fundamental Laws of 1906, which required the approval of the Duma for all civil legislation. It was true that articles 86 and 96 of this code were ambiguous in this area. The former required that laws pass the Duma and State Council, but the latter reserved to the tsar and his ministers the right to issue orders concerning the 'combat, technical and economic' affairs of the armed forces.[176] But the ambiguity inherent in this legal situation was fairly well clarified in a ruling of the Council of Ministers in 1909. This stated that the civil affairs of the Cossacks, if they did not deal with the organization of the armed forces of the Empire, were included in the category of authority that required the vote of the Duma.[177] Nevertheless as Kharlamov caustically observed, the Military Council, without submitting the matter to the Duma, had established the post of 'feldsher–akusher' (medic–midwife) to serve the Cossacks.[178] Was this the kind of issue concerning 'combat' that the laws reserved for the tsar? Similarly, the War Ministry had bypassed the Duma in establishing a new office of deputy ataman of the Don voisko and had fixed the pay of the stanitsa ataman.[179] It was particularly galling when an agency of the War Ministry arbitrarily ended one of the vestiges of self-government of a Cossack voisko, as the ataman of the Siberian voisko did in 1912, when he made the 'councillors' of the ataman appointive rather than elective. This produced a Duma interpellation, but no retreat by the War Ministry.[180]

Most Cossack deputies to the Second, Third and Fourth Dumas sought to replace the arbitrary authority of the War Ministry and its representatives in the voisko with some form of civilian Cossack self-government. This goal was linked to the revival of Cossack historical consciousness, the myth of the olden days of independence and democracy. Such a goal surely had no appeal to the tsar or the War Ministry, but in the wake of the revolution of 1905, the authorities showed an unusual desire to be agreeable to the Cossacks. In the Kuban, and then in the Don, situations developed in which the authorities countenanced the official revival of the words rada and krug to designate a body that was no longer a merely ceremonial affair. In both cases the authorities sought to hold representative assemblies on a one-time basis to deal with the distribution of additional land to ordinary Cossacks, an attempt to placate a long-standing grievance.[181] This gathering was originally called a 'consultative assembly', a term that had no historical evocations, but when it met (in the Kuban, 17 December 1906; in the Don, 8–20 December 1909) it quickly became known as the rada and krug respectively.[182] In the Don the authorities not only acquiesced to the revival of this name for this particular assembly but even accepted, on paper, the continuation of the krug as an elected assembly. The draft law that the meeting of 1909 adopted provided for a voisko krug, composed of two elected representatives per stanitsa meeting every three years in Novocherkassk. The krug was to exercise 'definitive' judgement on questions of Cossack land distribution.[183] Granted, this was a limited sphere of activity, but it did establish the principle of an elected Cossack assembly in the spirit of the days before tsarist control, as the Marshal of the Don nobility, A. P. Leonov, noted with pleasure at the end of the proceedings.[184] Had such an assembly become a reality it might have proved difficult to limit its concerns. This seems to have occurred to the War Ministry as an unpleasant likelihood, which it took steps to avert. First, the law came into force only on 26 February 1910, and it gave binding authority not to the krug but to the ataman of the voisko.[185] Moreover, this authority chose not to convene the krug, even though the law required that it meet every three years. This left elected bodies to transact the more or less current business concerning the land reserve of the voisko: a 'land council' for the voisko and one for each of its okrugs. In meetings of the voisko land council there were references to the anticipated meeting of the krug, but nothing happened.[186] Lest the members of the land councils become too difficult on this topic, a new law of 11 June 1912 gave the atamans the authority to confirm the elected members in office and to discharge them at will.[187]

Clearly the authorities were unenthusiastic about the establishment of a potent krug or rada among the Cossacks, but their misleading appearance of permissiveness concerning this matter encouraged Cossack Duma deputies to persevere in their efforts to pass legislation on Cossack self-government. The Cossack Group in the Second Duma made the first initiative in this direction. Only two months prior to the formation of this caucus its chairman, Shcherbina, had chaired the Kuban rada, where he appealed to the 'Bat'ka Otaman' (father ataman) to 'convert the first Cossack rada into a permanent one'.[188] And it was Shcherbina who on 25 February 1907 proposed to the Cossack Group a programme of reform centred on an assembly elected by the (male) Cossack populace of each voisko (krug in the Don, rada in the Kuban, and sbor or s'ezd in other voiskos).[189] This was a boldly optimistic proposal. It specifically stated that the civil administration of the Cossacks should be removed from the control of the War Ministry, and the Main Administration of Cossack Forces should be dissolved. In place of the old system there was to be a clear division between the state and local self-government. The link between the two was to be the ataman, who would represent the central government and supervise the decisions of the local government. But in the larger voiskos the ataman was to be elected by the assembly, in turn elected by general suffrage. In the smaller voiskos, the non-elected governor would continue to be ataman. Within the voisko, the assembly was to make 'final' decisions on a wide variety of matters: land distribution, finance, education, public health, food supply and such economic matters as fishing rights and irrigation. Just where this left the supervisory power of the ataman is not clear. The assembly was to elect the standing executive of the voisko, the 'board' and all other responsible officials, as well as the ataman. In the Don it would even elect the voisko military command. In all voiskos this elected assembly would share with the War Ministry the determination of the size of the annual call-up for the first turn. Cossack voiskos would receive the reformed judicial system of 1864 and the zemstvo, the latter including both Cossack and non-Cossack representation. Finally, as a gesture to the practice of the olden days of Cossack independence, priests were to be elected by their parishioners.

The Second Duma was dissolved before this draft could be submitted, but it must have struck a responsive note among Cossacks, for it reappeared in revised form in the Third Duma, even though only four of the Cossack deputies to this session had participated in its predecessor. With this turnover, the animosities that had split the previous Cossack Group were nullified. There was no new effort to address the general political issues of the day, and it was therefore possible to concentrate on several legislative proposals concerning specifically Cossack affairs. Thus, on 17 December 1908 the group supported the introduction of a bill on the establishment of voisko self-government, including an assembly (krug, rada, etc.) elected by all adult male Cossacks.[190] Again, this body was to elect in turn an 'economic board' which was to exercise substantial authority over civil affairs. The ataman, as in the earlier draft, would have only the power to supervise the legality of the actions of the elected authorities. Indeed, its role was to be strengthened in that the voisko assembly was given responsibility for supervision of the administration of the stanitsa. The new draft also established an elected okrug assembly, which would elect the civil administration on that level. On the other hand, the drafters of the new proposal were less optimistic than their predecessors about some major aspects of the change that the Duma might be expected to obtain from the War Ministry. The new draft did not propose that the ataman of the voisko be elected, nor did it mention the abolition of the Main Administration of Cossack Forces or the participation of the assembly in the determination of the size of the annual call-up. The idea of elected priests also disappeared.[191]

An 'explanatory note' accompanied the draft, attempting to present the legislation as a relatively modest reform which would bring about improved administrative efficiency and prosperity. It attacked the existing administrative system not for repressiveness but as an excessively complex arrangement requiring all legislation to pass through the offices of the ataman of the voisko, the Main Administration and the Military Council. Self-government allegedly would improve the prosperity of the Cossacks and save the state the large sums that it was currently allocating to subsidize the voiskos. The only reference to the olden days of Cossack independence came in an allusive way, while explaining that the cultural level and experience of the Cossacks (partly in stanitsa self-government) prepared them for the reform. The note even maintained that the proposed institutions differed only in name from those already established in normal guberniias.[192] Here the drafters acknowledged that, unlike the existing zemstvos, the proposed assembly would not be based on separate elections in several estates. They maintained that this egalitarianism suited the Cossacks, whose officers and bureaucrats were few and 'were considered to be the equals of the Cossacks'. All of this was an attempt at innocence, presumably to disarm conservatives. Avoiding the rhetoric of the romantic–democratic Cossack revival, the drafters minimized the very real democratism of their proposal. After all, the existing zemstvos were elected by separate groups on an inequitable basis, and they lacked the wide powers that these Cossack assemblies were supposed to gain.[193]

The legislative process in the Duma moved slowly, or at least it did on matters that lacked widespread political support. On 26 May 1909 the chamber approved the bill on Cossack self-government for submission to its commission on local self-government.[194] There it rested until 29 October 1909, when it received inconclusive discussion, finally getting the attention and approval of the commission at the end of discussions on 30 May and 2 June 1910.[195] The commander of the Main Administration of Cossack Forces attended this discussion, and at his insistence the commission added a proviso that the War Ministry must retain full control of the military service of the Cossacks. In conceding this, the backers of the bill added a second proviso: that the funds of the voisko (not individual Cossacks) pay for all the expense of active service.[196] Neither this condition nor the idea of democratic self-government among the Cossacks could have pleased the War Ministry. When the legislation was reported to the chamber by Kharlamov for first reading, the commander of the Main Administration refrained from any detailed attack, but merely asked that the Duma defer action until the War Ministry presented its own programme for the reform of Cossack governance. He hoped that this would be possible by the autumn, but it was not.[197] The self-government that he alluded to involved the adoption of the zemstvo for the voiskos of European Russia and some sort of watered-down version of the zemstvo in other voiskos.[198] Very likely the War Ministry hoped that the Cossacks' own bill would die in the Duma without a direct confrontation, and if so they were right. Although the Duma responded to this first reading with a voice vote declaring that the measure was 'desirable', nothing more was heard about it in the Third Duma. It was reintroduced in the Fourth Duma on 27 February 1913 with only a few editorial changes, but proceeded no further.[199] It seems probable that the basic problem was a lack of enthusiasm among the liberals and hostility on the right. The former were generally sympathetic to the expansion of self-government, but gave no evidence of commitment to any special privileges for the Cossacks. The latter, who applauded the statement that the War Ministry would introduce its own bill, were unfriendly to the democratic trend among the Cossacks. The Kadet deputy from the Kuban, Bardizh, summed up the problem that the Cossacks faced when trying to win support for any of their special-interest legislation: 'When a Cossack takes the floor one hears all around, "he's going to weep, he's going to plead" ', and when it comes to limiting debate on a Cossack proposal the right says, 'Well, enough. Kharlamov has already sobbed out his heart and we know all that.'[200]

If the proposals of the Cossack Group for local self-government were too ambitious to stand any practical chance of acceptance by the Duma and the government, there was an alternative and less ambitious means of enhancing decentralized Cossack self-rule: the zemstvo. This seemed a particularly plausible goal during the Third Duma because there was much activity, some of it fruitful, concerning the introduction of the zemstvo into the parts of the Empire that had not received it in the 1860s. The Duma favoured this trend, although conservatives in the State Council did not. In a celebrated political crisis in 1911, Premier Stolypin had to persuade the tsar to use special emergency powers to overcome conservative opposition and enact the legislation implanting a modified version of the zemstvo in six western guberniias.[201] The following year, without any major confrontation, Astrakhan and Orenburg guberniias received the zemstvo, but this excluded the Cossacks of those provinces. Their omission was welcome to the non-Cossacks of the Astrakhan and Orenburg, who for many years had wanted the zemstvo but who had always been told that first a way must be found to modify the system so as to include the Cossacks of the guberniia. In Orenburg this problem was resolved after a fashion by conducting a survey of opinion at the stanitsa level, which satisfied the authorities and Duma deputies that the Orenburg Cossacks wanted no zemstvo.[202] Also in 1912 the Duma passed a bill introducing the zemstvo into areas of Asiatic Russia that included the Siberian, Zaibaikal, Amur and Ussuri Cossacks. In these bills the Cossacks were to be represented, but the State Council never passed the legislation.[203]

The revived interest in the zemstvo for Cossacks centred on the Don oblast. Here there was now substantial support among Cossacks and non-Cossacks alike for the introduction of this institution. Even General Maslakovets, who had done so much to scuttle the zemstvo in

1879–80, had come around to supporting it when he chaired the commission to investigate the economic condition of the voisko in 1899.[204] Three successive atamans of the voisko in the early twentieth century, the assembly of the nobility, the assembly that elected justices of the peace and the oblast commissions of the Witte inquiry on agriculture, all concurred.[205] At one point the tsar himself seemingly supported the idea of the Don zemstvo. In 1904 the assembly of the Don nobility used the right of petition that all such bodies possessed and asked the tsar to give the oblast the zemstvo. Nicholas replied, 'I do not encounter any obstacle to the introduction of zemstvo institutions to the Don at the present time. I believe that the Don nobility, in raising this petition, is guided by feelings of the deepest love for its native region.'[206] Was the tsar dissimulating, or was he unaware of the obstacle that did remain, the military bureaucracy in the War Ministry and the Don administration? Encouraged, the nobles applied in January 1905 to the Main Administration for the introduction of the zemstvo, only to be informed that the tsar had meant to imply support for the drafting of special legislation to adapt the existing type of zemstvo to the Don. The nobles replied that this was a misunderstanding, that the existing type of zemstvo was suitable for the Don. But now the tsar declined to concur.[207] Whatever was on the tsar's mind, he did not interfere with the efforts of the military bureaucracy to prevent the introduction of the zemstvo in the Don. This successful rearguard action against Cossack liberalism lasted throughout the Duma period.

In 1905, following the tsar's favourable comments on the zemstvo, the Main Administration of Cossack Forces sought the opinion of local spokesmen who might be induced to adopt a conservative position, the atamans of the Don stanitsas. Some of these wanted to consult the ordinary Cossacks in the stanitsa sbor, but they were told (in the approximation of a contemporary journalist): 'Why make it so complicated? The oblast administration sends you questionnaires, you fill in the required information – and that's enough! What's all this about a "conference"?'[208]

The War Ministry seemed content to do nothing more on the issue, but in the Third Duma the question of the Don zemstvo reemerged under the auspices of a newly-formed 'Don Group'. Unlike the 'Cossack Group', this was a coalition of Cossack and non-Cossack deputies, ranging from the right to the Kadets and including both Duma deputies and members of the State Council. Under the leadership of Efremov this regional interest group instigated the introduction in the Duma of a legislative proposal bearing the signature of 77 deputies. This simply called for the installation in the Don oblast of the 1890-model zemstvo, adding special representation for the Cossacks, the large-scale horse-breeders who rented voisko land and the voisko administration. On 3 April 1908 the Duma readily accepted the principle of the proposal and referred it to a drafting subcommission of the commission on local self-government.[209] In this body the War Ministry representative maintained that he favoured the objective, but was in practice uncooperative and argued that there was a major problem in the desire of the Cossacks to deny the nobility the privileged position that they enjoyed in the normal zemstvo.[210]

Far from moving ahead with its own draft, the ministry actually attempted to concoct evidence that the Don Cossacks did not want the zemstvo. They did this through a new inquiry in late 1908, based on an elaborate plan intended to produce a negative response. First, each stanitsa ataman would select two Cossacks to go to their okrug administration and discuss the zemstvo question. When they returned to report their opinions to their comrades, the stanitsa ataman would distribute to 'literate, sensible and thrifty selected householders' a brochure 'On the Don Zemstvo' proposed by the administration. Only then would the stanitsa sbor consider the matter.[211]

The administration could not openly prejudge the outcome of this investigation, but it used covert pressure and slanted 'discussion' of the issue to try to defeat the zemstvo. 'It is completely impossible', wrote a stanitsa resident, 'to discuss the zemstvo. Anyone seen doing this is jailed, for anyone who supports the zemstvo is considered a "propagandist" here, and the command promises medals and promotion to uriadnik for catching such a propagandist.' Elsewhere a Cossack claimed to hear a stanitsa ataman tell a group of 'elders': 'Even though I shall stand for the zemstvo [the ataman at least had to propose the question], you, you see, will disagree.' The official brochure on the question emphasized that in the 1880s 'the Cossacks themselves' decided against the zemstvo, that they 'did not want to conduct local government [zemskii] matters through their delegates' because 'the government fulfilled their wishes'. Other articles appeared in the official newspaper, raising the spectre that the Cossacks would be overwhelmed by non-Cossacks.[212]

In the meetings of the sbor, the familiar theme that the Cossacks were in danger of conversion to a taxed estate reappeared. The local 'intelligentsia' in some cases were excluded from the meetings, and the ataman on occasion had recourse to parliamentary tricks. A local correspondent in the Aksai stanitsa reported that that ataman asked the assembly: 'Do we want such a zemstvo, as does Novocherkassk?' 'Agreed!; God grant it and soon! Sign the decision, Your Nobility! Agreed!', came the reply. But the ataman stalled and found some elders to oppose the zemstvo. 'Holy God Himself knows what will come of this zemstvo! It's either the work of the pany [nobles] or the khokholy [Ukrainians]; they say it's likely that you'll pay for land and for a cow and for a goose and for water!' Against the shouts of the pro-zemstvo forces, somebody called, 'Postpone the question to another time!' 'Postpone, postpone!', a few chimed in, convincing the ataman that the motion to postpone had passed. Three weeks later, after a campaign of propaganda, intimidation and bribery, the sbor voted against the zemstvo. In the Lukovskaia stanitsa a two-hour speech by the deputy ataman of the okrug produced a 91–17 negative vote.[213]

Nevertheless, only 50 of 125 stanitsas voted against the zemstvo, although 23 of the majority favouring the innovation did so with the proviso that the Cossacks receive two-thirds or three-quarters of the votes in the zemstvo assemblies.[214] Dissatisfied with this outcome, the Main Administration opined that the results of the inquiry might be misleading. Therefore Deputy War Minister Polivanov went to the Don in the autumn of 1909 to conduct his own investigation ... and found that many Cossacks opposed the zemstvo. The commander of the Main Administration concluded from this that perhaps the results of the voting in the stanitsa sbors had not provided a fair appraisal of popular sentiment. Perhaps the okrug administration had pressured the populace in favour of the zemstvo! This was certainly disingenuous, and the subsequent order of the War Ministry to General Fon Taube, the new Don ataman, was more so. He was to draft a zemstvo law for the Don, or 'if the introduction of zemstvo institutions seemed impossible at the present time', to explain why this was so, providing 'precise data' in support of the conclusion.[215] In fact Fon Taube did produce a draft, which the War Ministry rejected.[216]

The Don Group concluded that the order to Fon Taube represented a commitment by the War Ministry against the zemstvo, so they proceeded on their own.[217] By February 1910 the drafting subcommission completed its work, which passed the commission on local self-government on 4 December 1910 and the Finance Commission on 5 May 1911. The chamber adopted the measure, 'almost unanimously', on 9 March 1912.[218] In most respects this plan, which was supposed to come into effect in 1913, followed the zemstvo law of

1890, including supervision by the Ministry of Internal Affairs, rather than the War Ministry. But, to accommodate the Cossack population, the Don zemstvo was to have a special electoral curia which would give the martial estate a bare majority – 158 out of 315 seats in the oblast assembly. The peasants would receive only 38 seats, the landowners, subdivided into two groups according to wealth, 119. Unlike the original Duma draft of 1908, the voisko administration and the large-scale horse-ranchers were unrepresented. Another kind of accommodation of Cossack interest appeared in the portions of the bill dealing with fiscal matters. The stanitsas were to receive two substantial subsidies, which presumably would obviate the Cossack's objections to the zemstvo on the grounds that it was a new financial burden. One subsidy was to compensate the stanitsas for the fact that the normal zemstvo land tax was now applied to land that the tsar had presumably granted to the Cossacks tax-free. This was to equal the cost of schools, public health institutions and the like. The second subsidy was to compensate the stanitsas for the loss of another privilege that had once been granted to the Cossacks by the tsar, the right to sell alcoholic beverages. This was set at 230 000 rubles per year, which was scarcely likely to make the idea of the Don zemstvo more attractive to the War Ministry, short of funds as it always was.[219]

The War Ministry hardly could have been pleased by the passage of this bill, but it attempted to preserve the impression that it was not basically opposed to the zemstvo for at least some Cossacks and that it was working on its own legislation.[220] Kharlamov observed that the Duma had 'heard this more than once', and indeed the ministry was still claiming in 1912 and 1913 that it was making progress in drafting this legislation.[221] But always there were references to serious problems, and it appears that only the submission of the Duma bill to the State Council galvanized the ministry into making a specific proposal. Even this turned out to be a manoeuvre intended to sabotage the Duma bill rather than to install any kind of zemstvo among the Cossacks. The War Ministry submitted not precisely a rival bill but only a draft plan that was considered to be 'reference material' for the State Council when it considered the Duma bill. The War Minister claimed that this was done because the draft happened to be in the hands of the Council of Ministers when the Duma bill reached the State Council, so the ministers did not have time to consider the War Ministry proposal article-by-article and could merely approve it in principle. Therefore, the War Ministry draft was not placed before the State Council as a bill that might be passed, but merely as reference material, which might in practice undermine confidence in the Duma version.[222]

According to subsequent debate on the floor of the upper chamber, the War Ministry 'counter-draft', as one member called it, still resisted the subordination of the Don zemstvo to the civilian Ministry of Internal Affairs. Furthermore, the chair of the zemstvo assembly should not be entrusted to the oblast marshal of the nobility, a person who would almost certainly be a civilian, but to an ataman of an okrug, that is, a military officer from the oblast civil–military command, chosen by the voisko ataman. The Cossacks would have weightier representation relative to the peasants in the War Ministry version than in the Duma draft, but the Cossack representatives would be chosen by the election of two candidates on the stanitsa level, from whom the administration would choose one. The War Ministry departed from the Duma proposal (and the normal model) by eliminating the curia of the nobility from the Don zemstvo. One might assume that this class would be conservative and therefore highly agreeable to the War Ministry. But the past few years had demonstrated that the Don nobles included too many men who were attracted to the revival of the myth of the free Don. Their assembly had even embarrassed the military authorities by petitioning the tsar for the introduction of the zemstvo. So the War Ministry draft eliminated this element, substituting representatives of the operators of the vast horse-breeding ranches, which depended on land leased from the voisko. This small and wealthy group was indeed noble, but much more concerned about maintaining its highly advantageous deal than in myths of an independent Don. Finally, the War Ministry proposed not to turn over to the zemstvo the existing medical and veterinary facilities, and it envisaged no substantial fiscal subsidies to the voisko to mitigate the problem of raising new taxes to support the zemstvo.[223]

Only on 26 February 1914 did the State Council debate the passage of the Duma bill on the Don zemstvo. To avert this erosion of its civil authority over the Cossacks, the War Ministry determined to come out in the open in its opposition in principle to the introduction of the zemstvo among the Cossacks. In taking this stance the War Ministry made common cause with an important conservative official of the Ministry of Internal Affairs, A. S. Stishinskii. He was the chairman of the legislative commission of the State Council and therefore had the task of reporting the Duma bill to the upper chamber.[224] His chief motivation emerged by implication when he spoke of 'the recent time of trouble' when 'in the hands of the government the Cossacks were that terrible force which crushed the revolutionary hydra'.

Stishinskii and the voisko ataman of the Don, General Pokotilo, evidently planned a joint assault on the idea of a Don zemstvo. The former was lawyerly, sophisticated, the latter a bluff, patriotic soldier. Together they appealed for the rejection of the principle of a zemstvo in the Don oblast, without any discussion of particular articles in either the Duma or War Ministry version. This, said Stishinskii, was the recommendation of the majority of the legislative commission, and it carried weight with the conservative body that he was addressing, half of which had been appointed by the tsar. The War Minister, General Sukhomlinov, played only a minor role in the campaign, explaining rather incoherently that he did not want passage of the bill that his ministry had drafted because further consideration had showed that 'real Cossacks (not self-styled ones)' had informed him that the zemstvo was unsuitable for the estate.

Stishinskii opened his speech against a Cossack zemstvo with a characteristically devious point. The Fundamental Law (art. 57), he argued, required that the Duma could draft a law only with a specific demand by 30 members if the pertinent ministry had offered to draft that particular piece of legislation. The War Ministry had said that his people were drafting a law for the Don zemstvo, but the Duma went ahead with its own draft without bothering with the specific demand. Stishinskii proceeded to an equally devious argument to prove that the Cossacks did not want a zemstvo. They had opposed it in 1875–82, when it had 'failed', and they did so in the inquiry of 1908, a survey that was conducted 'without any pressure from the side of the command'. He acknowledged that the economic condition of the Don Cossacks was poor, but considered the introduction of the zemstvo merely a 'cliché'. 'Various agitators mainly from the left parties' had described to the Cossacks 'the golden mountains of zemstvo agronomical assistance', but the 'sound sense' of the Don Cossack realized that the new institution would lead to increased taxation. With a good deal of statistical demonstration concerning the cost of self-equipped military service and zemstvo taxation, Stishinskii argued that the zemstvo would destroy the Don Cossacks. The issue, he concluded, came down to this: 'will there or will there not be Cossacks in Rus?' He used this archaism to lead into a truly romantic, and cynical, peroration in which he stated that in a 'mercantile' age only people 'who measure and value everything by the ruble' (and who 'in the given case gladly join with the left elements of Russian society') believe that the Cossacks are an anachronism that should be ended;

> do not raise your hand against the Russian Cossacks, against this distinctive manifestation of Russian life, formed by the creative genius of the national soul, a manifestation the like of which exists nowhere except in Russia; no, do not raise your hand, for the Cossack is dear to each Russian patriot, for the Cossacks are necessary to Russia.[225]

With much less legal and oratorical elegance Ataman Pokotilo reaffirmed the argument that the Cossacks did not want the zemstvo. Muddling the questionnaire of 1905 and the inquiry of 1908, he attempted to discredit the pro-zemstvo conclusion of the latter by observing that ten of the stanitsas that had favoured it were inhabited by Kalmyks, 'half-savage, semi-nomadic' people who 'render service as Cossacks excellently' but many of whom 'can't even speak Russian'. Pokotilo admitted that the economic situation was bad, and he even asked for increased direct financial aid from the government. But not in connection with a zemstvo. As an alternative, he was drafting his own plan for some kind of Cossack self-government, one that would be adapted to the peculiar features of this society. He was vague about the form that this should take, but it should somehow work so that 'at the head will stand the Voiskovoi Ataman, who from time immemorial and, praise God, to this day stands tall in every Cossack voisko, which can only gladden one, because only thus can order and discipline be preserved in Cossack life'. The nearest approach to specifics concerning such a 'reform' was a general reference to the Ural Cossack system of 1874, which, it will be recalled, provided for assembly of representatives with much less authority than the usual zemstvo.[226]

The rebuttal of these emotional and tendentious arguments fell to a few pro-zemstvo liberals, such as Academician Grimm, and the Marshal of the Don nobility, V. I. Denisov. Calling for a reduction of passion, they denied that the zemstvo bill was a left-wing idea and argued that the majority of Don Cossacks had come to favour the zemstvo. It would not seriously increase the local taxes that the Cossacks were already paying and would improve the impoverished conditions of their life without destroying the Cossacks' martial qualities. Evidently they sensed that the chamber was stacked against their case, and one of the pro-zemstvo speakers moved to refer the matter to a special committee of 15, which (the mover no doubt hoped) would bring in a more favourable report than Stishinskii's and allow time to rally support for the zemstvo. But this motion lost (78 to 64) as did the Duma bill itself (87 to 51). The civil administration of the Cossacks thus remained under bureaucratic–military governance while the Russian Empire endured.[227]

4 Financing an Anachronism

Слава казачъя да жизнъ   Cossack glory means a dog's life.
собачъя

Cossack saying.[1]

Stishinskii may have believed that 'only people who measure and value everything by the ruble' considered the Cossacks an anachronism, but in fact the Imperial regime for many years appreciated the Cossacks precisely because they were supposed to be an advantageous economic proposition. In theory, the land and other resources that the tsars granted the Cossacks to enable the martial estate to provide self-equipped military service was not nearly as valuable as that service. Around 1870 the Main Administration of Cossack Forces attempted to calculate the cost to the state of the Cossack system and to compare this with the situation that would come about if the Cossacks did not exist as an estate and their lands were transferred to normal civil status. It maintained that such a change would bring the state about 4.2 million rubles per year in revenue, which the existing system sacrificed to Cossack privilege in one way or another. But the annual cost of providing a military force equivalent to the Cossack contribution would be about 10 million rubles. And if the regime expropriated the capital assets of the voiskos, it would gain a one-time sum of about 4.7 million rubles, but lose 19 million to build installations.[2]

This was indeed a measurement by the ruble, and it may have had some degree of validity in the 1870s when complications of economic modernization had not yet affected the Cossack system profoundly. The land and other economic privileges that the tsar had bestowed on the Cossacks still sufficed to enable the martial estate to provide its part of the bargain. But the regularization of the Cossack forces and the rising cost of arms steadily undermined this ability, and in an

154

increasingly modern economic setting it became questionable that the martial estate could sustain itself. The financial relationship between the tsar's regime and the Cossacks was intended to be fairly simple: the benefaction of land and other privileges in return for military service. But with the passage of time this became increasingly overlaid with complications, and the state had to play an ever greater role in financing the system. By the early twentieth century it might have been argued that the state would have profited by ending the Cossack system to permit normal development and taxation of the voisko land. But the events of 1905 demonstrated that the grave stresses of modernization in the Empire as a whole produced revolutionary consequences that, from the viewpoint of the monarchy, justified the continued existence of the Cossacks even if they were an uneconomic institution.

THE VOISKO AND STANITSA BUDGETS

In law each Cossack voisko was a separate, self-sustaining corporation. Not only were Cossack troops supposed to train and equip themselves mainly at their own expense, but also the administration that made possible the military service was supposed to pay its own way without drawing on the general revenue of the Russian Empire. To cover these expenses, each voisko was expected to rely on certain tangible assets and fiscal privileges that the tsars had awarded to it. In a general economic sense, these properties and rights constituted the capital of the voisko, but in the usage of Russian law and officialdom, the 'voiskovoi kapital' (voisko capital) meant the cash balance on hand, from which the bills of the voisko were to be paid.

As with military organization and civil administration, the financial affairs of the Cossacks were subject to a long-term process of subordination to the central government. Control was still quite loose when the Don statute of 1835 was enacted, even though it represented an important step towards increased supervision. At this time there were a number of separate and autonomous accounts, each called a 'kapital', in the Don administration, and the law did not deal with all of them. The most important, the 'military capital', was subject to certain guidelines, but was 'entrusted to the direct authority and accounting' of the ataman and voisko administration. The voisko merely had to show its books to the agency called State Control at the end of the year. Given the weakness of commerce and formal education in Cossack culture, it is no wonder that the St Petersburg authority, on closing out this system, said that there were 'extreme shortcomings' in the accountancy that it provided.[3]

The War Ministry addressed the task of regularizing the fiscal management of the Cossacks along with its attempted reform of military and civil administration. An important first step was the definition of the legal character of the voisko capital. The War Ministry in 1867 posed this question to the State Council in a form which implied a serious dilemma: should one 'consider the capitals [funds] of the Cossack voiskos as communal private property or as voisko treasury property?' The first definition implied limitations on the right of the state to impose its control on these funds, but to consider the funds as a mere species of state treasury assets would imply a violation of the myth of tsar and Cossack, the concept that successive tsars had granted the voiskos certain property and economic privileges for all time. The council hit upon a formulation that served the interests of the state while preserving the myth of Cossack privilege. The capital funds of a given voisko, it ruled, were 'the property of the whole voisko, conceived as a special state institution'.[4]

This paved the way for the preparation of a new, basic law 'On the Administration of the General Voisko Capital of the Don Cossack Voisko', which was issued in 1871 and became the model for similar laws in other voiskos the following decade.[5] The authorities in the Main Administration of Cossack Forces wished to systematize the fiscal practices of the Cossacks and place them under more effective central supervision. In the case of the Don, ten existing 'capitals' were abolished and replaced by a consolidated 'voisko capital'. This did not mean that henceforth each voisko would have only one fund. In 1890 there were in the Don 30 'special capitals', apart from the voisko capital, including a pension fund for officers and civil servants, which was important, and various philanthropic endowments, which were not.[6] But the voisko capital was indeed the fiscal centrepiece and, as the law said, it was 'exclusively under the authority of the War Ministry', although administered according to the rules for state institutions in general, as laid down by the Ministry of Finance. Beginning in 1872 the voisko had to submit an annual budget for the approval of the Military Council. The ataman of the voisko could make only small changes in this budget, although emergency expenditures of up to 3000 rubles might be made pending ministerial approval. The authorities were extremely concerned that the voisko run in the black. The law 'strictly forbade' borrowing in case of a shortfall, but then went on to say that if 'exceptional' circumstances required borrowing, the War Ministry had to approve. The cash balance of the voisko was held by the State Bank, which paid interest on the account. But the voisko endowment was by no means large enough to enable it to flourish as a rentier. In 1879, for example, 9 per cent of the Don voisko capital revenue came from interest.[7] In most voiskos, a much larger category of revenue was the one that was called a subsidy (subsidiia) or grant (posobie). This was not an outright gift (until 1895 when this principle was modified), for that would have violated the idea that the Cossacks were self-sustaining. Instead, the theory was that the state treasury granted cash to the Cossack voisko only in lieu of various traditional privileges that the tsars had awarded the Cossacks in the relatively remote past and had subsequently withdrawn.

The main case in point was the liquor trade. The 'vinnaia regalia' was one of the most valued privileges granted by the tsars to the Cossacks, and as late as the Don statute in 1835 it was reaffirmed and spelt out in some detail.[8] But the chronically impoverished state could not bear to leave this valuable resource untouched. In 1862 the state ended the right of Cossacks to manufacture and sell spirits, excepting the stanitsas, which were still permitted to maintain taverns. In compensation the voiskos received a flat annual grant in cash (in the case of the Don, 1 239 000 rubles) based on the average sales over the previous three years. Despite increasing sales over the following years, not to speak of inflation, this grant remained fixed. Only in 1901, as a result of the abolition of the right of stanitsas to operate taverns, was the grant increased, merely by 230 000 rubles in the case of the Don.[9] This new total compensation for the loss of the liquor trade, 1 469 000 rubles, did not come close to the profit that the state obtained by the turn of the century, about 7 million rubles, a sore point with the Cossacks.[10]

The state also paid seven voiskos (Kuban, Terek, Astrakhan, Orenburg, Siberian, Zabaikal and Semirechenskoe) compensation for the termination of the 'Society of Merchant Cossacks' that had existed in each voisko before 1870. Members had paid their respective voiskos a fee in return for exemption from military service until that year.[11] In seven voiskos the societies were then terminated, and the voiskos received small annual compensatory grants, ranging from 2000 rubles in the Astrakhan voisko to 69 200 in the Kuban. As in the case of the liquor trade, these were fixed sums.[12]

There also were a few so-called grants from the state treasury to the voisko that reflected various local peculiarities. For example, the Orenburg voisko had not enjoyed the right to engage in the liquor trade and was not compensated when the state took over this commerce, but in 1879 its voisko capital nevertheless received over half its revenue from state grants in compensation for the right to lease gold-mining rights on voisko territory, in lieu of a bygone tax collection that had once been paid to the voisko and special payments to support the maintenance of two military cordons in Central Asia.[13] In the case of the Don, an additional treasury grant appeared when the voisko annexed and took over the administration of Rostov and Taganrog.[14]

In the 1870s roughly half the revenue of the capital of the voiskos derived from the state grant and half from other sources. But, because the various forms of state grant were mainly fixed sums, they constituted only about a quarter of all revenue by the turn of the century.[15] The voisko could not raise a large proportion of its revenue by direct taxation of real estate, because the tsars in their charters had provided the Cossacks with exemption from taxation of this sort. But the voisko could tax privately-owned land, a levy called the 'posazhennaia plata' (literally, the 'per sazhen fee'). Before 1895 only non-Cossack landowners paid this, but thereafter members of the martial estate also paid in the exceptional case that they owned land as personal property and not as a communal allotment. With the coming of economic modernization, this became a considerable source of revenue in some voiskos.[16]

In most voiskos, the most important internal source of revenue was the rental of land, forests, fisheries and mineral rights. In the Don, which had a great deal of arable land relatively near to the populous parts of the Empire, the rental of reserve land played a particularly important role, constituting 21 per cent of all voisko revenue in 1882 and rising to a high point of 42 per cent in 1907. No other voisko was as dependent on the rental of reserve land. The Kuban voisko received over 20 per cent of its revenue from land rental in the first years of the twentieth century, but no other voisko ever attained this level, and at about that time only one other voisko, Astrakhan, received over 15 per cent in this respect.[17] Until the enactment of a new law on land use in all voiskos in 1869, revenue from rental of the reserve was inhibited in the Don by a law of 1851, which permitted rental only to Cossacks and only for hay-making or grazing.[18] The law of 1869 removed these limitations and in the Don revenue from land rental increased, but not as much as it should have, owing to the inept business practices of the voisko administration. An inordinate share of the profit went not to the voisko but, in the words of the War Ministry, to 'local capitalists who look on the land not as an object of cultivation but as an object of profitable speculation'.[19] These operators took advantage of the auctions at which the administration found it convenient to deal in a few large leases rather than many smaller ones. For example, in 1875 in one auction in the Don a non-Cossack merchant rented a huge tract of 32 000 desiatinas, a Cossack merchant 18 000, a Cossack officer 15 000 and a *Swiss* citizen 17 000.[20] Only the wealthy could bid on such large tracts, which they could then sublet in smaller parcels at a great profit, as much as 300 per cent according to one official estimate.[21] In some cases the speculators improved their margin by bid-rigging, and some parcels of land passed through several middlemen before being rented by an actual agriculturalist, often a peasant, not a Cossack.[22] By 1901 the War Ministry was sufficiently concerned by the situation that it authorized the voiskos to rent tracts up to 20 desiatinas to ordinary Cossacks and peasants from 6 to 12 years at no more than 10 per cent of the going auction rate, but this had little impact in practice.[23]

The voiskos leased forests and fisheries, to Cossack and non-Cossack. The resources and market opportunities for fish and lumber varied greatly. The barren Astrakhan, Ural and Semirechenskoe voiskos had no forest to rent, while the more easterly voiskos had enormous forests but no ready markets or adequate labour force until the last years of the Empire. For example, the Orenburg and Ussuri voiskos earned much less than the Don at the turn of the century, but by 1912 had climbed well ahead of all other voiskos in timber lease revenue. The Don by that time was suffering from encroaching deforestation, the result of substantial forest leasing in earlier years.[24] In fisheries, the Ural voisko was the biggest leasor, followed by the Astrakhan and Kuban. The Don had great fishery resources but the voisko did not rent them out, and other voiskos obtained little or nothing from this source.[25]

As for minerals, the only deposits that earned much revenue for the voiskos in the later nineteenth and early twentieth centuries were coal in the Don and oil in the Kuban and Terek. These were assets of great potential value, but the government was slow to permit these voiskos to derive much benefit from them.[26] In the Don, with its rich coal fields around Grushevsk-Aleksandrovsk, not far north of Novocherkassk, non-Cossacks were forbidden to enter the coal industry until

1864. A new Don mining law of that year sought to attract non-Cossack capital for the general economic development of the voisko by offering favourable terms. In place of the former royalty of one-half kopek per pud of coal extracted, only one-quarter kopek was levied. In addition to this royalty on coal mined, the voisko received a relatively small revenue from coal mining in the form of a flat fee required to open a mine and the rental of surface rights to the operators.[27]

Substantial oil production developed later in the Terek (Groznyi field) and Kuban (Maikop), but for some years the law authorized the voiskos to collect only a flat fee and surface rental rights, not a royalty on production. The introduction in 1894 of a royalty was a bonanza for these two voiskos. The petroleum revenue of the Terek voisko capital had been only about 16 000 rubles in 1894, but by 1896 it was 295 000 and over 2 000 000 in 1910.[28]

Although ordinary Cossacks as a group were not taxed by the voisko, a significant amount of income derived from fees paid by 'non-serving Cossacks'. In voiskos in which the abortive Miliutin reform of 1867 applied, this meant that those who did not choose to serve and were not conscripted by lot paid an annual fee. After the new service law of 1874 came into force, those who were considered unfit for service but fit for labour paid a fee, unless they provided labour instead. In the Don, members of the Society of Cossack Merchants also paid a fee.[29]

The definition of the expenses that the voisko funds were to cover lay with the officials in the War Ministry, even before the budget law of 1871 made this authority explicit. Considering the chronically straitened circumstances of the Imperial government, it is hardly surprising that the officials in St Petersburg were inclined to spend voisko funds rather than state treasury resources as much as possible. From its beginning in 1857, the office charged with the administration of the Cossacks was wholly supported by voisko funds. Each voisko was assessed a share of the total budget of the central office, the Don paying 20 per cent.[30] The Cossacks paid not only the salaries of the civil and military personnel who directed their affairs but also the wages of the office cleaning help, rent for the office space and something towards the maintenance of the building, which was simply the War Ministry. There was even a charge for material supplied by the Main Intendancy Administration to make uniforms for the clerks and a charge to cover the expense of awards for the bureaucrats and to subsidize the education of their children. The voiskos also paid for the

Temporary Committee for the Review of Cossack Statutes. The expansion of the central administration of the Cossacks increased the cost to the voiskos from 64 000 rubles in 1860 to 190 000 by 1900.[31]

The voiskos not only paid the War Ministry but also the accounting agency, State Control, which managed their fiscal affairs. Whenever an unusual activity of the state occurred in connection with the Cossacks, such as an inspection of some sort, the practice was to charge it to the voisko. A minor but particularly mean case in point occurred in 1904 when the State Control office in Stavropol sent some of its staff to the Kuban to see that the state was receiving its proper revenue from the liquor trade. For this the Kuban voisko capital was charged 480.25 rubles.[32] In addition, there were special payments by the voiskos to state educational institutions, military and civil, outside voisko territory, which maintained scholarships set aside for Cossack students.[33]

The voisko also had to contribute to the budgets of the state agencies that supervised their affairs on a regional level. For example, the Orenburg voisko not only paid for the peculiarly Cossack 'economic board' but also shared in supporting the general administration of the Orenburg guberniia.[34] The Don oblast was not subject to any such non-Cossack regional administrative body, but this voisko had to pay for the general costs of an oblast that in time contained a majority of non-Cossack residents. This included payment for all police expenses. Even the War Ministry thought it unfair that the voisko had to pay for the courts in the oblast, while the fines they imposed went to the state.[35]

Although the tsar's accountants did not classify it as a grant from the Cossacks to the state, a substantial share of the expenditures of the voisko that were not paid to St Petersburg were devoted to military readiness. In 1894, a reasonably representative year, it appears that the military spending of the Don voisko capital was about 20 per cent of all expenditure not paid directly to the state. The military contribution of the voisko capital included one-third of the salary of its active-duty officers until 1884 in some voiskos (1902 in others).[36] For years the salary of officers on off-duty status came entirely from the voisko, and in 1884, when this remuneration rose from half-pay to full for the Don, Ural and Orenburg officers, the War Ministry pleaded in vain for the state to assume the expense.[37] The voisko also had to pay half the cost of rifles and small arms for its troops, and it had to supply ammunition used in training on voisko territory.[38] It bore the cost of its internal military administration, including the staff of the voisko and its subdivisions, training camps for new recruits and members of the second and third turns, repair facilities and miscellaneous military buildings. The law of 1871 required ten pages to list the items that the Don voisko budget had to cover in the military area, including rental of rooms for the choir and meat for regiments on active duty. Those voiskos, such as the Don, which provided artillery units, paid for a separate artillery administration as well as other special expenses of this arm. In the Don a major horse-breeding establishment to supply remounts was paid for by the voisko, not to be confused with private military horse-breeding in the oblast.[39] This does not include the military expenses of the Cossack family or the stanitsa which had collective responsibility for his readiness.

In addition to these substantial external charges, the voisko had to finance its internal civil affairs. There were special Cossack schools and medical expenses, albeit modest in scale.[40] The cost of managing voisko resources partially offset income from them. In his report for 1890 the Don ataman noted that the voisko mining administration cost 15 739 rubles against rental revenue from the mines of 70 275. Some voiskos maintained a considerable forestry staff. Others had to spend funds on the regulation of fisheries.[41] There was even something for cultural activities, apart from churches and schools. The most notable institution was the secular choir, a traditional Cossack speciality.[42] By law the voisko could make loans of modest size, interest-free in cases of disaster, and in the early twentieth century this became a significant drain on its resources.[43]

Despite its complexities, the budgetary system established in 1871, which lasted as long as the Empire, attained a kind of success. In the decade before the introduction of this system, the ledger clearly indicated trouble. The aggregate cash balance declined from about 14.5 million rubles in 1860 to under 12 million in 1865 and crept back to its 1860 level by 1870.[44] From this point the aggregate capital of the voiskos climbed impressively until it peaked in 1906 at about 40 million. The decades 1870–9 and 1880–9 each witnessed gains of roughly 5 million rubles, and the 1890s 11 million rubles. This trajectory continued into the first six years of the new century. Although the upward trend was quite steady, it was slow in the 1870s, which led War Minister Vannovskii to boast in his report for 1890 that the situation of the capital of the voiskos had been 'highly unsatisfactory' at the start of his administration in 1881 but was now 'good' thanks to his stewardship.[45] In any case, the rise of the cash balance of the voiskos owed something to both restraint in spending and

enhancement of revenues. Even though the authorities in St Petersburg used the Cossack budgetary system to milk the voiskos, there was
a real concern for the solvency of the system. In the military sphere it
will be recalled that the War Ministry did not increase substantially its
levy of Cossack troops in the last quarter of the nineteenth century,
and was frugal in such matters as the supply of officers. As for civil
spending of the voiskos, total expenditures were kept under control,
especially with respect to such amenities as education, medical care
and agronomy. Until the twentieth century, the increase in revenue
did not come in any significant extent from the state treasury. In the
early 1880s the state subsidy decreased markedly, from 3.8 million
rubles in 1881 to 2.8 million in 1884. Rebounding slowly, the subsidy
regained its 1881 level only in 1902.[46] This was not entirely the policy
of the War Ministry. Periodically that authority proposed to the State
Council that the voiskos should receive an increased subsidy from the
state. In 1882 the new War Minister, acting on the report of the Don
ataman, maintained that decline in the previous four years of the
voisko capital, owing to pressures generated by the new law on
military service, required state aid. The ataman optimistically asked
for an increase of almost 70 per cent in the payment in compensation
for the loss of the liquor trade and an outright grant of 313 766 rubles, a
total of over 1 million rubles.[47] The state responded by giving the Don
not money but an investigation committee, which met in the autumn of
1882. Its report was that 'the situation cannot be considered critical'
and that, instead of an increased subsidy, the state should consider
taking over some of the administrative expenses of the oblast, the kind
of expense that the state would pay for in an ordinary guberniia. The
Main Administration of Cossack Forces allegedly was working on this
problem, but it appears that the only concrete measure was the
transfer of the cost of prisons in the Don from the voisko to the state.[48]
More helpfully in 1884 the state took over the payment of the full
salary of active-duty Don officers, no longer only two-thirds.[49] And
indeed the wisdom of the commission seemed justified in the
remainder of the decade, as the Don voisko capital grew by about 40
per cent.[50] In 1891, the War Ministry was so pleased with its fiscal
success in the Don that it proposed a monument to the greater glory of
Orthodoxy, religious and fiscal: a vast cathedral to dominate the Don
Cossack capital of Novocherkassk. This project dated back to 1827
but had been dormant for want of funds. The authorities now planned
to build a cathedral second in size in the Russian Empire only to the
Cathedral of St Isaac in St Petersburg. It budgeted 1.5 million rubles

for a ten-year period and succeeded in creating a large and rather ugly
neo-Romanesque structure that has withstood the ravages of Bolshe-
viks and Nazis.[51]

Although the state had rejected the idea of an outright grant to the
Don in 1882, and did the same for the Terek voisko in 1886, the
government overcame its aversion to this idea in 1895 because of the
chronic difficulties of the Zabaikal voisko. The War Ministry in 1894
suggested an annual grant of 26 000 rubles for five years, and the state
agreed the following year to 19 600 without any definite term.[52] Only
after approving this concession did the State Council yield on a request
that the War Ministry had also advanced in 1894 concerning the
Orenburg voisko. Here the series of deficits led the War Ministry to
propose substantial help, the reduction of 85 000 rubles per year paid
towards the cost of the civil administration of the area by the state plus
an outright grant of 25 000 a year for three years. While the
authorities procrastinated in making a decision, the situation
worsened, and in 1898 the State Council agreed to reduce the voisko
payment to the treasury by 85 000 rubles per year and to make a
one-time grant of 115 000.[53] In 1901 and 1904, respectively, the
Semirechenskoe and Siberian voiskos each received grants of about
16 000 rubles.[54]

The financial system of the voisko was in many respects replicated in
the stanitsa, although among the Ural Cossacks all financial transac-
tions were conducted by the voisko. Elsewhere, each stanitsa
maintained its own budget, with sources of revenue and items of
expenditure generally following the pattern of the voisko. But the
stanitsa was a more self-contained financial entity, neither receiving a
regular subsidy from above nor rendering direct payments to the
voisko. The laws on the governance of the stanitsa, despite the efforts
of the regime to increase its control on the lower levels, did not provide
for very close supervision of local financial affairs.[55] The stanitsa
assembly elected a treasurer and was empowered to check his accounts
and to authorize both expenditures and revenue-raising measures.
The voisko administration was vaguely authorized 'in case of need' to
advise the stanitsa or khutor on economic affairs, but the local level
was in large measure on its own. Indeed, the various voiskos, even in
the last years of the Empire, seemed to have trouble learning much
about what was actually going on in the fiscal affairs of the stanitsas.[56]

The stanitsa could raise revenue by the rental of its land; the
collection of a fee for the right of passage of a cattle drive or the right to
operate a mine; the levying of fines; the exaction of a payment from

Cossacks who were unfit for service but able to work; and, until 1901, the licensing of taverns. The stanitsa could also collect interest on its cash balance. In practice the largest source of revenue in most instances was land rental.[57] This, of course, diminished the amount of stanitsa land that was available for distribution to the Cossacks as their personal allotment.[58] In the Orenburg voisko, stanitsas also relied on their communal land in another way to raise revenue: they set aside some of the best land for communal grain-growing, selling the crop for the interest of the stanitsa.[59]

Until the right of the stanitsa to license taverns was ended in most voiskos in 1901, this was often the second largest source of revenue. The conversion of this privilege into a cash payment by the state to the voisko, which kept the money for its own budget, was a serious blow to the stanitsa and a subject of numerous complaints.[60] But this right was retained in the Zabaikal, Amur and Ussuri voiskos, where it was in some cases the largest single source of revenue.[61]

The Don and Kuban stanitsas chose not to exercise their right to levy a direct personal tax on their residents, while this practice was erratically practised elsewhere. In 1894 only the Amur and Ussuri reported that their stanitsas collected a capitation of 2.50 and 5.50 rubles, respectively, on all Cossacks between the ages of 17 and 55. In 1904, however, it was the Terek, Orenburg, Siberian and Zabaikal voiskos in which stanitsas raised funds in this way, and the implication is that the others had stopped this practice. In the case of the Terek, this source of revenue increased dramatically following the revolution of 1905, rising from about 8000 rubles in that year, to a range of 32 000 to 40 000 over the period 1907–10.[62]

In most stanitsas the largest expense, as far as incomplete data indicate, was basic administration, and specifically the salaries of local officials, including clergy. Sometimes the construction and maintenance of buildings and bridges took first place, and occasionally schools gained this distinction. Other categories of expenditure included the purchase of drugs for a local pharmacy, fire-fighting equipment and, increasingly, the purchase of military equipment and horses for Cossacks who could not do so themselves when their active military service began. The fragmentary data available show that this was the largest single expenditure of the stanitsas of the Terek, running a close second to the general administration in the Don and Kuban.[63] Evidently the various voiskos and their stanitsas applied diverse interpretations of need concerning Cossacks who were beginning their active service. Although the Don was, by the turn of the century, regarded as economically hard-pressed, its average contribution per Cossack going on active duty in 1904 was only 46 rubles, compared to 107 rubles in the Kuban, where the Cossacks were more prosperous. In that year Astrakhan contributed the high of 118 rubles per mobilized Cossack and Orenburg, certainly not a wealthy voisko, only 13 rubles. Thus in the voiskos in which the stanitsas shouldered a substantial part of the cost of military equipment, the very principle of Cossack individual self-help was diluted. As a result the total expenditures of the stanitsas of the Kuban in the 1890s and early twentieth century were about double that of the Don, despite the fact that the Don had the larger population.[64]

The stanitsa budget system operated in the black, the cash balance rising from 1.8 million rubles in 1882 to 10.6 million in 1902.[65] Thus, if one looked only at the bottom line of the voisko and stanitsa ledgers, one would conclude that the Cossack financial system was flourishing in the late nineteenth century and the first years of the twentieth. This, however, reflected not the prosperity of the Cossack people but the effective economic exploitation of the martial estate. To understand the seriousness of the disjuncture between the official financial order and the real economic circumstances of the Cossacks, it is necessary to consider the land on which the estate lived.

THE LAND AND THE LAW

The fundamental benefaction of tsar to Cossack was land. No other estate of the Empire received specific parcels of real estate as its corporate property. This provided the territorial basis for the special form of governance that applied to the Cossacks, and it represented the economic foundation of a populace that was increasingly dependent on agriculture for its livelihood and the financing of its special military obligations.

But did the Cossack voiskos actually own their territory? The charters that granted tracts of land to the Don and Black Sea voiskos in the 1790s did so in very general terms that hardly covered all the contingencies that might arise in a more settled and economically developed situation. The Temporary Committee for the Review of Cossack Statutes was by no means sure that the Cossacks had actually received from the tsars unconditional title to their land. One idea that the Committee entertained certainly did not take seriously the idea that the Cossacks had permanent title to land. This was the proposal that the law of 1866 that emancipated the state peasants should be adapted to the Cossacks.[66] Although not serfs of private landlords, the state peasants had been a class of bound labourers who had no title to their land. After emancipation, the communes of former state peasants compensated the state for the land that they received, parallel in principle to the redemption dues that the former landlords' serfs paid. Had the Cossack stanitsas received land on such terms, it would have made a mockery of their supposed tsar-granted right to their land. In fact, the Committee decided against applying the law of 1866 to the Cossacks, not because it would violate their rights but because it would interfere with the performance of their military obligations. The argument ran that if the Cossack stanitsas became the owners of land, this would entitle the Cossacks to sell the land to non-Cossacks, thus depriving the martial estate of the wherewithal to pay for their service.[67]

The consideration of such problems drew the Temporary Committee to the more general question of collective Cossack land title, which struck them as a dangerous pitfall, to be skirted if possible. The official account of the deliberations states that the Committee 'did not find it opportune to submit this question to special discussion'. The charters already existed, they argued, and in case of disputes it would be up to the courts to decide what the land rights of the Cossacks actually were. 'In any case ... it was all the more useless to predetermine questions of the rights of Cossack voiskos to land in that the state, as the supreme sovereign, had the right to dispose of these lands ...'[68] Clearly the bureaucrats were reluctant either to infringe rights that the autocrat might have intended to grant the Cossacks, or to undermine the future potential power of the state to make use of a valuable asset.

The ambiguity concerning the legal title of the Cossacks to the land that they had been granted surfaced in the annual reports of the War Ministry after 1880. In the Don and several other voiskos, private individuals at one time or another obtained legal possession of parcels of land.[69] This land remained within the boundaries of the territory granted by the tsars to a Cossack voisko, yet it was owned by private individuals. It might be argued that there were private enclaves within the voisko, but the bureaucrats did not commit themselves to this position, which would have implied a violation of the 'monarchial word' in granting in perpetuity to the Cossacks all the land within the boundaries of a voisko. The drafters of the annual reports simply listed separately the total size of the land of, for example, the Don, and its voisko and non-voisko components. How there could be land that was and was not Cossack corporate property remained a paradox.[70]

As the Temporary Committee had expected, a test case concerning the absoluteness of Cossack land-ownership did reach the highest court of the Empire in 1894. A person named Kalmykov attempted to assert his claim to private ownership of some land in the Don by right of prescription, 'squatter's rights'. At this time, the Senate rejected his claim. But in 1909 the War Ministry sought to make this ruling a law, arguing that, if voisko or stanitsa land could pass into private ownership by means of long occupation, this would violate the charter of 1793 as well as the Don statute of 1835. Perhaps they would have served Cossack interest better if they had left well enough alone, for the Council of Ministers rejected the proposed law and the tsar gave his approval to a ruling that Cossack land could not be exempt from the general law on ownership by right of prescription. In short, the tsar was unwilling to affirm without qualification the Cossack right to the land that he had supposedly awarded them.[71]

One aspect of the question of the fullness of the property rights of the voisko seems to have caught the attention of the Temporary Committee for the Review of Cossack Statutes when they revised the Don statute of 1835 with respect to land. According to that law, the land allotted to the stanitsas 'is considered the inviolable property [neprikosnovennaia sobstvennost'] of the commune of the Cossacks of each stanitsa ...' For the committee flatly to withdraw this seemingly unqualified assertion of ownership would be a violation of the tsar's promise, but the formulation evidently discomfited the drafters of the new law. They therefore found alternative wording, which introduced an element of ambiguity into the matter: now the land allotted to the stanitsa 'is the communal possession [vladenie] of the commune of each stanitsa'. Some sort of ownership remained, but the connotations of the new wording surely were intended to give future legal hair-splitters an opening, should the need arise. The root of 'vladenie' implies power over something, while that of 'sobstvennost'' refers to one's own self. And in any case, the awkward word 'inviolable' (neprikosvennaia) had vanished.[72]

In general, however, the land law produced by the Temporary Committee followed the main lines of the Don statute of 1835, which it considerably condensed and simplified. Enacted on 21 April 1869, it remained in force, with only minor changes, until the fall of the Empire, covering all Cossack voiskos, except the Ural.[73] Its basis was the division of Cossack land into three categories: for (a) stanitsas, (b) officers and civil servants (c) 'the needs of the voisko'. Thus the actual Cossack populace did not enjoy the right to all the land that the tsars had granted to the voiskos. A share of this resource was reserved for the officers, according to separate legislation, which appeared later at various dates for separate voiskos. Another share was placed at the disposal of the voisko administration to form a 'reserve'. Some of this land would be more or less permanently allocated to voisko forests, or to military reservations, or to other public needs; some of it might be transferred to the stanitsas to accommodate population growth; and some of it could be rented to provide revenue for the voisko budget. The share allotted to the stanitsa (the 'iurt') was to be calculated on the basis of 30 desiatinas of 'good' (udobnyi) land for each male Cossack, officer or civil servant living there.[74] On paper, this was a generous benefaction, derived from legislation of 1835, when land was still plentiful, relative to the population of the martial estate. If the law of 1869 had meant that each male Cossack of age 17 actually received 30 desiatinas, as Cossacks liked to believe, then Cossack family farms would have been impressive in size. For example, a multigenerational family with five males of at least age 17 would have the use of 150 desiatinas or 405 acres, a substantial family farm even in the United States in this period, and wealth beyond the dreams of Russian peasants. But the law referred only to the basis on which voisko land was to be awarded to the stanitsa, not to the size of the individual Cossack allotment. And the law did not expect this basis to hold up in reality. The third article of the law stated that 30 desiatinas was merely 'normal', and the fourth somewhat ominously discussed the steps that would be taken when the land per Cossack fell below 20 desiatinas: land would be transferred from the voisko reserve, expanding existing stanitsas or forming new ones, restoring the normal supply of land per capita. To accommodate this goal, the law required that the reserve be one-third of the total of stanitsa land, which implied that only moderate population growth could be covered, and nothing was said about what would happen when the reserve was gone.

Intimations that the 30-desiatina norm would not mean much in practice appeared in additional decrees concerning the application of the 1869 land law in certain voiskos. These decrees started with the premise that the varying quality of land made it unreasonable simply to apply a single norm for the per capita Cossack allotment. Therefore, the survey process should include the appraisal of land according to quality and the establishment of a hierarchy of categories. Thus in the Kuban, a region of excellent agricultural land, there were five categories. Where the best quality of land was involved, the per capita allotment was only 16 desiatinas; only in cases of the poorest land did the 30-desiatina norm apply. In the Astrakhan voisko the range was 15 to 80, reflecting widely varying conditions; in Orenburg, 21 to 29.[75]

According to the law of 1869, once a parcel of land was awarded to a stanitsa it could not pass into the possession of any private owner. The individual Cossack in a given stanitsa merely had the use of portions of its land. Each had the right to a household plot, on which he could own buildings and which he could rent out for a maximum of 24 years. And each had the right at the age of 17 to a 'pai' or equal share of farmland, which he could rent out for a maximum of 12 years. But his claim to this land was temporary. The law specified that a majority vote of the community in the presence of a quorum of two-thirds of the eligible voters could redistribute the land among its residents. The right to an allotment was awarded to officers and civil servants resident in a stanitsa, apart from additional land that they might receive under special legislation.[76]

The need for a special land law for the Ural voisko arose from the strong attachment of these Cossacks to the idea that their land belonged collectively to the entire voisko and could not be parcelled out to stanitsas. The administrators in St Petersburg dealt with this eccentric voisko in gingerly style, issuing a land law only in 1882. Even then the law was exceptionally brief, passing over the tripartite division of voisko land that was the basis for the general Cossack land law of 1869. Moreover, it was explicitly experimental, establishing trial land norms per capita for a three-year period, and in 1886 there was a revised version.[77] The Ural land law merely stated the amount of land that various categories of voisko members were entitled to utilize for agriculture 'without the right of transfer to another person': for ordinary Cossacks 25 desiatinas in the 1882 version and only 20 in the 1886 revision; ten for those under serving age or unfit to serve; 50, 75 and 100 desiatinas, respectively, for officers, staff officers and generals (and their civil service equivalents). In addition to this allotment, Ural Cossacks could rent from the voisko as much as 210 desiatinas per family at three rubles per desiatina. This was a steep price, profitable for the capital fund of the voisko, considering that the average rent per desiatina of land belonging to the reserve of the adjacent Orenburg voisko was only 0.14 rubles in 1885. But the Ural Cossacks derived a significant benefit from their land law, compared to the other voiskos. The Ural land that was not allocated to members of the voisko was not called a reserve and thus was not subject to rental by the administration to outsiders. Only Ural Cossacks could farm the land that the tsars had bestowed on their voisko.[78]

The legal position of Cossack officers with respect to land evolved separately. As noted previously, Don officers attained noble status through an edict of 1798.[79] Some members of this class acquired the use of large tracts of land, often trampling the rights of stanitsas. By 1823 the wealthier nobles of the Don, constituting less than 1 per cent of the population, occupied 27 per cent of the land. They built homes, planted orchards and woodlots, and above all settled serfs on their estates. Most of these bound labourers came to the Don as fugitives from serfdom elsewhere, especially the Ukraine. During most of the eighteenth century they were regarded as free peasants, working on a contract basis on the land of a Cossack noble. To assist the collection of the capitation or 'soul tax', the regime registered these labourers on the land of the noble with whom they had contracted, and then in 1796 made them his serfs. By the year of emancipation, 1861, there were about 280 000 males and females in this category in the Don, but only insignificant numbers in other voiskos.[80] Early in the nineteenth century the regime recognized that its support of the interests of the Cossack nobility was threatening the military objectives of the system. If the acquisition of land by the nobles was not checked, the ordinary Cossacks in the stanitsas could not provide the service that was required of them. Hence a commission was appointed in 1819 to consider legislative remedies in the context of a general systematizing of law on the Don voisko. After years of complex politicking, this produced the Don statute in 1835, which tried to put a stop to the acquisition of voisko land by the nobles. The land of the stanitsas henceforth was to be inviolate, but the nobles at this point received personal title to land under certain conditions. The boundaries of the stanitsas were to be surveyed, and nobles whose estates were within stanitsas had to exchange these estates for new allotments from free voisko land. The nobles' land was in all cases allotted on the basis of the number of male serfs who were counted in the 'eighth revision' (1834): 15 desiatinas per 'soul' (male) if the estate was already outside any stanitsa; 20 desiatinas if the noble had to exchange his estate within a stanitsa for voisko land elsewhere.[81] One contemporary stated that the requirement that some Cossack nobles vacate their estates and move to new land 'struck like thunder', and another wrote that some of them believed that they were entitled to all the land that they had settled. But, he continued, others, 'more reasonable, understanding the insecurity of their former ownership, were satisfied with the allotment of 15 or 20 desiatinas per revision soul, understanding well that securely and firmly consolidated ownership of less is always better than even a vast amount, held in temporary use'.[82] The statute of 1835 was a boon for the minority of nobles who owned a large number of serfs, yielding to these aristocrats the title to land that the tsars supposedly had granted to the Cossack voisko.[83] But the law was far from favourable to the interests of the larger number of Cossack nobles who had few if any serfs, in some cases getting along with labour-extensive cattle-raising. The majority of Don Cossack nobles became dependent on life tenure grants of land that the stanitsa in which they lived was required to make: 1500 for a general, 400 for a staff officer and 200 for a lower officer. They could buy this land at fixed rates, but for most of them this was impossible.[84] Indeed, the system was so unsatisfactory that in 1857 a new law was issued for 'estateless and small-estate officers'.[85]

This legislation was more generous towards the officers in that it added 100 desiatinas to the allotment of generals, established a new, 800-desiatina level for colonels, and provided for widows and orphans. But the allotments remained on a temporary basis, and the settlement of serfs was explicitly forbidden. Land was now granted in 15-year renewable terms (including retirement and the life of a widow), contingent on 'irreproachable' service. An advocate of the Don officers maintained that the law pressed many of them into 'extreme poverty, need and even heavy work!' So bad was their plight that he observed cases, especially in the elite regiments, in which ordinary Cossacks declined promotion to officer rank.[86]

The principal grievance of the Cossack officers concerning their land allotments was not so much the size as the impermanence of the title. In 1863 the committee that had been established in Novocher-kassk to review the Don statute of 1835 unanimously requested that the existing allotments be given to the officers as private property, and this proposal was adopted by the body which in 1865 took over the task of legislative reform, the Temporary Committee for the Review of Cossack Statutes in St Petersburg. In 1865 the commission proposed to the Military Council a draft that attempted to enable the officers to acquire their land allotments as personal property, in the Don through immediate gift of the existing allotments, elsewhere after the officer had served for 15 to 25 years, depending on rank. This plan visualized a finite amount of land available for permanent grants of officers (and their heirs, who had no obligation to serve), a million desiatinas in the Don and an unspecified amount of reserve land elsewhere. To provide financial security for officers who would be promoted after the exhaustion of this land fund, the draft called for a modest tax on the land grants in order to form a pension fund which would be used to pay pensions to these officers.

But the Military Council rejected this proposal, taking seriously the idea that the charters of the tsars committed the land to each voisko as a whole. On this principle, the Council even went so far as to order the commission to produce a plan by which Cossack officers would be compensated with cash, not land, and that land previously awarded to officers as their private property be returned to the collective ownership of the voisko. The Don ataman argued in response that if the officers were deprived of their land this would transform thousands of families into a 'dangerous proletariat'. He insisted that the officers receive title to their land through some means, and the War Ministry officials yielded on the principle. The Don authorities then drafted a compromise proposal that would have continued the temporary land grants for officers that already existed, with the right of purchase of these allotments by the occupants, a right that had existed in the 1835 statute, but was ended in the 1858 law. This proposal the Don ataman submitted to the War Ministry on 15 December 1869, but by that time the picture had changed fundamentally. Tsar Alexander ii, who was aware of the debate on this issue and who was probably lobbied by the Don magnates, on 1 September 1869 announced that he wished to celebrate the tricentennial of the formal founding of the Don voisko by giving the Cossack officers permanent title to the land that they previously held as temporary grants. In choosing this occasion, Alexander meant to regard this new benefaction as a symbol of the paternal relation of tsar to Cossack, though the particular policy in question might justifiably be considered a betrayal of the interests of the ordinary Cossacks in favour of the Cossack nobility. Certainly it violated the charter of 1793 concerning the donation of the land to the Don voisko for all time. It might be argued that the officer–proprietors were Cossacks, but they had now gained the right to sell their land to anyone.[87] Alexander's wishes reversed the thinking of the Military Council on the question of private ownership of land by Cossack officers. When next this body received legislation establishing this hereditary possession, they spoke not of the rights of the voisko according to the charter, but of the economic benefits that would flow from full proprietorship.[88]

The complexities of this issue prevented the Temporary Committee for the Review of Cossack Statutes from having any conclusion concerning officers' land to include in the general law on Cossack land when it was published on 21 April 1869. But with the tsar's decision on the basic issue of private ownership, the Temporary Committee was able to fill this gap fairly quickly, using as its basis drafts that had been submitted by both the Don ataman and the viceroy of the Caucasus, the latter concerning the Kuban and Terek voiskos. Both started with the principle of giving officers then on duty hereditary land title in return for some kind of payment that would establish a fund, the interest on which would provide a pension for retired officers and their dependants. The effect of this was to favour officers who were on active duty at the time the law was enacted (and their heirs), as compared with anyone who became a Cossack officer afterwards and whose antecedents had not been officers. Both categories would receive a salary on active service and pension on retirement, but only the first category would also own land which had come into the family as a grant from the voisko. Presumably the framers of the law did not expect this distinction to be a large problem, owing to the tendency of the Cossack officer corps to be a hereditary caste. Moreover, the new law did not abolish the right of officers to a temporary allotment of stanitsa land for 15 years per term, according to the law of 1857. Approved by the Military Council, these principles became law for the Don, Kuban and Terek voiskos on 23 April 1870 (just in time for the Don tricentennial) and for the Astrakhan, Orenburg and Siberian voiskos in the next few years.[89] In drafting the final version of the law the committee chose to call the payment that the new officer-landowners would make to the pension fund a 'tax' (oblozhenie) rather than a 'redemption' (vykup), the latter being the term proposed by the Don ataman. This distinction was intended to emphasize the generosity of the tsar in giving the land and the unconditional ownership by the officers. The tax itself was related to land quality, in the Don ranging from 12 kopeks per desiatina down to 3, in addition to a flat rate of 1.5 kopeks per desiatina which had been charged ever since 1835.[90] Additional revenue for the officers' pension fund was to come from a payroll deduction contribution by officers and from taxes on the land of peasants, emancipated in 1861. These were the former serfs of the Don nobles who had received permanent possession of settled land under the terms of the statute of 1835. Like serfs in normal guberniias, they received upon emancipation part of the estates on which they lived, 370 525 desiatinas in all by the early 1870s, when the process was complete. This peasant land became a category of voisko land which was not really voisko land in any sense, except for the payment of this tax to the officers' pension fund. Emancipation of the serfs did not, however, represent a new depletion of the land available to ordinary Cossacks, since the peasants' land was taken from estates that had already been alienated from the voisko by the statute of 1835. All told, in the early 1870s about 19 per cent of the land of the Don (2 795 490 desiatinas) was in the hands of officers (1.2 million in hereditary title and 1.1 million in temporary title) or peasants – a substantial diminution of the total land that the tsar supposedly promised to the Cossacks.[91]

This pattern did not, however, remain stable. As in the rest of the Russian Empire, Cossack noble landowners tended to be unsuccessful farmers, much of their land passing into the ownership of others. In the voiskos there was a limit on this, because only the land granted as hereditary property could be sold, although all noble land was subject to rental. By 1885 about 80 per cent of the land of the Don nobility was mortgaged, and much of this was sold to non-nobles because the former owners could not service their debt. Just what proportion of the hereditary land of the Don Cossack nobility passed into other hands is not established, but the Soviet historian Khlystov believes that transfer of land out of noble ownership was faster in the Don than in the average Russian guberniia. And his research indicates clearly that the new owners were rarely ordinary Cossacks. In the Orenburg voisko there were speculators who specialized in buying officers' land cheap and selling it dear. Much of this land, ran the Cossack complaint, passed into the hands of German colonists, peasants and (the choicest parcels) merchants.[92] The tsar, it seems, had neither honoured his promise to give the voiskos their land in perpetuity, nor had he rewarded the Cossack officers as richly as he had intended.

LAND TENURE IN PRACTICE

It was one thing to write law and quite a different matter to implement it. The Cossacks in the stanitsas seem to have been quite casual in their observance of many of the things that officers and bureaucrats put on paper in St Petersburg, and in particular the requirement of the 1869 law that the allotments of ordinary Cossacks (the pai) be equal. For many years before the new land laws, the stronger and more fortunate Don Cossacks extended their use of stanitsa land at the expense of their neighbours. Utilizing the tradition, appropriate to a frontier society in which land was abundant, that each Cossack could plough as much as he wanted, some Cossacks had taken large tracts for their use. Often this was accomplished simply by ploughing two or three furrows ('rarely as many as seven') around a plot. An ambitious Cossack could thus stake his claim to quite a lot of land, hiring peasants or poor Cossacks to work it for him. Although they could not own land, such wealthy Cossacks could accumulate major capital resources in the form of animals and implements. Kharuzin cites an unusual case of two brothers who worked over a thousand desiatinas, owning 75 harrows and 30 or 40 ploughs. Among poor Cossacks, in contrast, one found two or three Cossacks sharing one plough.[93]

By the 1860s it appears that the poorer Cossacks had started to press for a redistribution of stanitsa plough land on a more equal basis. It was a slow and uneven process, which depended on the traditional right of the assembly of the stanitsa to redistribute land. If there were references to the law of 1869, which required equal allotments, this did not reach the attention of Kharuzin. The first point that the poorer Cossacks tried to establish was that the wealthy did not have hereditary right to their tracts. In some cases the assembly voted that land left fallow for one to three years could be claimed by any member of the community, in other cases that nobody was permitted to use a plot for more than three years.[94]

But the crucial step that had to be taken if a stanitsa was to attempt the equalization of landholding was a repartition, which, according to the law of 1869, could be accomplished by a two-thirds vote of the assembly.[95] One obstacle to this was the persistence of the myth of the free Cossack of the frontier. Kharuzin encountered considerable support for the view that 'The land is not parcelled out, but one ploughs it freely, as our ancestors established from time immemorial.' Then there was the opposition of the wealthy element in the stanitsa, who often dissuaded others from repartition by means of rumours of imaginary dangers, above all that it would lead to the transfer of some of the land to non-Cossacks. The well-to-do often controlled the stanitsa administration and prevented the appearance on the agenda of repartition, even when the voisko administration urged it. As late as 1892 a correspondent in Kobylianskaia stanitsa reported that the oblast had sent the stanitsa officials a memo urging land equalization, but nothing had been done.[96]

Repartition required a survey of the land of a stanitsa, a novel and suspect procedure in the eyes of many Cossacks. Rather than hire a professional, some stanitsas attempted to do their own surveying, paying a small fee to elected surveyors from their midst. These used various simple and not very precise techniques, such as measurement by sight or by stretching a cord, which would pull a good deal longer on a damp day than a dry one. Boundaries ran 'from kurgan [mound] to kurgan' or along a furrow. In this spirit, disputes were often settled by having an old-timer walk the supposedly true line, carrying an icon. Sooner or later the stanitsas usually got around to hiring professionals, which did not please the wealthy Cossacks, who often tried to delay or influence the surveyors' work. Kharuzin knew one case in which some prosperous Cossacks got the surveyors drunk and stole the plans.[97]

The number of completed repartitions of Don Cossack stanitsas seems impossible to determine, because the voisko authorities did not systematically collect information on this. A survey of 1874 indicates that only a minority of the more than 100 stanitsas had carried out a repartition. In the early 1880s, when Kharuzin made his sojourn on the Don, he gathered that the process was gaining but was far from universal. A decade later, however, a local correspondent in Esaulskaia stanitsa on the Don reported that they had just held their first repartition. By 1900 an official inspector reported that stanitsas usually repartitioned every ten years in the Don voisko.[98]

When it had been carried to completion, the actual arrangements for the distribution of land varied greatly. The legal reference to 30 desiatinas per Cossack played no role in this, and reasonably so, because the law referred only to a basis of allocation of voisko land to the stanitsa – not the allocation of land within the stanitsa. Moreover, the stanitsa generally made separate allocations of ploughland, grazing land, hayfields and woodlots, using a different procedure in each case. It would have been impossible to arrange that the sum of these allocations work out to 30 desiatinas per capita. Some stanitsas awarded land only to 17-year-old males, others, ignoring the law, included 10-year-old males, or women, on equal terms with men, or made special rules for the share of a childless widow, and so forth. Some stanitsas partitioned their land into sections for each khutor and allowed the assembly of that hamlet to make the distribution, while others arranged everything on the basis of the stanitsa as a whole. In at least one case the stanitsa divided its male populace into 'desiatkas' (tens), actually varying somewhat in number, some representing kinfolk, others neighbourhoods. Each received an allotment of land which it subdivided into parcels that were distributed by lot. The number and dispersion of the plots in the share of a given Cossack varied widely. Some stanitsas sectioned their land into two or more areas, awarding each recipient a plot in each area as a matter of equality. A particular allotment might include plots 50 verstas apart, and occasionally further. The size and shape of the parcels could vary considerably. In a number of sample instructions to surveyors, collected by Kharuzin, there is no specific norm, but in three cases the width is given as 160 sazhens, with no stated length, while in another example the width is to be 30 sazhens by 150. Precision is impossible in these matters, because the survey lines, even professional ones, often meandered along roads, streams or furrows, or hopped from mound to mound or hole to hole. The interval between periodic repartitions of ploughland varied greatly, from 5 years to 17, although under 12 in most cases.[99]

Unlike ploughland, meadows were repartitioned annually, a long-established practice. This was sensible because of the annual variation in the quality of the grass crop in one place or another. Meadows tended to be more remote from settlements than ploughland, since the grass crop required fewer trips to husband. Usually the fields were known by name, and each Cossack would receive allotments in three or four fields in the interest of equality. The first step in the annual distribution process required the elders to ride around the meadows, no small trip, and evaluate the potential crop in each place. On this basis they would assign so many individual shares to each field. They would then bring up to date the list of those eligible to receive an allotment that year, deleting the deceased and adding males who had turned 17. The list was then divided into desiatkas. The assembly in which the actual distribution took place was one of the main social events in the year, usually occurring around Whitsun, the seventh Sunday after Easter. Vodka flowed copiously, quarrels flared noisily and in the confusion some Cossacks received no allotment, sometimes because they refused to accept an inconvenient location. The process lasted several days, sometimes a week. First, the heads of the desiatkas (the 'desiatniks' or tenth-men) would meet to determine by lot which fields their group would share in. The stanitsa ataman would announce the name of a particular field and the number of desiatniks who would share in it. Then cards bearing the name or number of each desiatnik would be shaken in a hat and the desired number drawn. The desiatniks whose groups were sharing a given field would then meet and subdivide the field in similar manner. There were variations on this theme in different stanitsas, some working on groups of 100 before dealing with the desiatkas, others breaking the desiatkas into groups of five before the individual share was allocated. Some desiatkas decided not to subdivide but to cut hay jointly. The individual allotments that were distributed in this time-consuming way were at best informally defined, using such landmarks as bushes, and it is no wonder that some of the recipients never could locate the share of hayfield that they received. Others found their allotments too far away, and Cossacks frequently swapped their allotments during this annual festival of strong drink and communal agriculture.[100]

In the Ural voisko the distribution of hayfields until about 1900 was peculiar, like so much concerning the Ural'tsy. Their system of meadow distribution was called a 'mowing contest' (kosit' udarom). At an announced time, each qualified resident would go to the meadow and look for a promising location, on which he would camp along with a maximum of two hired workers, who might be non-Cossacks. At the next dawn, on a signal from the authorities, or furtively, before the signal, the Cossack would define his allotment by mowing a swathe around the best and largest area possible. Sometimes this came down to a race between two rival mowers, each trying to continue his swathe across the path of the other to gain a larger area. On occasion this even led to the slashing of legs in the heat of a tight race. The areas defined in this way were then mown at a normal pace, and after a set number of days the remainder could be mown by any number of hired workers or mowing machines that the richer Cossacks might deploy.[101]

In the Don the use of meadows involved an additional form of communal activity. From early spring until late autumn the cattle, a significant part of the Don Cossack economy, had to be tended by herders to protect the crops. This was arranged in the spring through the joint hiring by neighbours of the necessary number of herders. The latter were sometimes Don Cossacks of the usual sort, sometimes Kalmyk Don Cossacks, and sometimes outsiders. The arrangement for sharing the cost of the operation among the owners of the cattle sometimes favoured the well-off, every owner contributing the same share of the herders' wages, regardless of the number of cattle he owned. Sometimes this was mitigated by an arrangement for feeding and even paying the herder in proportion to the number of cattle owned.[102]

The distribution of woodlots involved still another kind of communal procedure among the Don Cossacks, and a vital one, considering the scarcity of this resource. Indeed, Kharuzin found that ten stanitsas had no wood at all, and such humble growth as pussy willow was among the species of 'wood' that was carefully doled out where it did exist. Some stanitsas distributed shares of woodlot for a fairly long term, as much as 25 years, intending to encourage conservation through self-interest. Others used their woodlots in common, arranging for an annual cutting in which each member received by lot an area and even particular trees, which were marked in advance according to size, so that the individual Cossack would receive, perhaps, two of the 'first pai' (most desirable), two of the 'second pai', and so forth.[103]

Neither the efforts of the state, through its legislation, nor of the stanitsas, through various forms of repartition, could avert the rise of a serious land shortage, or at least a common conviction among Cossacks that there was such a shortage. Certainly the legal norm of 30 desiatinas of stanitsa land per male Cossack did not survive in the three westernmost voiskos, which comprised almost 70 per cent of the total Cossack population in 1890: the Don, Kuban and Terrek. With almost static land resources and rising population in these voiskos, the amount of stanitsa land per male Cossack that was deemed good for agriculture declined to about ten by the last years of the Imperial era – a third of the statutory norm.[104] The situation was somewhat better in the other voiskos, especially those that were still on a frontier, but of these cases only the Ussuri reported as much as 30 desiatinas of good land per male in the last pre-world war years. The others reported between 20 and 30 desiatinas, excepting Astrakhan, which reported only 12.8 desiatinas of good land per capita.[105]

In any case, the average Cossack allotment could not be determined simply by dividing the total iurt land by the number of male Cossacks. Not all were old enough to receive an allotment, nor was all the iurt distributed to individuals. Some of it was reserved for 'social needs', such as schools, roads and horse-breeding facilities. A considerable part was rented out to earn revenue for the stanitsa.[106] Only once did the War Ministry try to learn the size of the average allotment and then only in the Don. The report of General Maslakovets in 1899 showed that the average consisted of 11.3 desiatinas of ploughland and 2.5 of meadow, but this varied considerably within the voisko. The largest average allotment was in the dry and saline Sal'skii okrug (16 desiatinas of ploughland and 6 of meadow), the lowest in the relatively fertile and heavily populated Khoper okrug (9 desiatinas of ploughland and 0.6 of meadow). This seems approximately confirmed by other investigations of the period. Data on the average allotment in other voiskos are feeble, although a seemingly well-informed writer in 1904 maintained that in the Kuban the figure was 7.7 desiatinas, but as little as one desiatina in some stanitsas.[107] Whatever the correct statistics, it is clear that the size of the average allotment in the non-frontier voiskos was declining. Evidently some Cossacks were subsisting with no more land than the six desiatinas that was considered adequate for the average peasant family.[108]

The Cossack who received an allotment did not necessarily farm it himself, or even derive any economic benefit from it. He might choose to rent it out, as permitted by the land law of 1869, or the stanitsa might do so if the Cossack had been unable to pay for his military equipment and was indebted to the stanitsa for providing it, a procedure authorized by the law of 1891 on stanitsa administration.[109] Only at the end of the nineteenth century did the authorities attempt to learn about the extent and nature of the rental of allotment land by Cossacks. The head of the chancellery of the Don ataman attempted to gather statistics on rental during 1894–8. Incompleteness and inconsistencies in the results make detailed conclusions on the situation hazardous, nor did the authorities make it a practice thereafter to study the subject.[110] Nevertheless it is clear that a lot of renting was going on. The data seem to show that slightly over half the Don Cossack households rented out at least part of their allotment land. They also seem to show that the overwhelming preponderance of those renting (over 90 per cent) did so voluntarily and that only a small proportion (under 5 per cent) had all or part of their land rented by the stanitsa to repay loans. This seems confirmed by the report of the Don ataman ten years later (1909) that obligatory rental was increasing steadily, that it was 'in former times' 'exceptional' but had become 'common'.[111] It also seems safe to say that roughly half of all those households who rented out land retained some of it, although the data do not indicate how many partial renters retained any particular proportion of their allotment. Data on this subject in other voiskos are still less adequate, but two Soviet studies indicate that about 10 to 20 per cent of the allotment land in both the Terek and Kuban was rented out to repay loans from the stanitsas, and a commentator on the Orenburg voisko complained in the early twentieth century that Cossacks there heedlessly rented out their allotments, even down to their dwelling.[112]

There were various motivations for voluntary rental. The Cossack might, in the words of the Orenburg administration, be 'enticed by the possibility of obtaining without working the income from the land for a given time'. In some cases this might mean that the Cossack found some other form of work more agreeable than farming. To a certain extent, this depended on traditional non-agricultural activities, especially fishing, but it gained ground and diversified in areas affected by economic modernization. The stanitsa of Novocherkassk, the capital of the Don oblast, was a particularly striking case in point by the early twentieth century. A majority of its residents rented out their allotment and lived in Novocherkassk, Rostov and other cities of the oblast, in the capitals, 'and even some in Manchuria, India and other countries'.

The impoverished Cossack might rent because he lacked the draft animals to cultivate his allotment. Families who lacked this considerable capital asset sometimes formed small collectives to pool their animals and implements, but there remained cases in which rental was the only way of obtaining any return on the land. Similarly, there were cases in which a household lacked enough able-bodied workers, especially if one or more of the men were on active duty. A major consideration that encouraged rental was the substantial distance that often separated Cossacks from at least part of their land.[113] Generally the growth of population in the stanitsa did not result in the establishment of new settlements, dispersed more or less evenly over the territory of the stanitsa. To a considerable extent the Cossacks preferred to live in the existing settlements, while the land allotments crept out to the fringes of the stanitsa or khutor. There is no systematic statistical measure of the dispersion of Cossack allotments, but all contemporary discussions of Cossack agriculture agree that this was a serious problem by the end of the nineteenth century, and examples abound. In 1900 War Minister Kuropatkin found distances of up to 60 verstas (over 60 km) between home and allotment in the Don, but a Duma deputy claimed what seems to be a record of 300 verstas in the Terek voisko. Apart from such extreme cases, there is no doubt that many Cossacks held allotments that were far enough from their residence that it was more attractive to rent them out than to cultivate them in person.[114]

The rewards of renting allotment land could vary widely, and no records exist to provide an overall picture. Even within the Don oblast there was great variation, to which the Maslakovets commission did not do justice in estimating 40–50 rubles per year as the average rental of an entire allotment. One contemporary observer considers that the range is from 5 rubles to 100, while others estimate a difference of 400 to 750 per cent between the low rents and the high. Frequently circumstances or poor business acumen led the Cossack to rent at less than a fair market value. In 1880, for example, an observer of the Don reported that there were cases in which Cossacks who needed cash rented their allotments for ten years for a lump sum of only 25 rubles. A resident of Nizhne-Chirskaia stanitsa wrote in 1892 that some

Cossacks there had allotments on both sides of the Don and could not reach the ones across the river from their residence during the spring floods. Unable to farm them, they rented at low rates, only 20 kopeks per desiatina in some cases. In Gnilovskaia stanitsa the complaint was that 'kulak land-speculators' rented allotment land at about half its market value. Sometimes the rent was paid in kind at a low rate. In 1904 a Don writer complained that non-Cossacks traded land in return for only three or four shocks of grain from the harvest. In Orenburg voisko an observer wrote that Cossacks received only 'a pittance, five or ten rubles a year for an entire allotment'.[115]

Even on the high end of the scale, the Cossack who rented out his land would not receive much more than the average earning of an impoverished seasonal agricultural labourer in the Don oblast, about 40–60 rubles per year. This was hardly enough to live on, much less to equip a man for military service. But at least the Cossack who rented his allotment voluntarily received some return on the tsar's benefaction to him. This could not be said for his neighbour, who could not afford to pay for his military equipment and was equipped at the expense of the stanitsa. He had to give his allotment to the stanitsa to be rented out until the debt was paid. This was an arrangement that accelerated the pauperization of those who were already poor.[116] As an official inquiry noted, it was grievous luck to have two sons close in age. True, the Cossack received his allotment at the age of 17, but if the family could not accumulate the cash to equip him, that land would be taken over by the stanitsa. For example, a poor Cossack named Ia. N. Lagutin, after struggling as a farm labourer for years, turned 17 and received his allotment. This was rented out by his family during the next three years, but the pittance that they received from this did not pay for the young man's horse and equipment. These were provided by the stanitsa, which rented out his land to a wealthy Cossack. Four years later, when he returned from active service, the debt had not been fully repaid and his land continued to be rented out.[117] A still harsher example was the Kadykov family in Uriupinskaia stanitsa. When the only male in the family was still four years under serving age, the stanitsa rented out his allotment merely in anticipation of his inability to equip himself, which was well-founded considering that the household otherwise consisted of his aged grandmother, his mother, who was suffering from malnutrition, his wife and two sisters, aged six and eight. Only the philanthropy of the Red Cross saved them from starvation. In a similar case in Kremenskaia stanitsa the authorities also sold the family's barn, horse and cow.[118]

Not all stanitsas expropriated the entire allotment of an indebted Cossack. General Korochentsev, after making an inspection in the Don in 1899, wrote of Cossack families that had been driven to ruin because half their allotment had been taken from them, leaving them with less than an adequate resource. At least one stanitsa tried to mitigate such disasters by taking over only the hayfield portion, leaving the Cossack with ploughland but no way to feed his draft animals. The hayfield brought in only five or six rubles a year, which meant that the Cossack was unlikely to live to see the payment of his debt to the stanitsa. In the Don there were cases in which fathers of sons turning 17 would appeal to the stanitsa to keep the son's allotment in return for taking over responsibility for the cost of his equipment. Often the Cossacks who lost their land allotment because of indebtness to the stanitsa became 'batraki', poorly paid hired hands of their more prosperous comrades or non-Cossack farmers.[119]

But could not the voisko alleviate the situation by distributing its reserve land? The law of 1869 had provided for the creation of a voisko land reserve precisely to offset the pressure of population on the land at the disposal of the stanitsas. On paper, the amount of reserve land in the most troubled voisko, the Don, seemed quite substantial: in 1882 over 3 000 000 desiatinas. Even if one deducted approximately 1 000 000 desiatinas that were devoted to various public enterprises and unavailable for distribution, this left about 2 000 000 desiatinas, which was more than 20 per cent of the area previously given to the stanitsas.[120] The Kuban and Terek were not so fortunate. In 1890, when the pertinent figures became available, they had reserves that were equivalent to only 7 and 6 per cent, respectively, of their stanitsa land, and not all of this was 'free' because of commitments to public enterprises. In the Don, the administration tried to relieve the land shortage by forming new stanitsas out of the reserve land. A law of 1873 paved the way for this, specifying that Cossacks who lived in stanitsas in which there was less than 26 desiatinas per male should be able to resettle in new stanitsas, receiving 25 desiatinas there. In 1880 this was put into practice with the formation of three new stanitsas, which soon filled with volunteer settlers from the more crowded ones. Three more stanitsas opened in 1880–6, but did not attract many settlers. One was mainly poor, saline land, another lacked water, pastures and woodlots and was divided by the land of two private estates. Moreover, the authorities in St Petersburg sought to conserve the land by ruling that only males born by 1873 could receive the going allotment of 25 desiatinas. Thereafter a family would have to subsist on that allotment regardless of its growth. The ministry made the new stanitsas even less attractive in a ruling of 1898, which specified that the family allotment should equal the average amount of land per Cossack in the voisko, calculated in such a way that the result would be less than the 25 desiatinas previously offered.[121] Despite these conditions the three new stanitsas were 80–90 per cent full by 1902. The Don administration repeatedly requested permission to open more new stanitsas, but the War Ministry would not consent until after the revolution of 1905.[122]

Blocked in this attempt to activate the mechanism that the land law of 1869 had established, the Don administration on four occasions asked permission to attempt an alternative amelioration of the land shortage: to resettle some Cossacks from particularly land-poor regions to better-endowed areas. But the War Ministry objected to resettlement among the existing stanitsas on the plausible grounds that no stanitsas would admit to having more than enough land and that population shifts would cause dissatisfaction. Only on the basis of a thorough survey of respective quality of the land of the stanitsas could there be a fair redistribution of population, argued the War Ministry. And that, replied the Don administration, would take 37 years with the existing supply of surveyors, so nothing was done.[123]

The ministry was reluctant to transfer land from the voisko reserve to the Don stanitsas not only because the voisko budget depended on rental income from this source but because the budget of the army depended on the supply of relatively cheap remounts from the large-scale horse ranches that existed on Don reserve land. These ranches occupied 784 687 desiatinas, leased from the voisko, in the thinly-settled southeast triangle of the oblast, the Transdon Steppe. There had been horse ranches in this area since the beginning of the nineteenth century, generally along the river Manych'. The proprietors included the greatest names in the Don nobility, such as Platov, Martynov, Efremov and Ilovaiskii, so it is not surprising that their enterprises received legal confirmation in the Don statute of 1835. According to the law, these absentee landlords enjoyed a bargain rent of 1.75 kopeks per desiatina for tracts so large that the buildings of separate ranches were usually about 30 verstas apart. It required only a few hired hands to run the operations, the horses fending for themselves summer and winter, which permitted rampant horse-stealing by the nomadic Kalmyks.[124] Until 1865 the horses were sold mainly to the general public, but in that year Grand Duke Nicholas Nicholaevich, Inspector-General of the Cavalry, ordered the purchase of a few remounts from the Transdon Steppe as an experiment. He was justifiably concerned about the decline in the supply of remounts from the Ukraine as the result of the steady increase of population and land tillage in that region. There were doubts about the quality of the Transdon horses, and very few of them were ever used by the guards regiments. But these tough, relatively small animals, the breed of which was upgraded by the introduction of various new strains, such as Arabians, proved adequate for the ordinary cavalry. Army purchases of Transdon remounts grew rapidly, reaching over 2000 in 1870 and almost 4000 in 1890. By 1882 these remounts constituted 65 per cent of all those purchased by the army, only increasing slightly beyond this level in 1893. Increased demand substantially raised the price of a remount. A top-quality horse which went for no more than 60 rubles in the 1860s cost as much as 150 rubles by the early 1890s. But the cavalry had in view no alternative supplier, and the War Ministry supported the private breeders in various ways. Active-duty Cossacks patrolled the ranches to attempt to check horse-stealing, and the army supplied veterinary services.[125] In 1872 a new regulation for this enterprise raised the annual rent to three kopeks per desiatina and in 1899 an observer claimed that the Transdon Steppe would rent for two rubles per desiatina on the free market. The law permitted ranchers to use their parcels for raising cattle and sheep or for ploughland, as long as they were able to raise one horse per 12 desiatinas. The standard ranch supposedly held 200 head on 2400 desiatinas. The ranchers had the security of a 12-year lease, which was increased to 24 years in a revised version of the regulation in 1877.[126]

As 1901 and the expiration of the leases approached, the War Ministry accepted the opinion of the Don administration that the stanitsas would require the land occupied by the ranches, and the new law provided for terminal leases. But these were not short: 12 years in the western half of the area (closest to settled areas and relatively well-suited to agriculture) and 24 in the saline eastern half. And beyond this, all ranchers could have three years in which to wind up their operations. In recognition that the rental rate, which was not raised from three kopeks per desiatina, was far short of fair value, the state agreed to pay the voisko 538 000 rubles a year. This worked out to about 1.50 rubles per desiatina, counting both the rent and the state subsidy, which was close to the average rent of reserve land at the time.[127]

If the War Ministry was unwilling to find much land within the more westerly voiskos on which to resettle land-hungry Cossacks, they were willing to try to move some of these people to the more easterly voiskos, where land was relatively plentiful and the security of a frontier still uncertain. Apart from the 'great Siberian migration', sponsored by the civil authorities of the Empire, the War Ministry attempted to promote its own programme of Cossack resettlement in Siberia, and specifically the Amur and Ussuri voiskos. It first broached this idea in 1883 in a special conference concerning the defence of the Amur area, but nothing came of it because the former governor-general of the area took six years to provide the information that was required of him – and when he did respond, failed to provide the material needed. In 1893 the projected Transsiberian Railway reinvigorated interest in the transplantation of Cossacks from the west to strengthen the defences of the east, specifically against 'gangs of Chinese bandits' that troubled the area. There was broad support for this proposal within the bureaucracy, but much discord about financing it. The governor-general of the Priamur, apparently apprehensive about invidious comparison between peasant and Cossack settlers, proposed that the newcomers pay their own way, receiving an interest-free loan on arrival, as did peasants. The Ministry of Internal Affairs claimed, however, that its funds for loans were not large enough to cover Cossacks as well as peasants. The War Ministry, unwilling to take on any new expenses, maintained that the land shortage among Cossacks in European Russia was not such as to oblige resettlement, that any resettlement would be for the good of the Empire, not the Cossacks. This was not true, but saying so improved the chances that some other agency could be manoeuvred into finding the necessary money, an estimated 1119 rubles for a family of three adults and three children. This left it to the Siberian Railway Committee, chaired by Sergei Witte, to decide whether or not to dip into its 14-million-ruble fund for enterprises ancillary to the railroad to pay for whatever additional security some Cossacks would provide. On 18 November 1893 the committee agreed to appropriate 336 000 rubles for the 300 families, a total of 1767 people, of whom 975 were to be males and 318 aged 20–38. This was a fairly high price to pay per soldier, especially considering that the terms of the agreement excused the Cossack settlers from all military service except annual training assembly for five years. In a separate agreement the railway agreed to pay 86 000 rubles to move 150 land-poor Zabaikal Cossacks to the Amur, a much shorter and cheaper operation.[128]

For the Cossack, squeezed by the land shortage in the western voiskos, the terms seemed favourable. The state paid for transport via Odessa and the sea route, offered a 30-desiatina allotment (plus ten for each child), donated 144 rubles per family for food during the first year, and loaned each family 600 rubles for 33 years without interest. The first group, 187 Don and 50 Orenburg families, arrived in 1895, soon losing 73 of the children to disease, mainly measles. Good horses cost 250 to 300 rubles and cows 150–200, so the government aid did not reach very far. Some of the land in the Ussuri region was judged to be poor.[129] An unofficial report from an Ural Cossack who happened to visit the area in the course of a lengthy search for a legendary 'Belovodskoe tsarstvo', inhabited only by Old Believers, maintained that the settlers suffered starvation and death in some cases. Lacking clothing and housing, other than huts made from branches, settlers were permitted to live in military barracks only for the two coldest months of winter, and residents of Vladivostok were ordered not to house them on penalty of a large fine. When the settlers asked permission to return to their native voisko, the command regarded the petition as 'mutiny'.[130]

In the face of such hardships, it was a tribute to the impoverishment of the Cossacks in the western voiskos that additional volunteers kept coming in the next few years. By 1902 over 9000 settlers had been moved from the Don, Kuban, Terek, Orenburg, Ural and Zabaikal voiskos to the Amur and Ussuri. But this was an insignificant part of the population of the more crowded voiskos, few of whom had any intention of migrating anywhere. As a serious official student of the land problem wrote in 1904, resettlement in the Far East was 'exceedingly feeble', which one Don official simply attributed to 'the general undesire of the Cossack to pick up and move to a new place'.[131] As for the state, its willingness to invest in the resettlement operation testified not to its concern for the land problem but to the possible need, in the words of the governor-general of the Priamur, 'to smash any hostile attempt by the yellow Asian races' – to which Nicholas II responded in annotation: 'obiazatel'no' (obligatory).[132]

In sum, the actual use of the Cossack lands in the last half of the nineteenth century became a complex matter that the government neither understood fully nor regulated effectively. The authorities annually calculated the amount of stanitsa land per male Cossack, but they did not know the size of the average allotment, which might vary considerably within a voisko. Still less did they know of the amount of land that Cossacks, richer or poorer, actually cultivated for their own interest. This depended on the position of the Cossack in the rental market, a subject on which they never collected systematic data. The Cossack might be a heavy loser in this market, at worst renting out his land at no return at all in order to repay indebtedness to the stanitsa. Or he might be a substantial gainer, renting land, in some cases at a bargain price, from other Cossacks, from a stanitsa, from the voisko, from officers who held their land on a temporary basis, from nobles who held their land as private property, or from persons who had bought this property from them. And all of this might involve one or more middlemen. The Cossack who prospered in this rental economy might even become a landowner himself, purchasing voisko land that had passed into private hands through award to nobility.[133]

This situation encouraged the development of economic stratification among the ordinary Cossacks, not to speak of differentiation between them and the starshina, the aristocrats who had appeared in some voiskos before the mid-nineteenth century. The distribution of wealth among the various strata was never determined by the authorities, and it is probably impossible to reconstruct it today on the basis of the extant data. The most careful investigation of the old regime, the Maslakovets Commission on the Don, proposed a three-tiered model:[134]

	Group I	Group II	Group III
Percent of households	21.6	45	33.4
Number of pais per household	2.98	2.18	2.07
Number of pair of oxen	3.93	2.05	0.4
Head of horned cattled	10.55	4.9	2.1
Horses	4.77	1.8	1.0
Sheep	26.3	9.9	2.67

According to the commission, the first group could keep going economically, the second was in decline and the third constantly in debt to the stanitsa. Soviet scholars are committed to the idea that capitalism brought about economic stratification among the Cossacks, but they have not produced any systematic model of the results.[135] Perhaps the last word on the subject should lie with contemporary writers, official and unofficial, who proposed no systematic model but who believed that the system of land tenure had produced the 'rich' or 'kulaks' among Cossacks, as well as 'bobyly', 'batraki' or 'proletarians'.[136]

MAKING A LIVING

The martial estate could not survive and render its military service by
the tsars' benefactions alone. The labour of the Cossacks was equally
basic to the system. The provision of land allotments, the restrictions
on personal mobility while the Cossack was of serving age and sheer
tradition dictated that agriculture would be the principal livelihood of
the martial estate, but it was far from being the only one. The varied
natural conditions and the changing economic character of the Russian
Empire attracted substantial numbers of Cossacks to non-agrarian
occupations. The unimaginative formalism in the official collection of
economic data on the Cossacks was such that one cannot present a
clear, quantified picture of the different means of subsistence which
the Cossacks practised at various times, but the rough outlines of the
topic can be discerned.

In the main voiskos the predominant form of agriculture until
approximately the 1870s was cattle-raising. In regions of natural
grassland and low population density, this was rational, and particularly so before the construction of a railway network. In that period
cattle could be driven to distant markets on their own feet, particularly
by the 'Don cattle-drive route', which extended from the Don oblast to
Moscow and thence St Petersburg.[137] Animal husbandry also had the
advantage of requiring little labour, important in a society in which
many males were away on military service. Despite the grave impact of
famine in 1891, the cattle population of the Don and Orenburg voiskos
rose steadily until the opening of the twentieth century. Thereafter it
declined, reflecting the long-term shift to grain agriculture.[138] The
Maslakovets Commission found that by 1899 the sale of grain
contributed 39.6 per cent of Don Cossack household income, cattle
and cattle products 16.6 per cent. It also estimated that the amount of
ploughland increased 2.4 times in the last quarter of the century.[139]
The increasing population could not sustain itself on finite territory
simply by raising more animals. Grain production was a more
intensive use of the land, one that was inviting as foreign and domestic
markets improved. Moreover, the rental by Cossacks of their
allotment land accelerated the shift to grain. They usually started by
renting the most remote parts of their allotment, which had been hard
to get to and plough, and hence had been left to meadow, supporting
cattle-raising. But the renters were commonly peasants or kulaks who
wanted the rented land for grain cultivation. The total production of
grain by persons of all estates in all the voiskos did expand
impressively, from 5.2 million puds in 1872 to 40.5 million in 1902

and 65.8 million in 1912.[140] This was more than a twelvefold increase; the Kuban, which in 1907 surpassed the Don as the producer of the largest grain crop of any voisko, increased almost seventeenfold, the Don just under tenfold. During this period, population of these territories increased merely 3.6-fold, certainly indicative of a substantial growth in wealth per capita.[141] But how much of this relative prosperity found its way to the members of the martial estate? The official methods of collecting data become a serious difficulty at this point, for they offer only total figures for all legal estates and economic strata. The impression of contemporary commentators is that most Cossacks did not benefit greatly from the advance of grain agriculture because they were backward, undercapitalized farmers. The word 'rapacious' appears repeatedly in the contemporary observations about Cossack agriculture, along with 'primitive' and 'Asiatic'.[142] 'In fact Cossacks work the land poorly', wrote a Kuban officer. 'They sow weedy seed, harvest grain in shocks ... Many explain this by laziness and inertness', though he considered that it was largely a matter of ignorance.[143] A prevailing sin was heedless exhaustion of the soil. Usually the Cossack attempted to increase his crop simply by ploughing more land. 'As before, the slogan of the economy remains: [farm] more, even though [you do it] worse', wrote a critic of the Don in 1891.[144] When not farming this way himself, the Cossack often encouraged others to do so by renting out his land for a short term, often only a year, which provided no incentive for good technique.[145] If such land returned to Cossack cultivation, it was not likely to be good for much, for it received far too little fertilizer. The decline of animal husbandry, relative to tillage, contributed to this problem, but sheer ignorance was much to blame. The idea of fertilizing the soil was woefully absent, and one local correspondent reported in 1892 that the Cossacks simply dumped manure into the River Don.[146] As the demand for rental land increased, the practice of leaving fallow declined, so the need to replace nutrients was all the greater. As in Russian peasant agriculture, the allocation of land in strips led to inefficient use of land and labour. This problem was compounded among the Cossacks because the dispersion of allotments within the stanitsa tended to be much greater than that of peasant allotments.[147] Again as in peasant agriculture, the practice of periodic redistribution of allotments among Cossacks discouraged concern for the long-term fertility of the soil.

Apart from the deficiencies of Cossack grain farming, contemporary opinion also maintained that they failed to exploit the opportunities that existed for the development of such branches of agriculture as viniculture and tobacco. At the opening of the twentieth century, the Cossacks in the most specialized grape-growing area of the Don, the stanitsa of Tsimlianskaia, were still harvesting grapes from untrained, unpruned clumps, and they were not bothering to sort the grapes when making wine, a traditional Don product that had great and unrealized potential in the modern economy.[148] The production of grapes in the Don barely increased between 1870 and 1900, and between these relatively high points there were many years of partial crop failure.[149] The Terek and Kuban voiskos easily outstripped the Don as wine producers by the early twentieth century. While the Don produced an average of somewhat over 66 000 vedros in 1908–11, the Kuban produced over 918 000 and the Terek 1.7 million. The Terek wine was not very good, but cheap and therefore easily marketable, bringing in over 1 000 000 rubles a year. Unfortunately, official figures do not show the relative role of Cossack and non-Cossack cultivators, but the coincidence of the rapid increase in wine production and non-Cossack population suggests that the enterprising non-Cossacks played the major role.[150] The Kuban also grew a profitable tobacco crop, but the business was largely in the hands of ethnic Greeks.[151]

Cossack agriculture generally suffered from a deficiency of draft animals. Although the residents of Pavlovskaia stanitsa maintained that one had to have at least three pair of oxen to keep above the 'feeble' level, the report of the Maslakovets Commission held that only the upper fifth of Don Cossack households averaged four, while the bottom third had only 0.4 pair.[152] A survey of all the voiskos except the Amur and Orenburg in 1912 found that almost 20 per cent of Cossack households had no horse and only 36 per cent one horse.[153] In the Don, Kuban and Terek voiskos, at any rate, the numerous poor households tried to cope with this shortage by pooling what they had. In the Kuban such a collective was called a 'surpriaga', in the Don a 'combined plough'. The usual practice was to allocate ploughing time in proportion to the number of shares that each household contributed. A pair of oxen was one share, a plough one, a worker's (not to imply hired) help, one. Sometimes each share was worth 12 sazhens of ploughing on a strip that was assumed to be constant in width; sometimes a share was equated with a day's ploughing.[154]

Among the poorest Cossacks in the western voiskos there were many by the opening of the twentieth century who lacked either the land or the capital to farm in their own interest. Many of these became hired farm labourers for others, Cossack and non-Cossack farmers of some prosperity. The authorities did not interest themselves in gathering data on this matter, so it is impossible to determine how many Cossacks relied partly or wholly on wages for agricultural labour. Certainly it was no small proportion. A Soviet study maintains, without providing convincing evidence of its method, that in 1875 in the Terek voisko 39 per cent of the Cossacks were wage labourers.[155]

But not all the Cossacks who did not cultivate their allotment were in farming at all. The opportunities for alternative employment varied considerably, depending on one's location. In the late nineteenth century in Rostov okrug of the Don, 58 per cent of Cossack household heads worked in non-agricultural pursuits, while in the okrugs other than those near the Rostov area, the proportion was under 3 per cent. But even in these rural backwaters there were stanitsas containing towns large enough to provide non-agricultural work for a significant number of Cossacks. In the city of Novocherkassk, for example, in 1899, 17 per cent of the Cossack household heads worked in 'industry' – really such trades as blacksmith, carpenter, harnessmaker, cobbler, tailor and processors of agricultural products, candle and sausage-makers, for example. Further away from the large cities in Tsimlianskaia stanitsa, out of 432 Cossacks who rented out their allotments, 59 worked in commerce, 52 in skilled trades, 62 in 'personal service' (servants of the wealthy), and 239 did not live in the stanitsa. Some of the latter may have been farm labourers, but surely many had departed the stanitsa precisely to look for non-agricultural jobs. In 1899 the Maslakovets Commission estimated that there were 7000 Don Cossacks in factory labour and 2500 engaged as carters.[156]

Among the non-farming Cossacks, there were both the wealthy and the impoverished, but there are no data on the mix. There is, however, general agreement among contemporary observers around the turn of the century that the Cossacks played a relatively minor role in the commercial and industrial activity within the voiskos. There was an occasional exception, such as the millionaire Don Cossack Paramonov, a member of the Society of Merchant Cossacks who profited from the rise of the grain trade. But, according to the official agronomist of the Kuban and Terek, 'Any Cossack of the non-privileged estate [not a Cossack noble] who participates successfully in trade or industry, first of all dreams of liberating himself from the yoke that links him to the title of Cossack.'[157] On the whole, it was the non-Cossack population of the voisko territories, not the members of the martial estate, who benefited most from economic modernization. By the late nineteenth century, the Cossacks had lost almost all influence in the growing commerce of the Don, except in the city of Novocherkassk, the administrative centre, in which Cossack and non-Cossack establishments were about equal in number and income. In the oblast as a whole in 1894 there were 232 Cossack-owned commercial firms against 3097 non-Cossack, with receipts for the Cossacks of 2.9 million rubles against 91.4 million for non-Cossacks. In the vital grain trade, three Cossack-owned firms held only 6 per cent of the turnover against 27 non-Cossack firms. In the humble business of selling liquor (not included in the preceding), the Don Cossacks still owned 1071 out of 3231 establishments in 1894, but two years later only 898 out of 3122.[158]

The failure of the Cossacks to share in proportion to their numbers in the economic growth of their territories involved a peculiar aspect of the legal social order of the Russian Empire, the 'Society of Merchant Cossacks'. As noted previously, the state established the first of these in 1804 in the Don, making it an estate within the martial estate in all but legal title.[159] In the next 50 years comparable bodies appeared in the Kuban, Terek, Astrakhan, Orenburg, Siberian and Zabaikal voiskos. In return for a fairly modest annual fee (57.50 to 60 rubles), the members of these societies were exempt from military service, supposedly to develop the commerce of the voisko.[160]

This arrangement was highly advantageous to the Cossack merchants, but it was not conducive to economic development. Lacking capital, expertise and entrepreneurial drive, the Cossack merchants proved unable to fulfil the economic potential of the voisko lands. Nor could non-Cossack businessmen be totally excluded from these territories. The Don ataman recognized this in his reports for 1866 and 1867: 'The Merchant Society is far from occupying its appropriate place at present ...; although it is forbidden, non-Cossack merchants are settling in the land of the Don voisko, concentrating in their hands almost all of the local trade ...'[161] Recognizing the undesirability, from the viewpoint of the state, of obstructing economic development in order to protect the Cossack merchants, the regime wished to abolish the Cossack merchants. In 1863 there was a new Empire-wide law on the taxation of commerce and industry, and the ministers asked the Temporary Committee on the Review of Cossack Statutes to consider the application of this law to the voiskos. The committee's response in 1865 accepted the rationality of a uniform system of commercial regulation in the Empire but feared that the immediate end of Cossack trading rights would arouse dissatisfaction. They observed that, although the Ministry of Finance had proposed an annual subvention to the voiskos to compensate for the loss of the annual fees paid by Cossack merchants, this did nothing for all

Cossacks' loss of the right to trade without taxation. The result was a compromise law in 1870, which abolished all but one of the societies of merchant Cossacks, paying the voiskos compensation for the consequent loss of fees, and continuing the right of tax-free small-scale trade for all Cossacks.[162] While this saved the honour of the tsars, it had very little economic value. Very few Cossacks had the capital or the inclination to compete with non-Cossack merchants, and the latter now had much improved access to the voiskos. This was facilitated by a law of 1868 which for the first time permitted non-Cossacks to own buildings on voisko land.[163] The exception among societies of merchant Cossacks was in the Don voisko, where the institution was allowed to exist with no limit on its size, providing that the required levy of Dontsy appeared each year.[164]

Having made this concession to the Don, the authorities in St Petersburg showed scant interest in the actual survival of its Society of Merchant Cossacks. The new law of 1874 on Don Cossack military obligation offered no exemption for the merchants, although a regulation issued the following year did provide some privilege in this connection. A present member of the society was merely enrolled in the reserve; a young member (in practice, the son of a member, for membership in the society frequently ran in a family) could skip the preparatory category and go right onto active duty at the age 18. After completing active duty, members would have to attend only two training camps during their eight years in the second and third turns. This did not provide much of a motive to join the society, and its membership fell from 1104 in 1882 to 257 in 1886, with non-Cossacks taking over some of the business activities formerly in the hands of members of the society. Nevertheless, when Alexander III visited Novocherkassk in 1887, it was the society that paid for the erection of a temporary triumphal arch.[165] The voisko administration made some ineffectual efforts to reverse this trend in the 1880s, complaining that they had lost revenue from fees as membership in the society dwindled. When the new law on the society finally appeared in 1885, it was merely as a three-year trial arrangement, setting the maximum membership at 2000, and raising the fee to 150 rubles for those who had completed their military service and 300 for those who had not.[166] In 1893 the voisko administration succeeded in obtaining a reduction of the fee scale for those who were over age for the reserve (50 rubles) or for those of serving age who had put in their active duty (100 rubles). It even added a category, with a 200-ruble annual fee, for those who were excused from the completion of active duty and were enrolled early in the reserve, an arrangement that was now possible thanks to the surplus of eligibles over the required levy. But even with this inducement, membership declined to 203 by 1895.[167] Thus the Don retained the vestigial form of a special guild of Cossack merchants. It received no compensation for the abolition of this anachronism (unlike most other voiskos), but still saw almost all the profit from economic development slip into the hands of non-Cossacks.

There was one non-agrarian enterprise in which the Cossacks in certain regions succeeded in maintaining at least in substantial part their traditional role: fisheries. The grant of fishing rights in the charters of the tsars was one of the major traditional benefactions that the Cossacks received. In the early history of the Cossacks, fishing had surpassed agriculture as a means of sustenance, and in the later centuries it remained a major asset in a number of voiskos. The rivers Don, Volga, Kuban, Terek, Ural and Amur, and the seas into which they flow, as well as the Black Sea in the case of the Kuban voisko, provided all but a tiny portion of the catch. The most lucrative species, including the beluga, osetrina and sevriuga sturgeon, were called 'red' and yielded caviar, a major source of cash income. For their own consumption Cossacks preferred the humbler species that were usually called 'white'. The catches of various species varied vastly from year to year among the voiskos. For example, the Volga fisheries of the Astrakhan voisko supposedly yielded 6000 puds of red and 1000 of white in 1902, but 1000 of red and 40 000 of white in 1912, according to annual reports. In most years the Ural voisko led the way in total catch and was the voisko in which fishing made the greatest absolute and per capita contribution to the income of the Cossacks. In 1882, for example, out of a total fishing income of 4.7 million rubles in all the voiskos, 3.2 million accrued to the Ural'tsy. This relative wealth owed much to the huge harvest of caviar, over 6000 puds in 1882.[168] Among the other voiskos, the Kuban usually held second place in absolute terms, followed by the Don and Astrakhan. The Terek and Amur fisheries were definitely smaller, only beginning to be exploited. There are some complaints that the size of the catch in the major fisheries was in decline, owing to pollution, overfishing or silting, but the official figures, while including sharp fluctuations, do not conclusively substantiate this. The Don voisko reported a total of 125 000 puds of red and white fish in 1872; 192 000 in 1892 and 158 000 in 1912, with numerous rises and falls along the way. If the stock held up fairly well, this may be partly because the Cossacks were more judicious fishermen than farmers. Even in the 1870s, fishing in rich areas, such as the mouths of the Don and Ural rivers, was prohibited in order to protect breeding areas, and there were various seasonal limitations on fishing, which at least applied to commercial activity. As time went on, the authorities attempted to protect this resource with more complex regulations, purchased a steam-cutter to chase poachers on the Sea of Azov and instituted scientific study of the Don and Ural fisheries.[169]

Although a number of voiskos, which included a large majority of all Cossacks, possessed major fisheries, the value of this resource to these people was extremely uneven. Only in the Ural and Astrakhan voiskos did a substantial part of the total Cossack population do much fishing. The Ural voisko segregated its two northernmost (Iletskii) stanitsas from the fishing rights that were enjoyed by the rest of its Cossacks on the Ural River from the city of Ural'sk downstream. The main body of the Ural Cossacks derived about half their income from fishing, and on the lower course of the river the Cossacks, about 20 per cent of the total, did no farming at all. The same pattern applied to the stanitsas of the Don and Astrakhan that were located near the mouths of the Don and Volga. In the Don voisko, the stanitsas of Gnilovskaia and Elizavetovskaia dominated fishing and did little else; with Astrakhan voisko, this could be said of about half of that small community, the first otdel. Participation in the fishing industry was also limited by wealth. One needed capital to pay for boats, docks, sheds and other equipment. In some voiskos there were substantial fees for fishing rights, forming a considerable part of the revenue of the voisko in the Ural, Kuban and Astrakhan, and a minor source in the Terek, Siberian, Zabaikal and Ussuri voiskos. But the others, including the Don, collected nothing for this right, supposedly granted freely by the tsar. Sometimes, as in the Ural, this revenue came in the form of an excise on the catch; sometimes, as in parts of the Kuban, as a licence fee; sometimes, as in other parts of the Kuban, as a rental of a particular stretch of shoreline; and sometimes, as in the Astrakhan voisko, by renting rights to the whole summer fishing season.[170]

Fishing as a livelihood took diverse forms among the Cossacks. In the Ural voisko it was a well-organized operation involving the whole community, excepting the Iletskii stanitsas. Each spring the voisko administration constructed a substantial weir at Ural'sk, about 400 verstas above the mouth of the Ural River, blocking the upstream migration of the larger fish. As described by Korolenko around the turn of the century, it consisted of iron piles in the river beds, supporting beams holding iron grills. Cossacks on 'internal service' watched the river and reported the movements of fish, which in the autumn turned back from the weir and searched for places to plant their spawn and to spend the winter. In the spring and autumn, the Cossacks who came to fish elected a special 'ataman of fishing' who saw to it that the rules were observed and started each day's expedition on the river in small boats by giving a signal. This practice, called a fishing contest, paralleled the method and the terminology that the Ural Cossacks applied to their method of distributing haying rights and supposedly provided a high degree of equality of opportunity. In the winter the same principle applied to ice-fishing, the fishermen moving out in sledges on signal. This was a particularly animated occasion because the cold weather made it easier to ship the fish around the country, and the river banks drew crowds of merchant-buyers and sellers of all manner of goods, vodka among them. The whole practice drew the majority of the Ural Cossacks together in a way that was not matched in any other voisko. Korolenko believed that the communal spirit in these gatherings was 'more complete than in the primitive land commune'. But hierarchical and even bureaucratic elements were visible as well. Part of the river was designated only for the taking of fish as 'presents' to all manner of dignitaries, starting with the ataman of the voisko. All the fishermen supposedly gave a day to this enterprise.[171]

In the main fishing district of the Don, however, near the Sea of Azov, the fishing industry was much more a matter of individual entrepreneurship. In the stanitsa of Gnilovskaia, a boss would provide the capital to pay for a boat, shore camp, equipment and food. He would take into his service perhaps 15 to 17 workers, one of whom served as ataman, meaning foreman. One of the group remained ashore to cook, for the Sea of Azov is not so large that overnight trips were required. The proceeds of the undertaking were divided by shares, the boss taking perhaps as much as half of the total, the others one share each, except the ataman, who might get two or three. During the main fishing season, from Easter to Whitsun, the fishing grounds in the Don River itself were divided into sectors and distributed by lot among the various groups. Merchants assembled on the shore to bargain with the bosses, who had arrived on horseback long after the dawn departure of their workers, for the incoming catch. In another stanitsa, somewhat upstream and not as noted for fishing, the arrangements were still less egalitarian. Usually two well-off Cossacks would provide a boat, engaging about ten 'workers', who would divide equally a quarter of the catch, the entrepreneurs keeping three-quarters. In both of these situations the bosses were Cossacks, members of the estate to whom the tsar had granted fishing rights, but the ordinary fishermen were a mixed lot. War Minister Kuropatkin was justified in concluding after his visit to the Don in 1900 that 'Fishing is not organized for the profit of the whole voisko. This profit accrues only to a stanitsa and the non-Cossack population on the coastline.'[172]

In the Kuban voisko, the rewards of the right to fish, which supposedly applied to all Cossacks, in practice also benefited only a few who had some capital. The most profitable commercial fishing along the shores of the Sea of Azov and the Black Sea required the construction of permanent fish weirs or traps, called 'zavods' ('backwaters'). Alternatively, one could drag long nets in sweeps around schools of fish travelling along the shore, a method called 'naezdom' ('raid'), which meant that one was not continuously engaged in fishing. In 1881 there were only 676 fishing enterprises along the coast, and of these only 249 were the fixed variety, utilizing weirs. Altogether, this employed only a tiny portion of the total Kuban Cossack population, even if one allows for a certain number of partners and employees.[173]

Looming over every Cossack household, influencing fundamentally its level of prosperity or impoverishment, was the cost of military service. This was something that members of no other estate had to consider. A peasant family, for example, might lose the working power of a member for several years, but they did not have to lay out a large sum of cash to equip him. But the Cossack family (or failing that, the collection of families constituting a stanitsa) had to find a sum beyond the dreams of most peasants every time an able-bodied male attained manhood.

Around the turn of the century, estimates of the cost of equipping a Cossack for cavalry service ranged from 200 to 300 rubles. The lower estimates were from official spokesmen, who all acknowledged that there was a problem but did not wish to paint too bleak a picture. It is clear, however, that War Minister Kuropatkin's estimate of 200–250 rubles is too low. In the annex to his report one finds reference to specific cases of poor Cossacks who were equipped at the expense of their stanitsa, which paid as much as 294 rubles.[174] The most serious study of the Don Cossack economy, that of the Maslakovets Commission, concluded that equipment cost 122 rubles. This was fairly easy to calculate from the list of requirements and commissary prices. The price of horses was more variable, '100–120' but over 150 in some cases. Thus a total of at least 250 rubles was plausible as a typical expenditure.[175] At about this time two writers on the Kuban also estimated 300, one of them proposing 250 for the Terek.[176]

Nobody doubted that the cost had increased markedly in the late nineteenth century, partly because the new laws on military obligation required standardized equipment in good condition, and partly because the price of a horse had increased.[177]

A study of a sample of 24 peasant households in a Ukrainian town, by no means the poorest part of the Russian Empire, showed that at about this time the range of annual cash profit ranged from zero to 125 rubles per year, but only three households had a profit over 50 rubles and nine had less than one ruble profit. Clearly the idea of raising even 250 rubles at one time would have been horrifying and impossible for almost all peasants.[178] Although the typical Cossack presumably was better off than his peasant counterpart, the Maslakovets Commission estimated that the average Don Cossack made an annual profit of 14 rubles around the turn of the century, and this obviously made a cash outlay of 250 rubles a formidable burden. At the very least a household probably would be obliged to sell some of its draught animals or agricultural equipment or to rent out part or all of its land allotment.[179]

As we have seen, rental often was not a matter of choice but a measure that the stanitsa could take to indemnify itself for expenditures that it made on behalf of poor Cossacks.[180] Just how many Cossacks could obtain the required equipment only with the financial assistance of their stanitsas is unclear. The Maslakovets Commission believed that 56 per cent of the Don Cossacks received some aid, but this gives no idea how much. The sampling of Kuropatkin's inspection demonstrated how variable this could be. In the stanitsa of Uriupinskaia, for example, in 1899, 14 of the 28 Cossacks going on active service received some assistance, all but one of these for their uniforms and equipment (from 10 to 122 rubles) and ten for the horse as well (from 80 to 110 rubles).[181] In any case, a low level of aid rendered to Cossacks going on active duty might be a better measure of the stanitsa's success in wringing money out of its citizens than their prosperity. In the Orenburg voisko, for example, a local writer asserted that, beginning in 1893, stanitsas required the family of every male who was 16 to put a certain amount of money in a savings bank each year until he was 20, when he would have 105 rubles to equip himself.[182]

Nor did the financial burden to the family end when the recruit went off with his equipment and horse. Indeed the report of the Maslakovets Commission maintained that the burden was heavier for the Cossacks of the second turn who could not 'dispose freely of their personal labour, nor time, nor property'. This referred to the cost of maintaining a horse and equipment in the second turn and of attending a summer training camp at his own expense. The cost of keeping a horse that could pass inspection was a serious burden in a household such as those of the poorest third in the Don, which on the average owned only one horse. The temptation to use the animal for draft purposes was enormous, especially if one's original service mount had not survived four years of active duty in passable condition, obliging the purchase of a replacement. But, complained one writer from the Kuban in 1904, if the Cossack showed up for summer training camp with a horse that had the marks of a collar on its hide, the animal would be rejected.[183] One advocate of Cossack interest in the Duma maintained in 1911 that the total lifetime cost of Cossack military service, including lost labour, was 1600 rubles, a writer on the Kuban that a cavalryman there spent 1130 rubles and an infantryman 555, not counting lost labour. The Maslakovets Commission put the figure, not counting lost labour, at 950 rubles. Although the regime never really learned what proportion of the Cossack households could sustain such a burden, it was clear that it was in decline.[184]

STAYING AFLOAT

The Imperial government never relinquished the idea that the Cossacks were a self-sustaining martial estate, but in the closing years of the nineteenth century and the first 14 years of the twentieth century the regime relaxed its attempts to maximize Cossack payment of their expenses and to minimize state subsidies to them. This shift began in the 1890s as the regime became concerned about the economic viability of the martial estate and continued once the revolution of 1905 had demonstrated the potentially crucial role of the Cossacks as a domestic security force. Indeed, there was good reason to believe that the economic basis of the Cossack system was heading for collapse around the opening of the twentieth century, and it behooved the government of the tsars, if it wished to retain this peculiar instrument of power, to undertake economic rescue operations.

The first major step in this direction was not perceived as such, but merely as a short-term response to a disaster that struck a large part of the Imperial population, the great famine of 1891–2.[185] A disastrous drought in 1891 dealt the main blow to agriculture in a vast swathe of Russia running northeast from the Black Sea, but in the lands of the Orenburg, Siberian, Ural and Astrakhan Cossacks the harvests had been poor during the three previous years. All of these voiskos received aid in money and kind in 1891, especially the Orenburg, in which 255 000 Cossacks out of a total of about 350 000 were officially classified as needy. The disaster involved not only feeding humans but also farm animals, for the hay crop was especially hard hit. One Don correspondent reported that a shock of hay brought the unheard-of price of 15 rubles. Fugitives from the famine zone north of the Don brought typhus and cholera to the oblast, while rinderpest and glanders attacked undernourished cows and horses.[186]

Contrary to widely-held belief, the Imperial government devoted considerable resources to combat the disaster, achieving a respectable degree of success. Along with other parts of the stricken population, the Cossacks of Orenburg, Siberia, the Ural and Don received substantial aid in cash and kind (food for people and animals) in 1891–3. Indeed, the assistance was rushed with such haste and on such a scale that the accountancy system of the War Ministry lost track of it, and the figures provided in the annual reports are internally inconsistent.[187] It is in any case clear that the capital funds of the voiskos provided all that they could, and that this was not nearly enough, so the state treasury contributed heavily. Almost all of this aid was originally considered to be loans from the voisko capital or the treasury, repayable on relatively generous terms, three years without interest and thereafter up to ten years at 4 per cent in the case of one major loan to Orenburg. This voisko, the hardest hit, received 5 830 000 rubles in 1891–2 in loans from the state and used 820 000 from its own capital, while the annual voisko revenue, just before the disaster, was only about 400 000.[188] By the end of 1892, all the needy voiskos appear to have borrowed almost 9 000 000 rubles, including a relatively small loan from the Kuban voisko to the Orenburg in order to buy replacement draught animals, the first case of shifting funds from one voisko to another.[189]

Obviously repayment of this kind of sum, even on fairly easy terms, would threaten the solvency of the whole Cossack system. The state therefore undertook two major steps to reduce the debt, at the same time confusing their accounting. First, in 1893 the value of the loan was recalculated on the basis not of the cost of food actually purchased at famine-year prices but at average pre-famine prices, which cut the indebtedness of the Orenburg, Siberian and Ural voiskos by about two-thirds.[190] Second, Nicholas II celebrated his wedding in 1894 by repaying 'half' the debt incurred by the voiskos for famine relief. Evidently this was intended to mean that the portion of relief aid advanced from the capital funds of the affected voisko would be paid back from the state treasury.[191]

There were also some outright gifts. The Orenburg Cossacks, facing the loss of their entire stock of animals, received an emergency grant of 50 000 puds of hay and 1000 portions of horse biscuits. The Don received an outright grant of 100 000 rubles in 1892 with much fanfare concerning the mercy of the tsar. Supposedly this had a substantial impact on the Khoper okrug, in which most of the hardship was located, each needy Cossack family receiving an average grant of 33.50 rubles.[192] The state also made considerable contributions to combat cholera and animal plagues in the Don, Orenburg, Ural and Terek voiskos, where the outbreaks were worst. The largest expense was 400 000 rubles to combat rinderpest in the Don. This involved destroying a large number of animals, whose owners frequently did not approve of the sacrifice. In Krivianskaia stanitsa mutinous Cossacks refused to allow veterinarians to examine their cattle and arrested stanitsa authorities who tried to order compliance. Fearing a general Cossack disturbance, the administration called in regular troops and issued an official statement, which made frequent allusions to the will of the 'Gosudar' Imperator'. Another 100 000 of state funds went to the anti-cholera campaign in the Don, and 30 000 to the Terek. The Don, Terek, Orenburg and Ural voiskos provided 41 000 from their own funds for this purpose, even though it was clearly a matter of grave concern to the entire Imperial population.[193] In sum, the famine and epidemic relief dispensed to certain Cossack voiskos still reflected the parsimonious tradition that the Cossacks must pay their own way. But the severity of the crisis, especially in the Orenburg voisko, obliged the authorities to breach this principle, if only on a supposedly one-time emergency basis.

In the interval of approximately a decade between the famine of the early 1890s and the opening of the crisis of war and revolution in 1904, the War Ministry began to take seriously the idea that the Cossacks faced major economic problems. No doubt the famine itself helped prepare this realization, but it was questions about the military preparedness of the estate, especially the adequacy of Cossack horses, that led to the investigations of Maslakovets and Kuropatkin at the end of the 1890s and real awareness that something needed to be done. To be sure, it was not only the Cossacks who, among Russian agriculturalists, were a cause for concern around this time. Sergei Witte, the modernizing Minister of Finance, succeeded in establishing an Empire-wide investigation into Russian agriculture in 1902.[194]

Although the proceedings of this elaborate inquiry were understandably concerned first of all with the peasantry and did not always identify specifically Cossack problems, the guberniia-level committees of the Witte inquiry provided in several areas forums in which Cossack economic problems could be articulated in a way that could claim some official attention.

The burden of Cossack complaints has already emerged in the present study: inadequate land inadequately utilized relative to the burden of military obligation. As we have seen in connection with the evolution of Cossack military service, there was some attempt before the Russo-Japanese War to alleviate the problem by modestly reducing the military burden.[195] In considering ways of improving the supply side of the problem, official policy sought to overcome Cossack backwardness in respect to agronomical assistance. Non-Cossack Russia was no model of modernity in this respect, but at least the areas that had zemstvos enjoyed increasing access to the expertise of agronomists.[196] The War Minister, General Kuropatkin, in his report on his tour of the Don in 1900, strongly urged the development of agronomical aid in that oblast. This probably accounts for the decision to write into the law of 1901, continuing the rental of Transdon horse ranches, a clause requiring the expenditure on agronomy of 100 000 rubles of the increased state compensation paid to the Don. On this basis, the War Ministry approved a plan for four agronomical schools, four experimental farms and three instructors. But the project advanced at a leisurely pace, and it was not until 1905 that the government established the post of chief agronomist for the Don oblast.[197]

There were similarly tepid efforts to address the problem of land shortage, despite frequent allusions to this in the committees of the Witte inquiry. The official view of the Witte Commission was that distribution to stanitsas of the voisko reserve land, which was suggested in several of the committees, would not provide enough additional land to help much, only about one desiatina per male Cossack in the Don.[198] An alternative means of finding more land for the stanitsas, which appealed more to the War Ministry, was the purchase by the voisko of land that had passed into private ownership. This idea seems to have appeared first in the meetings of the Maslakovets Commission, with the proposal to finance the scheme with a government-guaranteed loan.[199] The War Ministry did work out a plan by which the oil-rich Kuban and Terek voiskos could begin in 1902–3 to spend between one million and two million rubles of their own funds to buy back privately-owned land.[200] But the Don enjoyed no such affluence. A local leader suggested that a government-guaranteed loan to the voisko would enable it to buy back over 350 000 desiatinas of Cossack land by about 1950 (yes, 1950).[201] But the War Ministry did not get beyond the stage of considering the problem in the Don before the crisis of 1905.

Both the improvement of Cossack agriculture and the expansion of the land available impinged on the question of credit, a sore point between the government and the ordinary Cossacks. For relatively small loans, particularly for the purchase of animals or equipment, there were almost no lending institutions. Some stanitsas in the Don that had healthy capital balances wanted to establish local banks, and one, Novo-Nikolaevskaia, succeeded in overcoming considerable official resistance in establishing its own bank in 1872. But the Don administration as late as 1891 considered that stanitsa banks were 'undesirable and untimely'.[202] As for larger funds that stanitsas or individual Cossacks needed if they were to buy privately-owned land, the problem was not only that they lacked such capital but also that their main competition, the richer peasants, had access to credit through the Peasant Land Bank, established in 1882. Although it was not the intention of the state, this institution in effect accelerated the transfer of land from members of the Cossack nobility who had received land as personal property. From the early 1880s to 1900, Cossack noble land ownership in the Don declined by almost 60 per cent.[203] Cossack delegates to committees of the Witte inquiry complained about the inequity of offering the peasants and not the Cossacks this kind of credit. Some simply asked that Cossacks be given access to the bank, which, however, would not have returned the land to communal Cossack ownership. Others proposed that the bank be closed down in the Don, or restricted to peasants already residing in the Don, or forbidden to make loans to buy land that was an enclave within a stanitsa.[204] But the state did nothing before the revolution of 1905. At least the War Ministry was sympathetic to one related complaint: that the economic decline of the Don, Kuban and Terek Cossacks was exacerbated by the 'flood' of non-Cossack settlers. As we have seen, these settlers rented Cossack communal land, bought privately-owned land, and dominated commerce and industry in the voiskos. The law of 1868 established the right of non-Cossacks to own homes and other buildings on the voisko land, giving these immigrants an accessible and secure base for their other economic activities. By 1890 the non-Cossacks were a majority in the Don, Kuban and Terek voiskos, attaining 80 per cent in the last-named.[205]

In the mid-1880s, the War Minister referred repeatedly to this problem, blaming it on the 1868 laws and asserting that the non-Cossacks 'exploit the Cossacks without restraint', taking over their land allotments and adversely affecting the ability of Cossacks to buy their military equipment.[206] Only a decade later did the ministry begin to consider possible legislative remedies, in particular giving the stanitsa assembly the power to block settlement of non-Cossacks in their territory. In a modernizing economy such restrictions were impractical and presumably would have met with serious opposition from the Ministry of Finance. No actual legislation emerged on this matter, except concerning the Jews. Given the anti-Semitic inclination of the regime, it is no surprise that they were the object of special restrictions with respect to settlement among the Cossacks. The War Ministry report of 1880 warned that Jews could 'exploit' Cossacks because the latter were tied down by military obligation, and that 'in a short time a considerable part of the land may pass into the hands of Jews'. In that year a law forbade the settlement in the Don of Jews, excepting those already there, physicians and university graduates.[207] This law was extended to the Kuban and Terek in 1892, leading to such absurdities as the court case of a surveyor, whose skills were badly needed, who converted from Judaism to Islam, evidently in order to live in the Kuban. He lost.[208] In 1899 the War Ministry reported that it was working on a law that would exclude Jews, presumably totally, from the Don, Kuban and Terek, but all that emerged was a ruling that they could not be members of the Cossack estate, which was not a serious issue in any case.[209]

In general, ameliorative measures had not made much headway when the Japanese War erupted in 1904, introducing a period in which the fragile Cossack economic system faced unprecedented stress. The impact of five years of mobilization of a substantial portion of the second and third turns required large outlays by the voisko, the stanitsa and the household. Had the legal and traditional norms of Cossack self-sufficiency been strictly observed, it is fair to suppose that widespread bankruptcy would have followed, most probably destroying the political reliability of this force just when it was needed most. It would be convenient for the historian if a policy document could be located that stated frankly: the regime is at hazard; without the Cossacks it is doomed; we must buy their loyalty without regard for the old ideas about self-sufficiency. Apparently no such direct expression survives, which is not surprising in view of the general reluctance of Imperial officialdom to admit that they were at the brink. There was, for example, a tacit understanding, even after the danger had receded, that one did not refer to a 'revolution', but merely 'troubles' (smuta). The essence of the situation was sufficiently clear to officials that the War Ministry secret report for 1914 could make the point that the Cossacks might be needed to suppress new upheavals merely by saying that the solution of their financial woes had 'enormous significance for the state'.[210]

The financial record of the time of crisis and its aftermath bears persuasive witness to the state's acceptance, albeit grudging, of the necessity of doing more for the Cossacks. Large sums of money for various Cossack needs appeared, beginning in 1904 and reaching a peak in 1906, when the strain of protracted mobilization coincided with the perceived need to maintain counterrevolutionary vigilance. It is next to impossible to produce a single summary figure for this outlay. Because of the desperate nature of the situation, the money spewed forth in diverse channels, sometimes as loans of doubtful collectibility, sometimes as grants that were not always adequately reported. The spirit of the change is in any case evident if one compares an order of 1902, collecting from the Don voisko 5872.60 rubles in compensation for mess tins that had been distributed to mobilized regiments in 1876, with the disbursement in 1906 of 2 million rubles of state money to replace the uniforms and equipment of Cossacks who had been mobilized for over six months.[211] During 1905–9 the War Ministry disbursed over 20 million rubles above normal entitlements in grants that were intended to end up in the hands of the rank and file. To determine the exact total would be a triumph of accountancy, for some of the disbursements came in small sums earmarked for such particular beneficiaries as four named Don regiments whose troopers received free sheepskin coats.[212] But these expenditures did not satisfy the advocates of Cossack interest, who maintained in the Duma that the increased state financial assistance was insufficient to cover the burden of mobilization of the second and third turns. 'We receive from women and children, old men and women who were left after the mobilization of the regiments', asserted the Don deputy Kharlamov in 1906, 'statements that without their breadwinners they may come to total ruin ...'[213]

It is plausible that the removal of a large part of the best manpower from the stanitsas would have a destructive impact on agricultural productivity, but it is not clear that Kharlamov was altogether correct. Families that could not cultivate their land because their men left for active duty could and presumably did rent out the land, although not necessarily for a profitable price. The sown area actually increased in most voiskos.[214] The crop, as usual, fluctuated from year to year and region to region, but there is no evidence of a general correlation between mobilization and decline. The Kuban and Terek harvested more grain each year in 1904–6 and the Zabaikal, after experiencing a decline in 1905, had an outstanding year in 1906. But adverse weather conditions produced poor crops in much of the Don, Astrakhan, Orenburg and Ural voiskos, clearly a regional weather pattern. In 1906 Orenburg harvested somewhat more than half the crop of 1904, the Don somewhat under half, Astrakhan about a third and the Ural voiska only 8 per cent. The state responded with a huge programme of loans, repayment of which was hardly plausible: in 1906 almost 1.3 million rubles; in 1907 almost 3.5 million; and in 1908 over 1.6 million.[215]

Another area in which the regime offered concessions to the Cossacks while the smell of revolution still hung in the air was land policy. In its most general – and cheapest – form this meant the issuance of charters reiterating the tsar's commitment to the donation of land to the Cossacks for all time. Previously Nicholas II had not found it necessary to issue any charters to his Cossacks, a matter that rankled. But in 1906 he graciously issued similar, ceremonial documents to six voiskos.[216] Far from reassuring the Don Cossacks, the charter that they received evoked the myth of tsar and Cossack in an unintended way. Widespread rumours that the tsar had promised them substantial rewards in land flew around the voisko. In the stanitsa of Arzhenovskaia the assembly solemnly affirmed that they understood that Cossack land would be increased to 25 desiatinas per capita. A still more optimistic and fanciful version was that 30 desiatinas per Cossack would be achieved when the tsar gave the Cossacks the land 'of the Mordvin', sending the latter to the Far East 'to scare the Japanese'. In the Orenburg voisko, Cossacks moved onto land held by officers or other proprietors, expecting that it would be given to them, and had to be evicted by force.[217]

Partly in response to reports of such expectations, the authorities moved rapidly to try to placate the Cossacks of the Kuban and Don. As noted in connection with administrative institutions, these voiskos were permitted to elect special assemblies to consider means of using their reserve land more helpfully. The Kuban rada of 17 December 1906 quickly accepted the proposal of the administration that it distribute the voisko reserve to the Cossacks, giving the land-poor mountain stanitsas 32 000 desiatinas and 110 704 to the rest of the voisko. The administration quickly set about this matter, and by 1910 the Kuban reserve was only 227 199 desiatinas, down from 1 044 630 in 1906.[218]

There was, apart from rumours of monarchial largesse, a substantial demand for the distribution of voisko reserve land in the Don. Between 1904 and 1907, 42 stanitsas made formal requests for additional space, and on 13 August 1906 three stanitsas were granted temporary use of some reserve land. But from that time until 1909 a mere 41 000 desiatinas had been distributed. According to a Don Duma deputy, the head of the Main Administration of Cossack Forces told him personally that the Cossacks already had enough land. One wonders, however, if he was not thinking partly about the problem of balancing the voisko budget if the reserve were not rented out. Just as an interpellation concerning the delay was passed in the Duma, the Don administration finally moved towards concession on this matter, convening on 8 December 1909 the elected assembly, which was soon called the krug.[219] The administration went to this assembly with a compromise proposal that fell short of simply distributing the entire reserve of land. At an unofficial meeting of part of the assembly, presumably delegates who were deemed receptive to official leadership, it was agreed in principle that half the reserve should no longer be rented out but should be partitioned to form new stanitsas. The other half would continue to be rented, but the revenue, instead of going into the general voisko budget, should go into a new land acquisition fund, which would buy up privately-owned land as it came on the market. Such land, once back in voisko ownership, would be awarded to needy stanitsas. This was a form of the law that had been established in the Kuban and Terek in 1902, but it was an innovation to propose to buy back alienated Cossack land by using rental income earned by the voisko land reserve.[220] In the short run, this had the effect of making less land available from the reserve for distribution to the stanitsas, but in the very long run it was theoretically better for the Cossacks. Once the buy-back operation was more or less complete, the stanitsas would receive not only the reserve land, no longer needed to raise funds for the operation, but also the considerable amount of land that had been taken from them for the benefit of nobles and officers.

When the proposal reached the whole assembly, a delegate from Veshenskaia stanitsa protested that it would take a century to buy all the private land in the Don by the means proposed. He suggested the establishment of a bank that would make loans to individual Cossacks who wanted to buy private land, securing such loans with their allotments. The ataman quashed this idea by noting that one could not use Cossack communal land as collateral (with the implicit possibility of foreclosure by a creditor) because it was inalienable. This was a nice irony, considering that the private land that the Cossacks were trying to purchase had once been promised to them for eternity by the tsar. This sore point seems to have been on the minds of a number of delegates who asked the ataman to have the charter of 1793 read aloud, which had the effect of reminding the assemblage that the whole issue would not exist if the tsars had kept Catherine's promise.

But this did not change the task facing the krug, which decided to use about half the reserve (not including the Transdon territory, which was never considered part of the business of the day) to form four new stanitsas, to which settlers could move from the most crowded areas, receiving a subsidy to defray their costs. The other half would indeed be rented out to provide revenue for a land purchase fund, which would be administered by elected 'land councils' on the oblast and okrug levels. As the draft law emerged, the new stanitsas were to embrace 423 513 desiatinas, the rented portion 533 687. This draft received War Ministry approval on 26 February 1910, and without awaiting action by the legislative bodies, the first meeting of the Land Council of the Don opened on 22 June of that year.[221] By the end of 1914 it had met twice annually and had conscientiously attempted to put into practice the intent of the legislation.[222]

Taking over the leasing of voisko reserve land, the Council by 1912–13 had an annual income of about 2.5 million rubles. With part of this substantial revenue it purchased land from private owners and from the Peasant Land Banks, which in 1909 had 30 000 desiatinas for sale.[223] Although this institution was not mentioned in the law, it played a significant role in the operation. At the request of the ataman, it ceased to sell land to non-Cossacks. In theory, the bank could now sell land to individual Cossacks, for in the Don and Kuban the members of the martial estate had in 1907 received legal consent to buy from the Peasant Land Bank. This could have been awkward for the goal of putting privately-owned land back in the voisko reserve, and the Don ataman secretly urged the bank to adopt a tacit policy of abstention from sales to Cossacks. There seems to have been no such formal decision, but for one reason or another only 4000 desiatinas had passed from the bank to individual Cossacks by 1914.[224]

Through 1916 the Land Council purchased from the Peasant Land Bank and from individual owners, such as 'the widow of a general', a total of 53 386 desiatinas.[225] This was not much in relation to Cossack needs, less than 1 per cent of the total land in the hands of stanitsas, but it added enough demand for land to force up the price.[226] The land acquired in this way consisted of relatively small properties that were scattered among existing stanitsas, none large enough to constitute a new stanitsa in its own right. Therefore the land that the Council purchased was rented out or given to adjacent stanitsas to permit them to establish new khutors, 22 of which had been formed by 1913.[227]

The other part of the operation of the Land Council was the establishment of four new stanitsas on the part of the former voisko reserve land which now was no longer rented out.[228] This change had some unwelcome side-effects. The removal of the land from the rental market forced up the demand for land to rent and greatly enriched the speculators who rented and then sublet voisko land. It also meant evicting from the formerly-rented land some 30 000 peasants who had been living on it: in some cases this led to violence and the destruction of property.[229] The new Cossack residents received 600 000 rubles for communal buildings and 60 000 in direct grants to families, paid by the Land Council. Nevertheless, one of the staunch advocates of the scheme, who visited the new settlements, the former Duma deputy Nazarov, found the condition of the migrants 'terrible'. Only the poorest had been accepted as settlers, the land constituting the stanitsas was arid and the amount of it available for individual allotments was not great, owing to the need to rent out much of it to meet communal expenses.[230]

Altogether the new khutors and stanitsas by 1915 provided 260 799 desiatinas of additional land for Cossack allotments, but this affected the condition of only a minute portion of the Don Cossack population. The successor to Ataman Fon Taube, General Mishchenko, did not share his predecessor's optimism about the whole scheme and in 1911 said that the purchase of private land was not a long-term solution to the agrarian problem in the voisko because the population and the price of land were both rising steadily.[231]

His view, shared by many observers of the Cossack land problem, was that the key to survival was not more land but increased productivity. Indeed, the Don Land Council devoted some of its funds to a study of the matter and also to some small-scale practical programmes, such as the control of harmful grasses and reforestation.[232] On the ministerial level there also was agreement that better farming techniques were vital to the survival of the

Cossacks, and in the last years before the First World War the state greatly expanded its interest in improving Cossack agriculture. The largest commitment was in the Don, which was to spend 160 000 rubles in 1909 on agronomy, increasing the sum annually until it reached 190 000 rubles by 1912.[233] All voiskos acquired, as part of their administrative staff, a professional agronomist, with a staff of assistants in the larger ones. In 1908 this collection of agronomists was substantial enough to warrant a convention in Novocherkassk, including the Don agronomical staff and colleagues from the Kuban, Terek, Astrakhan and Orenburg voiskos. Still, as the Don advocate Kharlamov put it, they were 'generals without soldiers' – a tiny force to deal with so large an area and population.[234]

One of their enterprises was the beginning of a network of experimental stations, at least in some voiskos.[235] Of particular interest was the strain of cold-resistant wheat that the Russian armed forces had encountered in Manchuria, a valuable plant that played a considerable role in the growth of North American wheat farming. Various experiments at introducing this seed to Cossack regions began, but only barely.[236] Other activities included measures to combat pests, such as the often calamitous invasions of locusts, and to develop modern cattle-breeding.[237] The introduction of agricultural machinery was a particularly important goal, which some voiskos attempted to foster by establishing publicly-owned stores that were supposed to sell equipment on favourable terms, others by establishing circulating funds from which Cossacks could borrow in order to purchase machines. But the amount of capital provided for these operations was modest and the credit limit to buyers was tight, 50 rubles in the Don and 200 in the Zabaikal.[238] Moreover, it was questionable that modern equipment could function economically in the strip system that prevailed in the distribution of the stanitsa land. Criticism of this tradition on economic grounds surfaced in the discussions of the Maslakovets and Witte Commissions on the Don and continued in the following years. With this in mind, the four new stanitsas established in the Don in 1910 were set up with the khutor system, that is, individual farmsteads surrounded by a block of land, rather than the traditional village surrounded by many, often remote, strips. But the Stolypin reform, which attempted to alter this tradition among the peasants, did not apply to the Cossacks, although it was in force among the peasants who lived on voisko land. The nearest that any voisko came to following this path on a large scale was a request of the Don ataman in 1911 to the okrug atamans under him to consider means of consolidating the strips into which the Cossack allotment was divided.[239]

One prerequisite for improved agricultural technique was better education for the Cossacks, whose Duma representatives frequently complained of the low level of financial support in this area. Voiloshnikov, the Social Democratic Duma deputy from the Zabaikal voisko, was particularly incensed by a remark that he attributed to the War Minister: 'What do you mean "school"? You know that we don't have enough cannon' ('Kakaia tebe "shkola"? Znaesh chto pushek ne khvataet').[240] Kharlamov of the Don maintained that three adjoining guberniias spent 28, 38 and 43 kopeks per capita per year on education, while the Don spent only 18. He also described a khutor agricultural school in his home area that closed after struggling for three years 'without textbooks, without equipment, having neither oxen nor horses nor ploughs'.[241] Despite such backwardness, the education budget of the Cossacks, like the Empire as a whole, increased markedly in the Duma period, by 47 per cent between 1904 and 1910. This produced a 34 per cent increase in the number of primary school pupils and a 51 per cent increase in secondary school students.[242] Given time, it seems predictable that the economy would have benefited from this kind of modernization. In the shorter run, however, there was a serious problem associated with the new level of investment in agriculture and education: it cost more than the traditional methods of financing could pay.

The squeeze that increased spending on welfare and economic modernization placed on the resources of the voisko painfully affected the aggregate of voisko funds. This figure reached its historic high in 1906 at 40.3 million rubles, then plunged to 28.6 million in 1908. The most critical point occurred early in that year when the Don voisko capital had only 215 316 rubles on hand.[243]

The officials of the War Ministry were loath to admit that they could not keep the Cossack system in the black. Published reports showed the total of voisko funds rebounding to a fairly robust 31.9 million rubles by 1913.[244] But this was misleading, partly a matter of accounting tricks. For example, in 1894 and 1904 only 15 per cent of all voisko funds was in the form of indebtedness of stanitsas to the voiskos, but by 1812 these doubtfully collectible debts constituted 28 per cent of voisko 'assets'.[245] In 1911 the Don showed a modest budget surplus, which was achieved only by counting famine relief loans to the voisko as 'income', which was not the normal procedure.[246] Above all, the oil wells of Groznyi continued to pump cash into the Terek surplus. In 1911 the royalty rate on oil was doubled, a government measure to assist Cossack finances at no expense to itself. Thus by 1913 about half of the supposed funds of all the voiskos, almost 16 million rubles, was in the coffers of this one small voisko. In 1912 the War Ministry violated tradition and loaned some of this Terek surplus to the 'completely exhausted' fund of the Ural voisko, over 200 000 rubles by 1914.[247]

In the Don and Kuban a considerable part of the financial problem was the loss of revenue from the rental of voisko reserve land, a result of the attempt of the regime to assuage Cossack land-hunger. In the Don this revenue declined from 2.6 million rubles in 1909 to 0.5 million in 1911, in the Kuban from 0.7 million in 1907 (the last year of the old system) to a mere 59 000 in 1912.[248] Otherwise the difficulty in voisko finance lay mainly in increased expenditure. Military costs soared during the period of emergency mobilization, rising from 0.9 million rubles in 1905 to 10.7 million in 1906, and receding only to 3.2 million by 1910. The education budget rose from 1.4 million to 2.3 million, medical costs from 0.8 million to 1.4 million, between 1904 and 1910.[249]

The secret annual reports of the War Minister, unlike the public ones, showed a growing awareness that the regime had to make major changes in this system to avert bankruptcy. Despite the appearance of an aggregate fiscal surplus for all voiskos, the annual deficits of those that were not running in the black were rising alarmingly: 0.7 million in 1909, 1.7 million in 1913. By 1912 the secret report acknowledged that 'the condition of the voisko capital of the majority of the Cossack voiskos is extremely poor'.[250] True, the Ministry of Finance clung to its traditional role as defender of solvency. As late as 1913, when the Orenburg voisko, stricken by crop failures in 1911 and 1912, appealed for assistance, the Deputy Minister of Finance responded with a sermon on thrift that would have gladdened the heart of Samuel Smiles. He observed that in 1903 an interministerial commission had considered the fiscal troubles of the Orenburg voisko and had concluded that only better management was needed. In particular the voisko administration should rent out more of the land at its disposal. The Orenburg ataman was incorrect to argue that this reserve land might be needed by Cossacks. Why, the Orenburg Cossacks, the deputy minister read in the annual War Ministry report, had 24 desiatinas per capita. He seems not to have realized that the actual allotment of the average Cossack was under ten desiatinas. The Council did in fact approve a loan to the Orenburg voisko but with a homily: 'Only the durable enhancement of the most important income categories in the voisko budget can secure the voisko the independent satisfaction of local needs and spare the state treasury significant expenses to cover deficits in the voisko budget.'[251]

In this grudging spirit the state doled out relatively modest grants to the neediest voiskos in 1909–13, Orenburg receiving the largest, 150 000 per year.[252] Zabaikal received 100 000 in three grants, and the Amur 34 700.[253] The deficits, however, continued, so in 1914 the state provided ten-year loans totalling 549 000 rubles to the Ural, Orenburg and Semirechenskoe voiskos.[254] Crop failures induced the state to grant much larger sums for emergency relief in 1911, the largest with a ceiling of 7.4 million rubles for the Orenburg and Ural voiskos, the Don receiving a much smaller loan of 0.5 million. In 1912 and 1913 follow-up loans totalling 477 500 went to the Orenburg and Ural voiskos.[255]

But none of this addressed the fundamental imbalance of revenue and costs in the Cossack system as it stood in its last years. One way of meeting the problem, which would not violate the theory that the voiskos were self-supporting, was to reduce their responsibility for 'the general expenses of the state'. Both the Don ataman and chairman of the Don nobility petitioned on this point, but the most audible advocates of reform on this issue were the Cossack Duma deputies. In 1911 they persuaded the chamber to back the general principle that the state should assume the general cost of government within the voiskos.[256]

The War Ministry spokesman in the Duma at first offered some resistance, maintaining that voisko capital was 'the property of the whole voisko, conceived as a special state institution'.[257] That is, voisko assets belonged to the state and should be used for state purposes. Not only Cossacks but also some other Duma deputies took exception to this interpretation, and went on to list a variety of state costs that the Cossacks had to bear, including courts, police, jails, surveyors, ecclesiastical bodies and the Main Administration of Cossack Forces.[258] The authorities were not unyielding. In 1909 the state ceased to collect from the Don payments for the maintenance of certain courts and administrative bodies and began compensating the Don for some other costs, including doctors', feldshers' and midwives' salaries and, most importantly, the Don ataman and his staff. This was a major improvement for the largest voisko, adding about half a million rubles in costs now assumed by the state.[259] Not only the Don, but all the voisko funds benefited by the decision in 1910 to reorganize the War Ministry, phasing out the Main Administration of Cossack Forces, transferring the work of this office to the General Staff. Starting in 1914, the voiskos would no longer have to pay for their bosses in St Petersburg, a gain of 266 290 rubles.[260] This was some help, but it did not satisfy the advocates of Cossack interest, such as Kharlamov, who in 1913 argued that seven voiskos paid over 5.7 million rubles towards the general expenses of the state, which continually evaded efforts to rectify this unfairness and thus balance the budgets of the voiskos. The head of the Main Administration of Cossack Forces, on the other hand, maintained that different atamans held diverse opinions on what was properly a Cossack expense and what a general expense of the state. He claimed that previously adopted fiscal changes would shift about 2 000 000 rubles to the state.[261]

Despite this public show of traditional miserliness towards the Cossacks, the War Ministry privately was moving towards the conclusion that the state should indeed take over more of the general costs of government in the voiskos. The secret reports to the tsar for 1912 and 1913 explicitly recommended a change in this matter and at last, on 20 May 1914, the War Ministry introduced in the Duma a bill that would transfer many 'general state expenses' from the voiskos to the state treasury. The Duma adjourned without taking any action, the First World War erupted and on 13 September 1914 the government passed its bill as emergency legislation. This resulted in state payments to the voiskos of over 8.5 million rubles, a vast sum relative to previous subventions, enough to put the voiskos in the black and even to permit some repayment of their indebtedness to the state.[262]

In the last prewar years the War Ministry also sought to assist the finances of the Don voisko by increasing the compensation that it received for the rental of the Transdon area to private horse-ranchers. In 1901, it will be recalled, these leases for the western part of the region were renewed for 12 years, to be followed by a three-year liquidation period preparatory to the return of the land to the voisko reserve. In 1909, as part of an aid package to the Don voisko, the compensation that the state paid to the voisko as a subsidy to the low rent paid by the ranchers increased by 840 000 rubles. At this time the War Ministry still operated on the assumption that the western, more arable part of the Transdon would revert to the land reserve in 1913.[263] But the same military considerations that had made the army the biggest buyer of Transdon horses worked against this transfer. The Russian Empire was at this time embarked on a new programme of military expansion for defence against Germany and the Dual Monarchy, and this required more cavalry than ever.[264]

A number of interests collided on this issue. First, there were the advocates of the Dontsy, who wanted a lot more money in compensation if any ranch leases were extended.[265] Second, there was the War Ministry, which wished to maintain the ranches but also wanted more money for the voisko budget. Third, there were the private ranchers, who wanted to continue in business at the existing bargain rates. Fourth, State Control and the Ministry of Finance were only mildly interested in the Don budget but greatly concerned that the state spend the minimum needed in buying remounts. Finally, there was Nicholas II, who in 1911 ordered the formation of a commission to consider the *expropriation* of the Transdon by the state so that it could continue as ranchland. Despite a protest from the 'autocrat', his ministerial employees ignored this command, which violated the charters that promised the Don Cossacks their land in perpetuity, including Nicholas's charter of 1906.[266] The ranchers had but one card to play. They could and did threaten to go out of business if their rents were raised too much. In most cases this seems to have been a bluff, which the War Ministry called in its negotiations with the ranchers. The draft of the new law on the ranch system included rental rates of 60 kopeks per desiatina in the western half of the Transdon, a huge increase compared to the former rate of 3 kopeks.[267]

The central conflict in the whole affair turned out to be between the War Ministry and the guardians of the solvency of the Empire, State Control and the Ministry of Finance. The result was stalemate. The War Ministry tried to use the issue of compensation for the ranches as a means of overcoming the deficits in the Don budget. The guardians of solvency succeeded in obliging the War Ministry to drop this idea in return for a promise – unfulfilled, as it turned out – to establish a separate commission to deal with the fiscal woes of the Don. There was, however, a joint commission of representatives of the War Ministry and the fiscal agencies which tried to find a fair rate of compensation for the voisko. The guardians of solvency offered a paltry increase of 350 000 rubles per year as a temporary measure. Negotiations became entangled with questions of legislative procedure. In 1912 the War Ministry argued that the new law on leases would have to appear as emergency legislation under article 87 because the old leases expired in 1913, too soon to get legislation through the Duma. The other agencies persuaded them to retreat from this line, noting that there was a three-year grace-period for the liquidation of the ranches built into the old law. But the War Ministry found another way to circumvent the Duma and the other ministries: the right of the tsar to pass purely military legislation under article 96 of the Fundamental Laws. This they used to establish a curiously incomplete law that only set new rental rates, without term, for the eastern part of the Transdon.[268] The Council of Ministers continued to press the War Ministry for a draft of the entire legislation, suitable for introduction into the Duma, but the War Ministry did not do so, presumably because they could not agree with the fiscal agencies on the rate of compensation for the Don. And so the matter drifted, unresolved.[269]

More serious than the condition of the voisko budgets was the impoverishment of the ordinary Cossack. The protracted mobilization for war and counterrevolution imposed a crushing burden on households that were barely meeting peacetime military obligations, often with communal assistance. The serious crop failures among the Cossacks during the period of mobilization and in 1911–12 testify to the weakness of the agrarian economy, even if weather and fishing conditions in the Ural River were serious factors. The population of the martial estate continued to rise, gaining 18.8 per cent between 1905 and 1912, but the land available to support it in most voiskos did not.[270] True, the Siberian voisko received 7.7 million additional desiatinas in 1907, and the stanitsa land of the Don and Kuban increased when a considerable part of the voisko reserve was transferred to Cossack farming. In both cases this reversed the long-term decline of stanitsa land per capita, but only for a few years. By 1912 the trend was down again.[271] Nor had improved agricultural technique compensated for the deteriorating land/population ratio. Even including the non-Cossack, presumably most advanced, portion of the economy, the average grain yield for 1908–13 stood at about 29 puds per desiatina in the Orenburg and Don territory, against 46 in Saratov guberniia, 74 in Orenburg and 71 in Kharkov.[272]

In 1914 even the arch-conservative defender of the traditional Cossack system Stishinskii acknowledged in the State Council: 'All the branches of local welfare and the economy of the Don oblast have long since been extremely unsatisfactory, in a condition that is desolate in the full sense of the word.' As for the ordinary member of the martial estate, his opinion might well have been summed up in the words of the Duma deputy who asked rhetorically, 'Where is Cossack privilege?'[273]

5 Conclusion

The outbreak of the First World War began the dissolution of the Cossacks and the Empire of the tsars. The martial estate was, of course, mobilized for combat with the foreign enemy, and it existed in some form for several years after the fall of the tsars. But the impact of the war, even while the military outcome remained unsettled, sufficiently disrupted the flow of the kind of records on which the present study is based that it is impractical to continue it past the beginning of hostilities.

Although this study has been organized topically in order to cope with the complexities of the Cossack system, it is clear that a common chronological development united the military, civil administrative and economic aspects of the system. In the era of Alexander II, the regime attempted to enhance its control over the voiskos through the modernization of their military service and governance. The notion that this process should lead to the gradual liquidation of the martial estate, Miliutin's project, was set aside when military exigency persuaded the regime that the process of modernization should focus on the creation of a regular Cossack military force. This thrust continued into the reign of Alexander III, and reached its most successful point approximately in the last decade of the nineteenth century, embodied in the improvements in the machinery of mobilization, the law on administration and the accumulation of healthy cash balances of voisko and stanitsa funds. But this success was based on excessive demands on the Cossack economy. By the opening of the twentieth century the regime was beginning to recognize this problem, which threatened the system in its military, civil administrative and fiscal aspects. Although the state made some efforts to address this problem, it is doubtful that it was willing or able to spend enough money to succeed, if indeed success was possible for more than a few years.

The Cossack system was an anachronism by the twentieth century, subject to serious stresses in addition to under-financing. The very concept of estates had disappeared or was becoming vestigial in most modern countries, and there was considerable recognition by educated Russians, even some conservatives, that their land was following this trend. Part of this pattern was the demand of a modern economy for a mobile population, capable of geographical and occupational flexibility. The Cossack estate was eroding in this process, as its own members sought livelihoods that took them away from their traditional agrarian setting and non-Cossacks flooded into voisko territories. There was widespread recognition among educated observers that the process they called 'raskazachivanie' or 'decossackization' was a major threat to the continuation of the Cossack sense of identity.[1]

The concept of a martial estate was a military as well as social anachronism. While legal social classes devoted to soldiering were common in many cultures in bygone eras, this form had vanished in modern countries. In particular it was impossible to sustain such a class as a financially self-financing military institution in the age of the machine gun. Industrialized warfare required greater expenditures than relatively backward agrarian villages could raise on their own. As cavalry, most Cossacks were also on the verge of obsolescence in 1914, even if few military leaders of that date realized how little opportunity was left for the armed horseman to play his traditional role on the battlefield.

But perhaps the horseman's tactical usefulness was not so obsolescent in one kind of war, the class conflict that had erupted in Russia's cities and villages in 1905. Although it was not the assignment that the War Ministry wished for its Cossack forces, cavalry could still do an effective job against poorly-armed and scarcely organized crowds. For this reason, there was considerable disposition within the Imperial regime in the years after 1905 to deny that the Cossacks were an anachronism. Stishinskii energetically condemned the view that 'in our merchantile age' one should 'consider an anachronism the vast military community that stretches along the banks of the quiet Don ...'[2] One might however argue that the value of the Cossacks as counterrevolutionary police depended precisely on their being a social anachronism. Their reliability would last only as long as their sense of identity and their belief in the myth of tsar and Cossack, with its valuable 'privileges'. By 1905 this tradition was beginning to disintegrate, but not as a simple process of Cossacks awakening to the realization that they were an anachronism. On the contrary, most

Cossack spokesmen, including professional men who themselves represented the process of 'decossackization', stoutly denied that they regarded the martial estate as an anachronism that should be disbanded.[3] In truth there was enough Cossack pride left that even liberals among them were unwilling to admit that the abolition of legal estates was a corollary of democratization. Instead of advocating the dissolution of the Cossacks they proposed an ideology that attempted to revive the myth of the free Cossack, merged with modern liberalism. In the Russian civil war and later among *émigrés* there was an attempt to overcome the inherent contradiction between particularism and democracy by asserting the idea of Cossack national identity and territorial independence.[4] But it was impossible to restore the conditions of the sixteenth or seventeenth century in the 'wild steppe', nor resist the power of the Soviet state.

If the persistence and even revival of Cossack consciousness, especially in the Don voisko, was a lost cause for Cossack liberals, it posed a serious problem for conservatives who would maintain the myth of tsar and Cossack. The very vitality of Cossack pride owed much to the release of growing indignation concerning the failure of the tsar to live up to his myth. There had always been grievances concerning what the Cossacks saw as excessive regulation and exploitation, but these had been fairly effectively suppressed in the nineteenth century. The rise of a small Cossack intelligentsia, the weakening of controls during the revolution of 1905, and above all the establishment of the Duma, expanded the Cossack protest against the established order in the martial estate. They could not obtain any significant legislative changes, not even the introduction of a zemstvo in the Don oblast, which would have been an additional forum for the propagation of the myth of tsar and Cossack. But the liberal 'kazakoman' (Cossackomane, or fanatic advocate of the Cossack cause) accelerated the dissolution of the anachronism that the conservatives hoped to preserve as a bulwark against future revolutionary outbreaks. It is no wonder that in February 1917 the Cossack units in the capital and elsewhere showed no zeal to fight for the tsar.

Historians in and out of the Soviet Union have had a good deal to say about the prospects for the Imperial regime in the early twentieth century.[5] Some Russian liberal historians in emigration, reflecting their hopes in the Duma era, have maintained that the First World War destroyed an opportunity for non-revolutionary political and social transformation. The prevailing Soviet view, which many Western scholars share, is that the old order was in any case on the brink of revolution before 1914. The present study should not attempt to settle this matter, concerning which there are numerous complexities and cross-currents. But it should make this sufficiently clear: the Cossacks had in the revolution of 1905 proven their importance as a counterrevolutionary police; they would be badly needed in any future upheaval; the regime did not or could not take adequate steps to gratify the economic demands of the Cossacks; in sum, the Cossack system was in dire straits and this anachronistic military caste was no longer one of the strengths of the regime but one of its serious vulnerabilities.

Sources and Abbreviations

The following list indicates most frequently used sources for the present work, marking with an asterisk those for which full publication data appear in P. A. Zaionchkovskii (ed), *Spravochnik po istorii dorevoliutsionnoi Rossii*, 2nd edn. (M, 1978). The abbreviations given are used in the following footnotes.

LAWS AND STATE PAPERS

Denisov
: *Doklad Oblastnago Voisko Donskago predvoditelia dvorianstva ocherednomu sobraniiu dvorian' 10 dek. 1907 g.* (SPB, 1908).

GDSO
: *Gosudarstvennaia Duma. Stenograficheskie otchety.* *

GSSO
: *Gosudarstvennyi Sovet. Stenograficheskie otchey.* *

Kaufman
: A.A. Kaufman, *Svod trudov mestnykh komitetov po Kavkazu, Oblasti Voiska Donskago, Sibiri, Stepnomu Kraiu i Turkestanu* (SPB, 1904)

Kuropatkin
: *Otchet o sluzhebnoi poezdke Voennago Ministra v Oblasti Voiska Donskago v 1900 g.* (SPB, 1900).

Leonov
: *Otchet Oblastnago Voiska Donskago predvoditelia dvorianstva A. P. Leonova* (Novocherkassk, 1910).

Maslakovets
: *Doklad sostoiashchago v rasporiazhenii Voennago Ministra Generala Shtaba General-Letenanta Maslakovtsa* (SPB, 1899).

OZSM
: *Osobyi zhurnal Sovetov Ministrov* (SPB, 1906–11).

PSOGD	*Prilozheniia k Stenograficheskim Otchetam Gosudarstvennoi Dumy.* *
PSZ	*Polnoe sobranie zakonov Rossiiskoi Imperii.* *
PVSS	*Protokoly Voiskovogo Soveshchatel'nago Soveshchaniia 8–20 dek. 1909 g.* (Rostov-na-Donu, 1915).
Shcherbov	*Doklad o rezultatakh komadirovki nachal'nika Glavnago Upravleniia Kazachikh Voisk General' letenanta Shcherbov-Neferovicha v 1900 v Oblast' Voiska Donskago* (SPB, 1902).
SPRKV	*Sbornik pravitel'stvennykh rasporiazhenii po kazach'im voiskam,* 51 vols (SPB, 1870–1915).
SVP	*Svod voennykh' postanovlennii.* *
SZ	*Svod zakonov Rossiikoi Imperii.* *
TMK	*Trudy mestnykh komitetov* (Osoboe soveshchanie o nuzhdakh sel'skokhoziaistvennoi promyshlennosti), 58 vols (SPB, 1904).
VDVM	*Vsepoddanneishii doklad no voennomu ministerstvu,* 53 vols (SPB, 1862–1915).
VOOVD	*Vsepoddanneishii otchet voiskovogo nakaznogo atamana o sostoianii Oblasti Voiskago Donskago,* 49 vols (Novocherkassk, 1866–1915).
VOVM	*Vsepoddanneishii otchet o deistviiakh Voennago Ministerstva,* 54 vols (SPB, 1858–1912).

PERIODICALS

DOV	*Donskie Oblastnie Vedemosti*
DR	*Donskaia rech'*
NS	*Novoe slovo*
RB	*Russkoe bogatstvo*
RI	*Russkii invalid*
RM	*Russkaia mysl'*
VE	*Vestnik Evropy*
VS	*Voennyi sbornik*

BOOKS

Babychev, D. S., *Donskoe trudovoe kazachestvo v bor'be za vlast' Sovetov* (Rostov, 1969).

Baluev, P. S., *Statisticheskii obzor torgovopromyshlennoi deiatel'nosti kazach'ego naseleniia Oblasti Voiska Donskago za piatiletie s 1894–1898* (Novocherkassk, 1899).

Baluev, P. S., *Istoricheskiia i statisticheskiia opisaniia stanits i gorodov poseshchaemykh G. Voennom Ministrom pri ob'ezd Ego Prevoskhoditel'stvom Oblasti Voiska Donskago v 1900 g.* (Novocherkassk, 1900).

Biriukov, I. A., *Istoriia Astrakhanskago Kazachia Voiska*, 3 vols (SPB, 1911).

Bogdanovich, M. I., *Istoricheskii ocherk deiatel'nosti voennago upravleniia v Rossii v pervoe dvadtsati-piatiletie blagopoluchnago tsarstvovaniia Gosudaria Imperatora Aleksandra Nikolaevicha (1855–1880 gg.)*, 6 vols (SPB, 1879–80).

Borodin, N. A., *Ural'skoe Kazach'e Voisko. Statisticheskoe opisanie*, 2 vols (SPB, 1891).

Chistov, K. V., *Kubanskie stanitsy. Etnicheskie i kul'turno-bytovye protsessy na Kubani* (M, 1967).

Efremov, I. N., *Otchet izbirateliam I. N. Efremova o deiatel'nosti v kachestve chlena III Gosudarstvennoi Dumy 1907–1912*, 3 vols (SPB, 1907–12).

Eroshkin, N. P., *Istoriia gosudarstvennykh uchrezhdenii dorevoliutsionnoi Rossii* (M, 1968).

Futorianskii, L. I., 'Kazachestvo v sisteme sotsial'no-ekonomicheskikh otnoshenii predrevoliutsionnoi Rossii', *Voprosy istorii kapitalisticheskoi Rossii. Problema mnogokladnosti* (Sverdlovsk, 1972).

Kharuzin, M. N., *Svedeniia o kazatskikh obshchinakh na Donu* (M, 1885).

Khlystov, I. P., *Don v epokhu kapitalizma* (Rostov, 1962).

Khoroshkhin', M., *Kazachi'i voiska* (SPB, 1881).

Medvedev, *Sluzhba Donskago Voiska v sviazi s ego ekonomicheskim polozheniem* (M, 1899).

Petrovskii, A. I., *Donskie deputaty vo II-i Gosudarstvennoi Dume. Istoricheskaia spravka* (SPB, 1907).

Pokrovskii, A., *3-i Donskoi Kazachii Ermak Timofeeva Polk. Proshloe za sto let* (Vilno, 1910).

Savel'ev, E. P., *Ocherki po istorii torgovli na Donu. Obshchestvo donskikh torgovykh kazakov 1804–1904* (Novocherkassk, 1904).

SVM, D. A. Skalon, *Stoletie Voennago Ministerstva*, 13 vols (SPB, 1902).*

Svatikov, S. G., *Rossiia i Don* (Vienna, 1924).

VKD, *Voiskovoi krug na Donu 8–20 dek. 1909 g. (Voiskovoe soveshchatel'noe sobranie)* (Rostov, 1910).

VRKV, *Voiskovaia rada Kubanskago Voiska zasedala v g. Ekaterinodar 1–17 dek. 1906 g.* (Ekaterinodar, 1907).

Zasedatel'eva, L. B. *Terskie kazaki* (M, 1974).

Zaionchkovskii, P. A., *Voennye reformy 1860–1870 gg.* (M, 1952).

Zaionchkovskii, P. A., *Samoderzhavia i russkaia armiia na rubezhe 19–20 stoletie 1881–1903* (M, 1973).

Zolotov, V. A., 'Agrarnaia politika tsarizma po otnosheniiu k kazachestvu v 1907–1917 gg', *Uchenye zapiski Rostovskogo Universiteta,* Istoricheskii-filologicheskii fakultet, t. 21, seriia 'Istoriia SSSR', vyp. 3 (1952).

Zolotov, V. A., *Istoriia Dona, Epokha kapitalizma* (Rostov, 1974).

Notes and References

CHAPTER 1

1. The same scene was depicted in prints that often hung in Don Cossack courts; Kharuzin, 309.
2. SVM, XI/1, 260, 395–7, 564–6. N. V. Galushkin, *Sobstvennyi ego Imperatorskago Velichestva Konvoi* (San Francisco, 1961) frontispieces.
3. SVM, XI/1, 566. He had visited the Ural voisko in 1890; N. A. Simonov, *Kratkaia istoriia po 1-go Sibirskago kazachiago Ermak Timofeeva Polka* (Omsk, 1907) 137–49.
4. Galushkin, op. cit., frontispiece, 9.
5. SVM, XI/2, 341–426.
6. SVM, XI/3, 503–11; XI/4, 433–41; SPRKV 1912, nos. 414, 446, 447.
7. VDVM 1894, 210.
8. E.g. DR 3 May 1892.
9. SPRKV 1904, no. 29; revised 1904, no. 127.
10. SVM, XI/2, 352, 414; SPRKV 1904, no. 15; 1907, *passim.*
11. SVM, XI/2, 341.
12. Korolenko, RB, 1901, no. 10, 179.
13. V. V. Mavrodin, *Krest'ianskaia voina v Rossii 1773–1775. Vosstanie Pugacheva* (L, 1961) III, 353.
14. VKD, 140.
15. Kuban Army Museum and Muzei L. Gv. Kaz. Ego Velichestva Polka.
16. See below, pp. 173–4.
17. SVM, XI/1, 589–96, 653–5, 748–9.
18. S. Vil'chkovskii, 'Prebyvanie Gosudaria Imperatora v Pskove 1 i 2 marta 1917 goda', *Russkaia letopis'*, III, 178; Galushkin, op. cit., 316.
19. The most extended version of the argument that ancient Cossack liberty should be regarded as an ancestor of modern liberalism is provided by Svatikov. For an estimable introduction to the full sweep of early Cossack history, Philip Longworth, *The Cossacks, Five Centuries of Tubulent Life on the Russian Steppes* (New York, 1969).
20. SZ, IX.
21. M. N. Tikhonov and P. P. Epifanov (eds), *Sobornoe Ulozhenie 1649 g.* (M, 1961) VII, i; VIII, 1; X, 31, 92, 124, 159, 266; XI, 2; XVI, 50;

XVIII, 10, 50–3, all of which seem to refer to Cossacks personally in the service of Muscovy, parallel with 'strel'tsy', and none of which reflect any attempt to regulate the affairs of a voisko. The first attempt to do this appears to be PSZ I, 262.

22. Svatikov, 199.
23. SZ, IX, no. 671.
24. Bruce W. Menning, 'A. I. Chernyshev: A Russian Lycurgus', *East Central European Society and War in the Era of Revolution: 1775–1856* (New York, 1982).
25. PSZ II, 8163.
26. SVM, XI/1, 287–98.
27. This is the main theme of A. P. Pronshtein, *Zemlia Donskaia v XVII veke* (Rostov, 1961) and V. A. Golobutskii, *Chernomorskoe Kazachestvo* (Kiev, 1956) and Bruce W. Menning, 'The Emergence of a Military–Administrative Elite in the Don Cossack Land, 1708–1836', in W. M. Pinter and D. K. Rowney (eds), *Russian Officialdom* (Chapel Hill, 1980) 130–61.
28. Svatikov, 197–209.
29. Robert E. Jones, *The Emancipation of the Russian Nobility* (Princeton, 1973).
30. SVM, XI/1, 320–30.
31. SZ, IX, no. 28.
32. Svatikov, 264–5; the legal establishment of the office of marshal of the Don nobility came about as an offhand result of the establishment of a pension fund; see below, p. 174.
33. SVM, XI/1, 330–1.
34. Ibid., 529. See p. 195 below on the abolition of this institution in most voiskos. It never existed in the Ural voisko.
35. SVM, XI/1, 64–5.
36. E.g. PSZ III, 30003.
37. SPRKV 1869, no. 69.
38. PSZ III, 12066; SVM, XI/1, 743–4.
39. N. M. Korkunov, *Russkoe gousdarstvennoe pravo* (SPB, 1909) 275.
40. Kuropatkin, 40; Shcherbov, 40.
41. SVP, X, 1205.
42. SZ, II, 1–639.
43. E.g. the major law on stanitsa administration, PSZ III, 7782.
44. Golobutskii, op. cit. An estate called the 'Malorossiiskii Cossacks' survived, but it was merely vestigial and its members were not Cossacks in the sense of the 'martial estate'. SZ, IX, nos. 608–702.
45. SVM, XI/1, 11–12, 14–15, 65–79, 90–117, 130–48, 224–54, 359–93, 55–63.
46. Svatikov is the most sustained discussion of this point.
47. Ibid., 97–109.
48. PSZ I, 7525.
49. Pronshtein, op. cit., 295–307.
50. John T. Alexander, *Autocratic Politics in a National Crisis. The Imperial Russian Government and the Pugachev Revolt* (Bloomington, 1969); Mavrodin, op. cit.

51. Bruce W. Menning. 'The Case of the Reluctant Colonists; Mutiny among the Don Cossacks, 1792–94', *East Central European Society and War in the Pre-Revolutionary Eighteenth Century* (New York, 1982). Pronshtein, op. cit., 323–50.
52. Pronshtein, op. cit., 238–45.
53. Denisov, 14.
54. Pronshtein, op. cit., 33–5.
55. Owing to changes in the survey there are major and minor fluctuatiuons in the reported areas of the voiskos. In this chapter, rounded figures from VOVM 1912 are used. As late as 1910 the War Ministry reported that its survey data on the voiskos were 'incomplete and obsolete'; VOVM 1910.
56. VOVM 1860, 1910.
57. Kharuzin, xxxv.
58. On Buddhists, P. S. Baluev (1900) 11; on Old Believers, Khoroshkhin', 151; VOVM 1862, 1910.
59. F. A. Shcherbina, *Istoriia Kubanskogo Kazachiago Voiska* (Ekaterinodar, 1910); SVM, XI/1, 90–9.
60. Golobutskii, op. cit., glava 4.
61. Bogdanovich, I, 269.
62. PSZ I, 17056.
63. SVM, XI/1, 232–6.
64. The Kuban was larger than the Zabaikal in survey data reported in most years, but the size of the latter voisko was in fact undetermined and fluctuated in VOVM between three million and ten million desiatinas, the higher figure dating from 1910 and after.
65. *Vseobshchaia perepis' naseleniia Rossiiskoi Imperii 1897 g.*, LXV, 238–9; SVM, XI/1, 650.
66. Khoroshkhin', 151; VOVM 1910 shows only 14.6 per cent.
67. Guenter Stoekl, *Die Entstehung des Kosakentums* (Munich, 1953) 147–61; SVM, XI/1, 3, 5.
68. Biriukov, vols I–III (map in vol. II).
69. Korolenko, RB, 1901, no. 10, 1902; no. 12, 195.
70. Kostenko, VS, 1910, no. 10, 314; V. Vitebskii, *Raskol v Ural'skom Voiske* (Kazan, 1877); VOVM 1862, 1910.
71. Alexander, op. cit., 44–52.
72. *Materialy dlia geografii i statistiki Rossii, sobranie ofitserami General'nago Shtaba* (SPB 1866) XXII, 73–83; below, pp. 45–7.
73. Khoroshkin', 125–6, 150; Bogdanovich, I, 271–3.
74. Until the abolition of the Bashkir voisko in 1861 it exceeded Orenburg in population.
75. VDVM 1882, 166–7.
76. It is not clear if these were ethnic Chinese or some other group from within the Chinese Empire. SPRKV 1869, no. 69.
77. PSOGD, IV/1, no. 422, 1–3.
78. SPRKV 1871, no. 56; SVM, XI/1, 256–7, 384–9.
79. In the summer of 1917 a meeting of Cossacks of the Enesei requested that they be established as a voisko, but nothing came of this; A. P. Ermolin, *Revoliutsiia i kazachestvo* (M, 1982) 18; on service see for example VOVM 1910, 130.

80. SVM, XI/1, 252–4.
81. Ibid., 389–93, 556–8.
82. See below, pp. 186–8.
83. VOVM 1862, 1912. In 1863 there were in all over 3 000 000 Cossacks, but many of these were about to be transferred to other estates upon the abolition of certain voiskos.

CHAPTER 2

1. L. Listopadov (ed), *Pesni donskikh kazakov* (M, 1949) II, 233.
2. Zaionchkovskii (1952) 18, 33; Bogdanovich, III, 282.
3. Khoroshkhin', 288; in 1911 the Cossacks constituted 2.5 per cent of the population and 7.1 per cent of the armed forces, PSOGD, III/5, no. 125, 8.
4. PSZ II, 8163.
5. E.g. SPRKV 1868, no. 108.
6. Khoroshkhin', 279–80; Bogdanovich, III, 276; Kharuzin, 197–308.
7. See below, pp. 42–3.
8. Khoroshkhin', 256.
9. Bogdanovich, I, 324–5.
10. *Otchet o deistviiakh Voennago Ministerstva* (SPB, 1860) 378–9.
11. VDVM 1862, 109–10; SVM, XI/2, 167–71.
12. SVM, XI/1, 406–7.
13. Ibid., XI/1, 397–403; the most important work on the military colonies, including their dissolution, is Alan D. Ferguson, 'The Russian Military Settlements, 1810–66' (dissertation, Yale University, 1966); on Sukhozanet, E. Willis Brooks, 'Reform in the Russian Army, 1856–61', *Slavic Review* (Spring 1984) 63–82.
14. SVM, XI/1, 407-8.
15. SVM, XI/1, 410–11; the official reason for the creation of the committee for the Caucasian voiskos in St Petersburg was that the recent creation of the Kuban and Terek voiskos were still in the process of organization, but one suspects that it had something to do with Miliutin's desire to gain a greater degree of control over the reform.
16. VOVM 1863, 9; Krasnov, RV, 1865, 350–1.
17. SVM, XI/1, 410.
18. VOVM 1859.
19. VOVM 1860.
20. Bogdanovich, I, 319.
21. SPRKV 1866, no. 109.
22. PSZ II, 31619.
23. SVM, XI/1, 462.
24. PSZ II, 31619.
25. SVM, XI/1, 466.
26. VDVM 1863, 98–9.
27. Ibid., 99–100; Zaionchkovskii (1952) 81.

28. SPRKV 1864, no. 91; VDVM 1863, 110–11; on the evolution of this body, see below pp. 92–3.
29. SVM, XI/1, 416.
30. Ibid., 467.
31. Ibid., 471; on the role of the Military Council, see below p. 85.
32. PSZ II, 44787, 48607, 49995, 50706, 50822.
33. SPRKV 1868, no. 42.
34. The duration of the Miliutin plan varied among the voiskos that experienced it: Orenburg 1867–76; Kuban, Terek 1870–82; Siberian 1871–80; Astrakhan, Zabaikal 1872–8.
35. Bogdanovich, III, 252.
36. Khoroshkhin', VS, 1873, no. 3, 142–3.
38. SPRKV 1886, no. 15.
39. Bogdanovich, V, 245; he notes that 'The reporting of the movement of the Cossack population is highly imprecise ...'
40. SVM, XI/1, 471–3.
41. Forrest A. Miller, *Dmitri Miliutin and the Reform Era in Russia* (Charlotte, 1968) 182–230; Zaionchkovskii (1952) 254–337.
42. Zaionchkovskii (1952) 285.
43. Ibid., 286.
44. S. M. Solov'eva, *Zheleznodorozhnyi transport Rossii vo vtoroi polovine XIX v.* (M, 1975) 296.
45. SVM, XI/1, 471.
46. Khoroshkhin', 248.
47. Bogdanovich, V, 197.
48. VDVM 1870, 124.
49. VDVM 1872, 235.
50. PSX II, 53943, 54588. The ustav was included in SZ, IV, nos. 409–502 (1897 edn); the polozhenie appeared in SVP, X.
51. SVM, XI/1, 475.
52. PSZ II, 56187, 58365, 59834, 60140, 61183.
53. A law of 1883 (PSZ III, 1317) permitted departure from the Cossack estate if a given voisko had enough men to meet its levy, but population figures in VOVM indicate that this was rarely practised.
54. PSZ III, 28043.
55. SPRKV 1876, no. 306.
56. Khoroshkhin', 296; VOVM 1894, 1906. It is possible that the much higher percentage of exemptions in the later years includes those excused on other grounds, especially poverty, but the report does not make this clear.
57. This form of reserve was the 'second turn', discussed below p. 40.
58. 'MLE', RB, 1904, no. 5, 3–4.
59. The number of Cossacks excused on this ground is hard to determine in official reports, but Khlystov (1962) 274, states that Don archival material reports that it had reached 26 per cent of the eligibles by about 1900. It was almost certainly much lower 20 years earlier and remained much lower in most voiskos.
60. The War Ministry did not consider exemptions in these categories sufficiently numerous to bother with, although the presumption must

be that with increasing involvement in education an ever-larger number of Cossacks did benefit from these provisions.

61. SPRKV 1912, no. 13; a regulation of 1901 attempted to tighten up on this practice, requiring the Cossack who avoided field service to take the place of the Cossack whom he 'hired' in the reserve training, SPRKV 1901, no. 38.
62. Zasedatel'eva, 269; a standard cavalry regiment was authorized 38 batmen.
63. But no actual military activity occurred in the first years of this category. In a sense the cycle of military service began at the age of 17, when the Cossack received his land allotment in anticipation of his enrolment the following year.
64. Until 1887 the replacements joined their regiments in May, thereafter in March or April; VDVM 1887, 164; 1889, 195.
65. SPRKV 1875, no. 124.
66. Kharuzin, 90–1, 182–5, 382–3.
67. See above, p. 17.
68. See below, pp. 197–8.
69. Borodin, 727; Kostenko, VS, 1878, no. 10, 311.
70. Borodin, 732; Khoroshkhin', VS, 1873, no. 3, 127–322.
71. Kostenko, VS, 1878, no. 9, 159–64; Korolenko, RB, 1901, no. 10, 179.
72. August Haxthausen (Frederick Starr, ed), *Studies on Interior of Russia* (Chicago, 1972); also Khoroshkhin', 132–3.
73. Lenin Library, Fond D. A. Miliutin, Karton 14.2, listy 147–9 (through the courtesy of E. Willis Brooks).
74. VDVM 1875, 179.
75. PSZ II, 53236; Borodin, chap. IX.
76. VDVM 1875, 175–6; Korolenko, RB, 1901, no. 10, 191, reports an unofficial Cossack story that the crux of the dissatisfaction was the requirement of a new oath; SVM, XI/3, 275.
77. PSZ II, 53237; below pp. 97–8.
78. VDVM 1875, 178–9; SVM, XI/1, 468, 483–5.
79. Borodin, 735–6, 762.
80. SVM, XI/1, 485–93; XI/3, 276–302; VDVM 1882, 16405; 1884, 204–5.
81. Borodin, 757–9.
82. Ibid., 754–9.
83. VDVM 1882, 162–3; 1883, 226–7; SPRKV 1910, no. 285.
84. PSZ II, 60046.
85. SVM, XI/1, 302; a modern version appeared 1860; *Stroevyi ustav kazachikh voisk,* revised 1862.
86. SVM, XI/1, 303.
87. Krasnov, VS, 1880, no. 7, 140.
88. PSZ II, 46669; 54944; 54946; Bogdanovich, V, 183.
89. PSZ II, 48948.
90. SPRKV 1889, no. 12; VOVM 1882, 1904; the army as a whole was reduced in 1882, Zaionchkovskii (1973) 124.
91. VOVM, years indicated.

92. VOVM 1873, 1903; in 1883 and 1894 2 per cent of the Cossack population was on active duty.
93. VOVM 1880, which did not report the population in the age group of the first turn, but for the whole combatant category age group.
94. SPRKV 1885, no. 140.
95. VDVM 1886, 197; PSZ II, 2867.
96. VOVM 1890–9.
97. Ibid., 1898.
98. Ibid., 1890.
99. Zaionchkovskii (1973) 123; Khoroshkhin', 307.
100. PSZ II, 53943, shtat; the arrangement of sotnias, regiments, etc., appears annually in VOVM.
101. An example of the rare exception to the rule that sotnias from different voiskos did not serve in the higher-level unit was the Kuban–Terek composite division, Bogdanovich, V, 228. On the conversion to larger vzvods, ibid., V, 246; VDVM 1885, 238–9; 1886, 195; 1887, 163–9. The change was achieved partly by reducing Cossack forces in the Kazan military okrug.
102. VOVM 1895; SPRKV 1875, no. 139.
103. These matters are covered annually in the military section of VOVM.
104. Galushkin, op. cit., opposite 10 contains a highly detailed chart of the evolution of the composition of the konvoi. Also 141–51.
105. Khoroshkhin', 267; SVM, XI/1, 494, 624.
106. SVM, XI/1, 497, 626; see below p. 82.
107. VDVM 1884, 199; VOVM 1895 shows an additional three sotnias assigned to the Don oblast for the same purpose.
108. SPRKV 1866, no. 48.
109. VOVM 1864.
110. SPRKV 1875, no. 124.
111. Based on VOVM 1864–1903, which however is not uniform in its system each year and omits these data in 1872–80.
112. SPRKV 1888, no. 16.
113. Listopadov, op. cit., II, 277.
114. PSZ III, 5859.
115. VOVM 1890s; some of these regiments had only four sotnias.
116. Ibid.; SVM, XI/1, 740.
117. VOVM, years indicated.
118. Zaionchkovskii (1973) 34.
119. Bogdanov, III, 277–8; V, 227; SVM, XI/1, 636.
120. Bogdanov, I, 293.
121. SPRKV 1865, no. 107; 1867, no. 54; 1869, no. 12.
122. SVP, X, nos. 16–21; Domozhirov, VS, 1911, 36–7.
123. VOVM 1901, or any year.
124. SVP, X, nos. 609–28.
125. 'S.M.', VS, 1895, no. 10, 352–3.
126. Zaionchkovskii (1952) 209.
127. VOVM 1891.
128. Kuropatkin, 37; Maslakovets, 14; Medvedev, 20; Shcherbov, 32;

VOOVD, 1900, 13–14.

129. *Istoriia Semirechenskago Kazachiago Voiska* (Vernyi, 1909) 796–9.

130. SPRKV 1882k, no. 7; 1885, no. 108; 1889, no. 15; PSZ II, 53943.

131. SPRKV 1900, no. 170; 1903, no. 291. Actual examples of the standard Cossack uniform were on display in Musée Royal de l'Armée, Brussels, until at least 1967, and I believe are still there.

132. SPRKV 1866, no. 33.

133. L. G. Beskrovnyi, *Russkaia armiia i flota v XIX veke* (M, 1973) 306.

134. Bogdanovich, V, 213; Svatikov, 356.

135. Bogdanovich, V, 213–15; SVM, XI/1, 517.

136. Beskrovnyi, op. cit., 313–17.

137. Ibid., 317.

138. SVP, X, nos. 340–1; Khoroshkhin', 257; Cossacks with various levels of education were promoted to uriadnik after as little as two months or as much as one year.

139. PSZ II, 53943, shtat.

140. Bogdanovich, I, 294–9, 342. The exam for Cossacks was easier than for others, omitting history and geography.

141. Zaionchkovskii (1952) 221–53.

142. Khoroshkhin', 257–9; Bogdanovich, III, 259–61; V, 209–10.

143. Zaionchkovskii (1952) 244; Bogdanovich, V, 211; SVM, XI/1, 683.

144. Khoroshkhin', 259–61.

145. VDVM 1882, 151; 1883, 233–4; 1888, 154.

146. Zaionchkovskii (1973) 219; VDVM 1873, 157, on Cossack officers in particular.

147. Bogdanovich, I, 341; on the award of land, see below pp. 171–2.

148. PSZ II, 53943, shtat.

149. SVM, XI/1, 505, 729–30.

150. Following a reform of 1884 (PSZ III, 2399) that abolished the army rank of major and the Cossack rank of pod'polkovnik, the equivalents were:

Army	Cossack
podporuchik	khorunzhyi
poruchik	sotnik
shtabs'-rotmistr'	podesaul
rotmistr'	esaul
podpolkovnik	voiskovoi starshina
polkovnik	polkovnik

151. This seems to have provided sufficient incentive to keep most Cossack officers in the career, however modest its rewards. In the 1870s only 1424 officers resigned out of a total force in the 3500–4000 range. Khoroshkhin', 260; VOVM, years indicated.

152. SVP, X, nos. 178, 240, 249, 254, 263, 268, 272; Medvedev, 14; 'A.M.', VS, 1895, no. 10, 346–7.

153. SVM, XI/1, 629; SVP, X, nos. 240, 249, 263, 268, 272

provide for a few surplus officers serving not in the first turn but in the voisko administration.

154. Ibid., no. 580; VDVM 1895, 243.

155. SVP, X, no. 387; 'A.M.', VS, 1895, no. 10, 346–63; Serov, VS, 1900, no. 11, 155; Domozhirov, VS, 1911, no. 11, 53.

156. Bogdanov, V, 153.

157. VDVM 1880, 189–90; Krasnov, VS, 1880, no. 4, 396–409; no. 5, 163–76; no. 6, 332–40.

158. SVM, XI/1, 514–15.

159. Khoroshkhin', 302–5; Krasnov, VS, 1880, no. 6, 332.

160. Krasnov, VS, 1880, no. 4, 407.

161. SPRKV 1888, nos. 16, 177.

162. VDVM 1890, 151; 1891, 146; 1895, 245; *Obzor deiatel' nosti Voennago Ministerstva v tsarstvovanie Imperatora Aleksandra III 1881–1894* (SPB, 1903) 285; SVM, XI/1, 619–21.

163. SPRKV 1894, no. 253; 1895, no. 178.

164. Ibid., 1888, no. 27.

165. VOVM 1890s; e.g. in 1898 there was a surplus of 32 675, of whom 13 712 were in the Don.

166. PSZ III, 8534.

167. VOVM 1905.

168. PSZ III, 9196; SVM, XI/1, 177–238.

169. VDVM 1894, 217–18.

170. However, in the Kuban and Terek a few additional junior officers were assigned to the voisko administration to assist in mobilization. SVP, X, no. 244.

171. VDVM 1896, 224–5; SPRKV 1902, no. 9.

172. VDVM 1892, 170; 1893, 213–14; 1894, 220; 1895, 226–7; PSZ III, 14097.

173. SPRKV 1901, no. 169; PSZ III, 27894. In the Kuban and Terek voiskos the results were poor. VOVM 1912 shows only ten stanitsa horse-breeding stations in the Kuban, out of more than 200 stanitsas, and none in the Terek.

174. PSZ III, 6626; rewritten and extended to other voiskos except the Zabaikal 1905, PSZ III, 26528; DOV 27 Mar, 10 Apr 1891; DR 4 Jun 1891.

175. VOVM 1890–9.

176. Kuropatkin, 7.

177. Maslakovets, 61, 114, 116; SPRKV 1898, no. 67 shows the membership: Maslakovets, representative of Main Administration of Cossack Forces, of Don oblast administration, eight of Don nobility, eight of stanitsas, one of Society of Cossack Merchants.

178. Kuropatkin, 113.

179. PSZ III, 18978. The former system was not renewed upon the expiry of the five years, PSOGD, III/5, no. 125, 7.

180. PSZ III, 19758. On the cost of a horse, see below p. 199.

181. Ibid., 24132; SPRKV 1904, no. 274. According to laws of 1904 and 1906 (24132, 26924), the infantry from certain Kuban stanitsas

were to receive 50 rubles per capita. These various enactments were consolidated in 1906 (29195), adding the Siberian voisko.

182.   Ibid., 23765.
183.   SPRKV 1904, nos. 465, 531, 578.
184.   VDVM 1902, 86.
185.   SPRKV 1904, no. 465.
186.   Ibid., no. 201.
187.   In the chaos of the war the Priamur military district, which was adjacent to the theatre of operations, was unable to submit a report to the War Ministry at the end of 1905 (VOVM 1905). The above estimate of the forces from the Don, Kuban, Astrakhan, Ural and Orenburg voiskos that were transported as far east as the Priamur okrug, whether or not they saw combat, is based on the report in VOVM 1905 for the total number of cavalry and infantry sotnias in that okrug, less the number that the Siberian, Zabaikal, Amur and Ussuri voiskos contributed after mobilization of the second and third turns. Even several years after the war the details do not seem to have been clarified, for they do not appear in the official history of the war, *Russko-iaponskaia voina 1904–1905 gg.*, 9 vols. in 16 (SPB, 1910). This massive work does, however, identify the Don Division, VI, 30.
188.   SPRKV 1905, nos. 230, 376, 382, 393, 536; 1906, nos. 447, 448.
189.   VDVM 1906, 165–7.
190.   SPRKV 1906, nos. 417, 459, 561, 501, 507, 535, 537, 541, 545, 551, 578.
191.   Ibid., 1906, nos. 168, 448, 449, 461.
192.   Ibid., 1906, no. 336.
193.   Ibid., 1906, nos. 228, 387, 473.
194.   SPRKV 1907, nos. 118, 120, VDVM 1907, 118.
195.   William C. Fuller, Jr., 'Civil Military Conflict 1881–1914 in Imperial Russia' (dissertation, soon to appear as a book, Harvard University) 230–7.
196.   VDVM 1908, 103.
197.   SPRKV 1905, nos. 201, 230, 376, 382; 1909, no. 257.
198.   Ibid., 1906, nos. 376, 387, 447, 473.
199.   Ibid., 1905, nos. 201, 230; 1907, nos. 142, 162.
200.   VOVM 1903, 1905, 1907, which was the final year in which this data appeared, probably excluded thereafter for security reasons, VDVM 1906, 165–7, states that 52 700 were mobilized from the second and third turns. If added to the first turn previously on duty, this would yield a total strength of only 106 000. Evidently there was considerable confusion in the War Ministry.
201.   VOVM 1903, 1905.
202.   Ibid., 1903, 1905, 1906. Of these okrugs, only Moscow had more Cossacks on duty in January 1906 than January 1905, presumably a reaction to the December 1905 insurrection.
203.   *1905 god v Moskve* (M, 1955) 103.
204.   DOV 26 Feb 1906; Biriukov, II, 859.
205.   Biriukov, II, 858.

206. Pokrovskii, 90–1.
207. V. Obninskii, *Polgoda Russkoi Revoliutsii, Sbornik Materialov k istorii Russkoi Revoliutsii (okt. 1905–apr. 1906 gg.)* (M, 1906) 18.
208. *1905 god. Revoliutsionnoe dvizhenie v Odesse i Odeshchina* (Odessa, 1926) 166–7.
209. VDVM 1907, 118–19; SPRKV 1906, no. 216.
210. Biriukov, II, 842, 885; Roberta Manning, *The Crisis of the Old Order in Russia. Gentry and Government* (Princeton, 1982) 177, 195; Leopold H. Haimson (ed), *The Politics of Rural Russia, 1905–1914* (Indiana, 1979) 45.
211. VDVM 1907, 118.
212. DOV 16 Jul 1906; 21 Jul 1912.
213. E.g. Kriukov, RB, 1907, no. 4; 'S. Ia. A-n' (Arefin), RB, 1906, no. 12; see below, p. 207.
214. Biriukov, II, 860.
215. Babychev, 34–7, 46; John S. Bushnell, 'Mutineers and Revolutionaries: Military Revolution in Russia, 1905–1907' (dissertation, soon to appear as a book, Indiana University, 1977) 308–10; L. F. Muzhev, *Kazachestvo Dona, Kubani i Tereka v revoliutsii 1905–1907 gg.* (Ordzhonikidze, 1963) 43–79.
216. V. A. Petrov, *Ocherki po istorii revoliutsionnogo dvizheniiia v russkoi armii v 1905 g.* (M, 1964) 345–6.
217. Muzhev, op. cit., 53–8; Kh. I. Muratov, *Revoliutsionnoe dvizhenie v russkoi armii v 1905–1907 gg.* (M, 1955) 239.
218. Sergei Starikov and Roy Medvedev, *Philip Mironov and the Russian Civil War* (New York, 1978) 14–15.
219. Muratov, op. cit., 16–17, maintains that protest strikes by workers averted the death penalty for Kurganov and his comrades; Starikov and Medvedev, op. cit., 16–17.
220. SPRKV 1907, no. 391 and many others; Pokrovskii, 99; on gramotas, see Chapter 1, note 6.
221. SPRKV 1906, no. 24.
222. Pokrovskii, 95.
223. VOVM 1905–7; SPRKV 1905, no. 107; 1906, no. 30.
224. SPRKV 1897, no. 32.
225. DOV 7 Mar 1906; 1906, no. 2; Pokrovskii, 91.
226. SPRKV 1906, nos. 27, 74, 272.
227. PSZ III, 26274, 39915. In 1909 the one training camp that inductees were to attend before starting the first turn was cut from four to three weeks, excepting the artillery, which remained four (PSZ III, 32105). But later in the year the four-week camp was restored (33345).
228. In 1901 a regulation forbade the assignment of Cossacks of the first turn to regular duty until they had finished two months of training with their unit, which implied a low regard for pre-induction training. SVM, XI/1, 728.
229. Zolotov (1952) 53; DOV 25 Mar 1912; VOVM on cancellation of training assemblies.

230. RSZ III, 30428; SPRKV 1811, no. 1; 1912, no. 417.
231. VDVM 1908, 107; on the reduction of service for non-Cossacks, PSZ III, 27818.

CHAPTER 3

1. Kriukov, RB, 1907, no. 4, 44.
2. PSZ III, 48207.
3. Eroshkin, 203.
4. Fuller, op. cit., 369; *Voennoe Ministerstva. Alfavitnyi ukazatel'* (SPB, 1904) 9–13.
5. SPRKV 1882.
6. For full data on the *Code of Laws* and *Code of Millitary Laws*, P. A. Zaionchkovskii (ed), *Spravochnik po istorii dorevoliutsionnoi Rossii. Bibliograficheskii ukazatel'* (M, 1978) 25–36, 238–41.
7. Eroshkin, 203.
8. See above, pp. 31–2.
9. SVM, XI/1, 414, 417–19.
10. Ibid., 419.
11. Ibid,.., 417; SPRKV; *Destvuiushchiia irreguliarnykh voiskakh postanovleniia*, 3 vols (SPB, 1879); SVM, XI/1, 417.
12. *Sistematicheskii ukazatel' postanovlenii po kazach'im voiskam* (SPB, nd).
13. SVP, chast' 3, kn. 9, 10 (SPB, 1907); SVM, XI/1, 709–13.
14. RI, 1858, no. 7; SVM, XI/1, 402–3. Alexander Nikolaevich became heir upon the death of his brother.
15. SVM, XI/1, 422; the first full legal description of the office appeared in 1869, PSZ II, 46611.
16. SVM, XI/1, 427.
17. SPRKV 1910, no. 31.
18. PSZ II, 46611.
19. SVM, XI/2, 180–2, 153–209. SPRKV 1910, no. 31.
20. Anon., VE, 1875, no. 7, 370.
21. SPRKV 1984, no. 304; 1867, no. 73, 144; 1873, no. 4; 1899, no. 96; 1894, no. 365.
22. Anon., VE, 1875, no. 7, 370.
23. VOVM 1870, 1898.
24. SPRKV 1901, no. 9.
25. VOVM 1898, 1904.
26. SVM, XI/1, 779–816; XI/2, 1–152.
27. PSZ II, 32553; 44412; 46611; III, 1104. In 1857 there was one representative from each of the following: Don, Caucasian voiskos, Orenburg–Ural–Bashkir–west Siberian (jointly), east Siberian.
28. See above, pp. 31–2.
29. PSZ II, 50692.
30. See above, pp. 34–5.
31. *Doklad po glavnomu upravleniiu kazachykh voisk 25 avg. 1888 g.* This abolished the Temporary Committee and awarded regular seats for

three of its former members on the Committee of the Main Administration. Previously they sat there under provisions of PSZ II, 44532, which permitted invited special delegates from the voiskos to participate with a vote in the deliberations. PSZ II, 50692 merged the chancellery of the Temporary Committee with the section of the Main Administration, that is, one of its standing offices.

32. PSZ II, 14976. SVM, XI/1, 696–8.
33. Bruce W. Menning, 'The Socialization of the Don Cossack Host Prior to the Reign of Nicholas I' (dissertation, Duke University, 1972) 172.
34. See above, p. 32.
35. On the application of the concept of 'general administration' in this context, SZ, II, nos. 219, 265. 362, 455, 502.
36. In some cases the same official bore a third title, commander of the military okrug.
37. PSZ II, 42058.
38. Eroshkin, 229–332.
39. On the reformed courts in general, Samuel Kucherov, *Courts, Lawyers and Trials under the Last Three Tsars* (New York, 1953) 43–50. Because Orenburg guberniia had no zemstvo to elect justices of the peace, special legislation established an appointive court, PSZ II, 58457, which dealt with Cossacks and non-Cossacks.
40. See below, pp. 155–64.
41. PSZ II, 42058; SVP, IX, nos. 183–232.
42. The Orenburg model was applied to other voiskos as follows: 1867, Semirechenskoe (PSZ II, 44845); 1868, Siberian (PSZ II, 46830), Ural (PSZ II, 46380); 1869, Kuban and Terek (PSZ II, 47847); 1872, Zabaikal (PSZ II, 50822); 1879, Amur (PSZ II, 60140); 1889, Ussuri (PSZ III, 6200).
43. The Kuban and Terek voiskos received the new courts, including justices of the peace, in 1866 (PSZ II, 43880); Orenburg and Astrakhan received the courts excepting justices of the peace in 1866 and justices of the peace in 1878 (PSZ II, 58457); the more easterly voiskos received the new system only in 1896 or 1898 (PSZ III, 12932, 15493). Because there were no zemstvos, justices of the peace were appointed.
44. SVP, IX, nos. 309, 369.
45. But in 1895 the 'uchastok', with a commander, was established as a subdivision of the Amur voisko, taking over both police authority and the military authority elsewhere associated with the otdel (PSZ III, 11650).
46. PSZ II, 53237. The norm of representation was two deputies per stanitsa until raised to four in 1911 (PSZ III, 36016).
47. There was one partial exception. In the Siberian and Zabaikal voiskos, assemblies of officers and men with civil service rank elected representatives to the economic board (PSZ II, 50760, 53314), until these were abolished in 1913 (see below, p. 141).
48. See above, p. 46.
49. He appointed a 'senior member', two councillors and the voisko physician, architect and surveyor, all of whom might vote in its meetings, the latter three if the business at hand concerned them (PSZ II, 61181, 61182).

50. *Sbornik protokolov s'ezdi vybornykh ot stanichnykh obshchestv' Ural'skago Kazach'iago Voisko za 25 let* (Ural'sk, 1900) 950 and in general.
51. PSZ II, 48387.
52. The word 'voiskovoi' was added to the title of General Grabbe as a personal honour in 1865, then to his successor on that basis, then in 1868 as a permanent fixture (PSZ II, 42542, 43787, 45640). The rights of a governor-general were confirmed by PSZ II, 42542.
53. PSZ II, 44048, 48276.
54. PSZ II, 54756, shtat, provides details on staffing.
55. PSZ II, 6493, 48276; III, 4397.
56. PSZ II, 48370, 52034.
57. PSZ II, 48370; Svatikov, 365; on zemskii nachal'nik, Eroshkin, 235.
58. I. V. Efremov, *Donskoe zemstvo* (SPB, 1912) 70.
59. PSZ II, 47019. In 1880–4 three successive governors of Astrakhan guberniia held the post of ataman, but this was an anomaly and not a matter of right; SVM, XI/2, 224.
60. VDVM 1884, 189.
61. Ibid., 1885, 225–7; 1886, 183; 1887, 152; PSZ III, 5076, 5077.
62. VDVM 1885, 226–7.
63. PSZ III, 3058, 4130, 5076, 5077.
64. GDSO 20 Mar 1910, 1315.
65. VDVM 1885, 227.
66. See below, pp. 123–5.
67. SPRKV 1896, no 29. The Don, Kuban and Terek voiskos had enjoyed this right previously because their atamans as such were considered the equivalent of a governor or governor-general, but the others reported on the Cossacks to the War Minister. SVM, XI/1, 719–20.
68. Terrence Emmons and Wayne S. Vucinich (eds), *The Zemstvo in Russia. An Experiment in Local Self-Government* (Stanford, 1982) especially Kermit McKenzie, 'Zemstvo Organization and Role within the Administrative Structure', 79–132.
69. Anon., VE, 1875, VII, 360–1; SVM, XI/1, 414, 433.
70. SPRKV 1866, no. 30; one delegate from each of the seven okrugs from the nobles with estates, the same representation for those without estates; two from the Society of Cossack Merchants, one ordinary Cossack from each of six okrugs; five peasants; one Kalmyk.
71. SVM, XI/1, 434.
72. VDVM 1869, 10–11.
73. Ibid., 1870, 124.
74. Anon., VE, 1875, VII, 362.
75. Ibid., 363–4.
76. PSZ II, 54758; VDVM 1875, 168.
77. In a sense, the Kalmyks constituted a curia of their own, for they had a separate okrug-level assembly which did not send any delegates to the oblast assembly.
78. PSZ II, 56507.
79. VOVM 1881, 80.
80. Lagunov, RB, 1909, no. 11, 131.

81. Eremeev, RB, 1880, no. 11, 52, 61; Lagunov, RB, 1911, no. 11, 127, 131; SVM, XI/1, 435–7.
82. Svatikov, 380.
83. Eremeev, RB, 1880, no. 11, 61–2; Lagunov, VE, 1910, no. 4, 280; RB, 1909, no. 11, 127.
84. Both 'zemstvo' and 'zemskie povinnosti' are related to the word for land (zemlia), but the latter term referred to taxes that predated the zemstvo and were not peculiar to the system of self-government.
85. PSOGD, III/5, no. 125, 14–15.
86. Lagunov, RB, 1909, no. 11, 121–2.
87. Ibid., 122–5.
88. Ibid., 129–30; and the reply of the zemstvo to its critics, 119–20.
89. Ibid., 131; VDVM 1880, 173; 1882, 156; Eremeev, RB, 1880, XI, 51; Lagunov, RB, 1909, no. 12, 56; no. 11, 132.
90. VDVM 1880, 173; PSOGD, III/5, no. 125, 22.
91. Svatikov, 382–3; SVM, XI/1, 436–7; Lagunov, RB, 1909, no. 12, 56–70.
92. Lagunov, RB, 1909, no. 12, 72–3; Svatikov, 383.
93. VDVM 1882, 156–60; Svatikov, 383–4.
94. Lagunov, RB, 1909, no. 12, 75–7.
95. PSOGD, III/1, no. 268, 1341–2.
96. Svatikov, 383–4.
97. PSZ III, 759.
98. PSOGD, III/5, no. 125, 20–1; GSSO 26 Feb 1914, 1366–7; SPRKV 1882, no. 35; GDSO 12 May 1913, 1945–6; TMK, vol. 50, 137–8.
99. VDVM 1882, 160; 1884, 196; 1885, 232; Lagunov, VE, 1910, no. 4, 279; SVM, XI/1, 721. As late as 1891 the War Ministry secretly mentioned the desirability of introducing the zemstvo to the Kuban. VDVM 1891, 141.
100. L. G. Zakharova, *Zemskaia contrreforma 1890 g.* (M, 1968); VDVM 1894, 208; SVM, XI/1, 721–2.
101. I. N. Efremov, *Donskoe zemstvo 1912 g.* (op. cit.) 79; PSOGD, III/5, no. 125, 28; Lagunov, VE, 1910, no. 4, 279. In 1914 the then ataman of the Don maintained that he did not know why the commission of 1903 had been disban d, but a member of the State Council who had been involved with the commission said that it was disbanded precisely because it favoured the zemstvo. GSSO 26 Feb 1914, 1359, 1370.
102. VOOVD 1900, 5.
103. SVM, XI/1, 589–90.
104. Ibid., 591–6.
105. Eroshkin, op. cit., 240–1.
106. PSZ III, 4466.
107. Annual War Ministry reports show an increase of state subsidies to the Don oblast from 1.2 million rubles in 1886 to 1.4 million in 1890, which may not have covered increased administrative costs associated with the enlarged territory.
108. VOVM 1897, 169.
109. VDVM 1893, 206; 1894, 204; SZ, II, no. 2.

110. PSZ III, 4853; Zolotov (1974) 24; SVM, XI/1, 598–9.
111. PSZ III, 37337; SZ, II, no. 2.
112. Khoroshkhin', 64–8; SPRKV 1867, no. 13; 1891, nos. 203, 294, 299; 1892, no. 259; 1894, nos. 337, 458, 489.
113. PSZ II, 8163.
114. DR 30 Apr 1892.
115. PSZ II, 48354; VDVM 1883, 217–18; SVM, XI/1, 456–7. However, this law was applied to the Ural voisko only in 1870, and with two modifications: the appointment from above of the stanitsa ataman and the direction from above of stanitsa finances (PSZ II, 53237).
116. GDSO 20 Mar 1910, 1316.
117. Kharuzin, 286–326.
118. Although the post of 'esaul' as an assistant to the ataman of the stanitsa disappeared in the 1870 law on stanitsa governance, this term seems to have persisted in use in preference to the term 'pomoshchnik', which lacks any specific Cossack associations and which appears in the law.
119. PSZ II, 48354.
120. PSZ II, 58557.
121. VDVM 1883, 218–19; DOV 18 Dec 91; *Svod proektov polozheniia ob obshchestvennom upravlenii stanits kazach'ikh voisk, predstavlennykh nachal'stvami sikh voisk* (SPB, 1888) 17; SVM, XI/1, 572–3.
122. D. Serov', VS, 1900, no. 9, 146–8; DR 1892, Jan. *passim.*
123. PSZ III, 2050; Kharuzin, 290; SVM, XI/1, 584, 576.
124. The stanitsas of the Ural and the peasant volost assembly already adhered to the principle of one-in-ten representation.
125. SVM, XI/1, 575.
126. *Svod proektov polozheniia ob obshchestvennom upravlenii stanits kazach'ikh voisk, predstavlennykh nachal'stvami sikh voisk* (SPB).
127. SVM, XI/1, 584–5.
128. Ibid., 718.
129. DOV 10 Dec 1891.
130. PSZ III, 7782.
131. L. G. Zakharova, op. cit.
132. GDSO 10 May 1910, 1314.
133. SPRKV 1906, no. 13, provided that if a stanitsa ataman or honorary judge was promoted to the lowest officer rank he automatically joined the estate of 'pochetnyi grazhdanin' (honorary citizen), although this presumably did not end his membership in the Cossack estate.
134. See above, p. 102.
135. SPRKV 1894, no. 229; SVM, XI/1, 581; see above, p. 72.
136. DOV 1 Jan 1892.
137. DR 5, 16 and 28 Jan, 6 Feb, 5, 27 Aug 1892; Kharitonov, NS, 1896, I, 180: The law specifically permitted the election of Cossack nobles to stanitsa offices (provided that the office was not subordinate to one filled by a non-noble), whereas nobles did not fill elective offices in peasant volosts.

138. Howard P. Mehlinger and John M. Thompson, *Count Witte and the Tsarist Government in the 1905 Revolution* (Bloomington, 1972) 241–312; S. M. Sidel'nikov, *Obrazovanie i deiatel'nost' Pervoi Gosudarstvennoi Dumy* (M, 1962) 7–114.

139. *Petergofskoe soveshchanie o proekte gosudarstvennoi dumy pod lichnym predsedatel'stvom Ego Imperatorskago Velichestva. Sekretnye protokoly* (Berlin, nd).

140. PSZ III, 27425.

141. PSZ III, 26662.

142. PSZ III, 27318, 27758, 27806.

143. PSZ III, 26662, prilozhenie.

144. Arefin, RB, 1906, no. 12, 147; Kriukov, RB, 1907, no. 4, 43, 45; Arefin, *Donskoe kazachestvo prezhde i teper'* (M, 1907).

145. Arefin, op. cit., 148–50; Svatikov, 477.

146. Cossack deputies to the First Duma, with voisko and factional affiliation: Don, M. P. Arakantsev (KD); V. A. Kharlamov (KD); K. I. Afanas'ev (KD); I. N. Efremov (Dem. Ref.); F. D. Kriukov (Trudovik); A. M. Skasyrskii (Party of Peaceful Renewal); M. N. Savost'ianov (Party of Peaceful Renewal); I. M. Vasiliev (Party of Peaceful Renewal); I. Ia. Kurkin (Party of Peaceful Renewal); Kuban, K. L. Bardizh (KD); P. A. Grishai (KD); N. G. Kochevskii (KD); Orenburg, M. I. Sveshnikov (Trudovik); T. I. Sedel'nikov (Trudovik); S. S. Vydrin (non-party); Ural, N. A. Borodin (KD); Terek, P. P. Dimirov (non-party). In several cases the deputy was not a Cossack in the most literal sense, but was understood to represent the Cossacks. For example, Skasyrskii was a 'landowner' and probably a Cossack noble, Afanas'ev was a priest but of Cossack background. Sources: *Gosudarstvennaia Duma. Ukazatel'k stenogtaficheskim otchetam 1906 g.* (SPB, 1907); *Novyi entsiklopedicheskii slovar'*, vol. 14 (SPB, nd); Svatikov, 493–4. Vydrin and Dimirov were the non-party deputies who voted for interpellation.

147. F. D. Kriukov, in *K desiatiletiiu pervoi Gosudarstvennoi Dumy. Sbornik statei pervodumtsev* (SPB, 1916) 157–72; Kriukov, RB, 1907, no. 4, 26–7; for additional analysis of the election in the Don oblast, see Terrence Emmons, *The Formation of Political Parties and the First National Election in Russia* (Cambridge, 1983) 320–1.

148. Kriukov, RB, 1907, no. 4, 34.

149. This minor conservative grouping was not wholly agreeable to the regime. Three of the four Don Cossacks associated with it signed a request for an interpellation of the Minister of Justice concerning the prosecution of some railway and post-telegraph employees who joined the October General Strike in 1905 in the Don oblast. GDSO 23 May 1906, 531–2.

150. GDSO 2 June 1906, 962–5; 13 June 1906, 1309.

151. SZ, I, no. 96.

152. GDSO 2 June 1906, 961.

153. Ibid., 963–4; 13 June 1906, 1309, 1323–4, 1330, 1334; Kriukov, RB, 1907, no. 4, 31–3, 40.

154. GDSO 2 June 1906, 962–3; 13 June 1906, 1307–34.
155. Kriukov, RB, 1907, no. 4, 26–31. The style suggests that the instructions were not composed by ordinary Cossacks. Also DOV 8, 15, 16 Oct, 21 Dec 1906.
156. GSDO 13 June 1906, 1316–20, 1328–9.
157. See above, pp. 75, 207–8.
158. F. D. Kriukov in *Vyborgskii protsess'* (SPB, 1908) 198; Svatikov, 509.
159. Cossack deputies to the Second Duma, with voisko and party affiliation: Don, M. P. Arskantsev (KD); M. S. Voronkov' (KD); K. P. Kakliugin (KD); A. F. Panfilov (KD); A. S. Petrov (KD); A. I. Petrovskii (KD); I. I. Ushakov (KD); N. V. Fomin (Trudovik); V. A. Kharlamov (KD); Kuban, K. L. Bardizh (KD); P. G. Kudriavtsev (KD); F. A. Shcherbina (Popular Socialist); Orenburg, I. V. Zaplatin (Trudovik); P. P. Vopilov (KD); Ural, F. A. Eremin (KD); Terek, M. A. Karaulov (KD); Siberian, I. P. Laptev' (Democratic Reform); Astrakhan, A. G. Poliakov (moderate right); Zabaikal, S. A. Taskin'; Semirechenskoe, Ia. I. Egoshkin (non-party). Sources: *Gosudarstvennaia Duma. Uazatel' k stenograficheskam otchetam. Vtoroi Sozyv.* (SPB, 1907), *Novyi entsikopedicheskii slovar'*, vol. 14.
160. Petrovskii, 15–20. He states the instruction from Migulinskaia said that many stanitsas would like to send instructions on 'the misery and needs' of the Cossacks but 'the administrative authorities strictly watch out for this'.
161. *Novyi entsiklopedicheskii slovar'*, vol. 14, 941–2; Petrovskii, 123; *Gosudarstvennaia Duma. Vtoroi Sozyv. Zakonodatel'nyia zaiavleniia* (SPB, 1907) 244, 246.
162. On 24 Feb Arakantsev was elected secretary and Petrovskii secretary.
163. Petrovskii, 123–4.
164. Ibid., 136.
165. This was true at the time the statutes were proposed, 14 March, but two additional deputies appeared in April. Petrovskii, 134.
166. Literally 'Cossackomania'. E.g. Borodin, RM, 1907, VII, 114.
167. OGSO 23 Mar 1907, 450–1. The Cossack Group also introduced a bill on military service, which never reached debate. *Gosudarstvennaia Duma. Vtoroi Sozyv. Zakonodatel'niia zaiavleniia* (SPB, 1907) 244–5.
168. PSZ III, 29242.
169. Ibid.; the Orenburg contingent of electors was reduced by separate legislation, PSZ III, 29242. The new law obliged the Don electoral assembly, like most guberniias, to send one deputy from the landowners' curia and one from the city curia, which meant that the Don Cossacks were in practice deprived of two deputies.
170. DGSO 8 Mar 1913, 2100–1; Svatikov, 555.
171. The count is debatable. Pyrkov was an okrug marshal of the nobility, which presumably indicates that he was a Cossack noble. On the other hand, A. A. Nazarov, a KD deputy to the Third Duma, is not counted as a Cossack because he was a 'factory-owner', but he showed a keen interest in Cossack welfare (Svatikov, 552; below, p. 211). This count also assumes that Savvateev and Cheriachukin of the Fourth Duma were Cossack nobles.

172. Cossack deputies to the Third Duma, with voisko and party affiliation: Don, M. S. Voronkov' (KD); I. N. Efremov (progressivist); I. F. Kadatskov (moderate right); M. I. Kir'ianov (rightist); P. F. Kravtsov (moderate right); A. K. Petrov (moderate right); P. R. Pyrkov (KD); V. A. Kharlamov (KD); Astrakhan, M. G. Lebedev (Octobrist); Amur-Ussuri, N. A. Man'kov (Octobrist); Zabaikal, A. A. Voiloshnikov (SD); Orenburg, S. I. Shemetov (progressivist); Kuban, K. L. Bardizh (KD); Terek, E. I. Tikhonov (Octobrist – replaced in 1908 by N. V. Lisichkin', Octobrist, then Nationalist); Ural, F. A. Eremin (KD). Sources: *Novyi entsiklopedicheskii slovar'*, vol. 14.
173. Cossack deputies to the Fourth Duma, with voisko and party affiliation: Don, M. S. Voronkov (KD); I. N. Efremov (progressivist); E. D. Loginov (progressivist); A. P. Savvateev (KD); V. A. Kharlamov (KD); F. V. Cheriachukin (KD); Astrakhan, E. K. Ermyovskii (non-party); Amur-Ussuri, I. M. Gamov (KD); Zabaikal, S. A. Taskin (KD); Orenburg, M. I. Kanashev (progressivist); Kuban, K. L. Bardizh (KD); Terek, M. A. Karaulov (non-party); Ural, F. A. Eremin (KD). Source: *Novyi entsiklopedicheskii slovar'*.
174. GDSO 10 Mar 1910, 1324; Svatikov, 551.
175. GDSO 20 Mar 1910, 1313–16, 1321; 1312; also 3 May 1906, 113, and 13 June 1906, 1312.
176. Ibid., 20 Mar 1910, 1317; the theme is reinforced in Leonov.
177. OZSM 1909, no. 79. In 1913 Cossack Duma deputies attempted to introduce legislation that would have transferred to the Duma even the determination of the annual call-up, but this came to nothing. PSOGD, IV/1, no. 169.
178. GDSO 8 May 1912, 802.
179. Ibid., also 12 June 1913, 1925.
180. PSOGD, IV/1, no. 288.
181. See below, pp. 208–11.
182. VRKV; VKD. The Kuban assembly consisted of 506 deputies, two per stanitsa, while the Don had only about 110, one per stanitsa.
183. PVSS, 61; stanitsas with less than 1000 people and the cities of Rostov and Taganrog were to send one delegate each.
184. VKD, 144.
185. PSZ III, 33143.
186. PVSS, 95, 113.
187. PSZ III, 37272.
188. Svatikov, 539; F. A. Shcherbina, *Istoriia Kubanskago Kazachia Voiska*, op. cit., vol. I, opposite 654, photograph of the delegates to the Rada, all wearing the cherkeska, many with a kinzhal (dagger) and in general allowing the viewer no doubt that they regard themselves as Cossacks.
189. Petrovskii, 112–18, 125–6; Shcherbina drafted the document, and a committee of Shcherbina, Kharlamov and Karaulov revised it, while another committee of Arakantsev, Petrovskii and Kakliugin drafted what proved to be the divisive preamble.
190. PSOGD, III/2, no. 116. The proposal was signed by 67 deputies, including ten Cossacks. Why the remaining Cossacks did not sign is unclear. One of the non-signers was Kharlamov, who surely supported

the measure and did sign a similar proposal in the Fourth Duma (PSOGD, IV/1, no. 168). One non-signatory was from the moderate right, but so was one signatory.

191. PSOGD, III/2, no. 116. Another change was the proposal, which was imprecise, of some sort of joint Cossack and non-Cossack assemblies in areas in which the population was too mixed to permit purely Cossack bodies.

192. Obviously the existing zemstvo institutions were neither as democratic in origin nor as powerful as the ones proposed for the Cossacks.

193. PSOGD, III/2, no. 116, 1–2.

194. PSOGD, III/3, no. 49, 1.

195. PSOGD, III/2, no. 116; on 20 March 1910 the Duma included in its 'formula of transition' attached to the War Ministry budget a general statement in favour of removing Cossack civil governance from the War Ministry (GDSO 20 Mar 1906, 1336).

196. PSOGD, III/3, no. 504, 3; GDSO 5 Jun 1910, 3590.

197. GDSO, 3590–1.

198. When it emerged, the War Ministry draft proposed an emasculated version of the zemstvo; see p. 000 below.

199. PDOGD, IV/1, no. 168.

200. GDSO 5 Jun 1910, 3591; 20 Mar 1910, 1332–5; 8 May 1912, 813–14, 830–6.

201. George Tokmakoff, *P. A. Stolyin and The Third Duma* (Washington, 1981) 123–89.

202. PSZ III, 37238, 37239; GDSO 23 Jan 1912, 827–8. But it is likely that the authorities distorted their findings to reach this conclusion about Cossack opinion. See PSOGD, IV/1, no. 38, 16, which states that a 'preponderant' majority of the Orenburg Cossacks favoured the zemstvo. The opposition of the Orenburg administration to giving them the zemstvo is confirmed in TMK, vol. 27, 69–70.

203. GSSO 26 Feb 1914, 1334; Svatikov, 534–5.

204. Maslakovets, 62; Efremov, 53; PSOGD, III/5, no. 125, 23.

205. Leonov; GSSO 26 Feb 1912, 1352; Lagunov, RB, 1910, no. 4, 279; Efremov, 53; Svatikov, 537–8; TMK, no. 50, 137.

206. GSSO 26 Feb 1914, 1352–3.

207. Denisov, 12–13.

208. Lagunov, RB, 1910, no. 4, 283. In 1914 the then ataman of the Don, General Pokotilo, told the State Council that 45 of 125 stanitsas opposed the zemstvo in the questionnaire, despite the pro-zemstvo inclination of the administration. But he is highly tendentious on the whole matter and confuses the questionnaire with a different inquiry of 1908 (GSSO 26 Feb 1914, 1357).

209. Efremov, 49; PSOGD, III/7, no. 268, 2340–8.

210. Efremov, 58.

211. Lagunov, RB, 1910, no. 4, 282.

212. Ibid., 284–7; in the State Council the Don ataman asserted that the atamans of the stanitsas were under orders to favour the zemstvo, but this was rebutted by another member of the State Council who

was a witness to the proceedings in the Khoper okrug (GSSO 26 Feb 1914, 1357, 1371).

213. Arefin, RB, 1906, no. 12, 149; Lagunov, VE, 1910, no. 4, 290–1.
214. Lagunov, VE, 1910, no. 4, 292; GSSO 26 Feb 1914, 1336, 1352, 1371.
215. Lagunov, RB, 1910, no. 4, 296.
216. PSOGD, IV/1, no. 38, 10.
217. The War Ministry representative told the Duma subcommission on the Don zemstvo that the ministry had not made up its mind on the issue, that the wishes of the populace were not the only side, another 'not less important side, the voisko command, had not yet spoken'. With some contradiction he then asked the Duma to stop work on the project because the War Ministry was preparing its own draft on the Don zemstvo (Lagunov, RB, 1910, no. 4, 294–5).
218. GDSO 15 Feb 1912, 2164–5; 9 Mar 1912, 628–30. The votes for and against were not recorded, but Kharlamov claimed that it was almost unanimous (PSOGD, IV/1, no. 238, 9). The full text of the Duma bill on the Don zemstvo appears in GDSO 9 Mar 1912, 726–32, a detailed commentary by its authors in PSOGD, III/5, no. 125, 25–38.
219. On the voisko financial system, see below, pp. 155–64.
220. According to Kharlamov, the bill proposed only consultative powers (GDSO 5 June 1910, 3590–1).
221. GDSO 30 Jan 1912, 1236–8; PSOGD, IV/1, no. 38, 2.
222. PSOGD, IV/2, no. 38, 13.
223. GDSO 26 Feb 1914, 1349, 1371.
224. His considerable importance as a conservative leader in this whole period is well documented in Manning, op. cit.
225. GSSO 26 Feb 1914, 1332–45, 1354–5.
226. Ibid., 1355–62.
227. Ibid., 1345–55, 1378–9, 1387.

CHAPTER 4

1. Babychev, 24; Kharuzin, xxvi.
2. Khoroshkhin', 299–300.
3. PSZ II, 8163; VDVM 1873, 145.
4. PSZ II, 44370; SVM, XI/1, 541.
5. PSZ II, 49768, 55482, 55483, 55919, 57516, 58573, 59029, 59838, 59228; III, 5710. The prodolzhenie of 49768 contains a long list of expenditure and revenue categories. The following discussion is based on this source, confirmed by many samples of annual voisko budgets appearing in the annual reports of voisko atamans (e.g. VOOVD), Biriukov, DOV, Borodin and related material in the annual volumes, 1870–1914 of VOVM.
6. VOVM 1890.
7. Khoroshkhin', 236; the range was 26 per cent of income from interest in the Orenburg budget to 5 per cent in the Terek.

8. PSZ II, 8163, prodolzhenie II.

9. PSOGD, III/1, no. 125, 10–11, 75; Medvedev, 13–15; PSZ II, 19742, 19758. The Zabaikal, Amur and Ussuri stanitsas retained the right to operate taverns, 1904.

10. GDSO 13 Dec 1907, 960; TMK, vol. 50, 312, 315, 411–12; Maslakovets, 62; *Postanovleniia okruzhnykh Voiska Donskago komitetov po vyiasneniiu nuzhd sel'skokhoziaistvennoi promyshlennosti* ... , 13, 285.

11. See below, p. 194.

12. SPRKV 1870, no. 121.

13. Khoroshkhin', 237–8.

14. See above, pp. 110–12.

15. Khoroshkhin', 236; VOVM 1896, 1904.

16. PSZ II, 45785; SPRKV 1884, no. 26, sets the rates for the Don, others follow. VOVM budget reports do not show this as a line item; presumably it is in 'miscellaneous', which grew substantially.

17. VOVM, years indicated.

18. PSZ II, 25388.

19. PSZ II, 46996; SPRKV 1901, no. 98.

20. Khlystov, 20.

21. TMK, vol. 50, 415.

22. Khlystov, 19.

23. SPRKV 1901, no. 98; in practice this reform was only applied in one okrug of the Don (Khlystov, 22).

24. VOVM, years indicated; as late as 1904 the Amur received only 46 000 rubles from this source.

25. VOVM 1870–1912.

26. There were also salt works in most voiskos, but these were exploited mainly for the personal use of Cossacks, a traditional privilege, and did not contribute to the voisko budgets (VOVM, any year).

27. In Grushevskii itself, the royalty of half a kopek remained, but half of that went to a fund for roads, drainage, etc. In 1864 the voisko itself paid for a drainage project (SPRKV 1865, no. 51). The law on coal mining in the Don is PSZ II, 40666. VOVM shows that coal production rose more than threefold in 1870–90, while revenue to the voisko did not even double.

28. PSZ III, 10738; SPRKV 1898, no. 193; VOVM, years indicated.

29. Above, p. 38; VDVM 1894, 211; SVM, XI/1, 477; Khoroshkhin', 253.

30. PSZ II, 32553.

31. VOVM, annually, PSZ 49678, prilozhenie.

32. Ibid.; SPRKV 1904, 345. The voisko had to collect and transmit to the central treasury any standard taxes, such as the 'soul tax', that applied in its boundaries to Cossacks or, usually, non-Cossacks, but this did not pass through the voisko budget (e.g. VOOVD 1900, 22).

33. E.g. SPRKV 1867, nos. 52, 73, 98, 139.

34. Above, pp. 96–7.

35. VDVM 1876, 149; 1882, 148; SPRKV 1881, no. 133.

36. Don, Ural and Orenburg officers were paid wholly by the state after 1884 (PSZ III, 2209); Kuban, Terek, Semirechenskoe, Siberian and Astrakhan after 1902 (SVM, XI/1, 730); Zabaikal, Amur and Ussuri were always paid by the state.
37. VDVM 1884, 203.
38. Above, p. 61; SPRKV 1898, no. 317.
39. PSZ II, 49768, prilozheniia.
40. E.g. DOV 18 May 1891.
41. VOOVD 1890, 45; SPRKV 1882, no. 118; 1897, no. 103; 1881, no. 60.
42. E.g. SPRKV 1872, no. 56; 1890, no. 216.
43. PSZ II, 49678; SPRKV 1881, no. 209; below, 369.
44. VOVM 1860–70.
45. VOVM 1870–90; VDVM 1890, 147.
46. VOVM, years indicated. For a comparison, to the disadvantage of the Don, of that area and nearby guberniias, DGSO 12 Jun 1913, 1920–1.
47. VDVM 1882, 149–50.
48. VDVM 1882, 149–50; 1883, 213–14; 1884, 186–7; SPRKV 1889, no. 61; SVM, XI/1, 664.
49. PSZ III, 2210.
50. VOVM 1881, 1890.
51. SVM, XI/1, 262; VDVM 1886, 190–1; 1891, 144.
52. VDVM 1886, 190–1; 1894, 211; 1895, 235.
53. VDVM 1894, 212; 1898, 168–9.
54. PSOGD, IV/1, no. 591; SPRKV 1904, no. 513.
55. PSZ II, 48354; III, 7782.
56. The annual VOVM demonstrates this by producing only scanty data on the subject, see especially the complaint in 1890; numerous complaints in VOOVD on poor reportage from stanitsas (e.g. 1895, 20; 1911, 20).
57. VOVM annually. On land, 1904, showing 1.1 million rubles from land rent out of a total stanitsa revenue of 2.8 milion; Kuban, 2.3 million out of 4.5 million, among other examples.
58. Arefin, RB, 1906, no. 12, 131; TMK, vol. 50, 119–20; RI 1903, no. 191.
59. VOVM 1904; this produced about 48 000 rubles revenue, about 7 per cent of the total in Orenburg stanitsas.
60. VOVM 1894, 1896–8. Data are inadequate for other voiskos. Arefin, RB, 1906, no. 12, 131; TMK, vol. 52, 683.
61. E.g. Zabaikal in VOVM 1904 and both Zabaikal and Ussuri, 1910.
62. VOVM 1894, 1904 (in the latter year Orenburg raised about 18 per cent of its stanitsa revenue this way); Zasedatel'eva, 266.
63. VOVM 1904; Maslakovets, 96, shows salaries of officials and aid to poor Cossacks going on active duty, each consuming a little over 20 per cent of stanitsa expenditures.
64. VOVM 1890–1904.
65. VOVM, years indicated.
66. PSZ II, 43888.
67. SVM, XI/1, 530–1.
68. Ibid., 537.

69. PSZ II, 8163, prilozhenie, and below pp. 171–3.
70. The paradox appears in VOVM after 1890.
71. SVM, XI/2, 657; SPRKV 1909, no. 58; 1909, no. 13. In 1913 some Cossack Duma deputies attempted to introduce a bill that appealed to the sanctity of the tsars' charters and exempted Cossack land from the law on prescription, but it never came to a vote (PSOGD, IV/1, no. 243).
72. PSZ II, 8163; 46996.
73. PSZ II, 46996; on the Ural voisko, below, p. 170.
74. An exception was the Kalmyk Cossacks, for whom the norm was 40. The parish church was to receive 300. The famous allotment of 30 desiatinas per Don Cossack did not appear in the main law of 1835 (PSZ II, 8163), but in a follow-up the same year (PSZ II, 8172).
75. SPRKV 1869, no. 48; others follow until 1914 (on the Semirechenskoe voisko), SPRKV 1914, no. 316.
76. There were some minor exceptions concerning private possession, relating to virgin forest that had been cleared in the Caucasus and the Far East; there were special provisions concerning widows, unmarried daughters and sons under the age of 17.
77. PSZ II, 661; 3670.
78. PSZ II, 22192; over a third of Ural voisko revenue came from this source in 1900 (VOVM).
79. See above, p. 9; *Istoriia Dona s drevneishiikh vremen do Velikoi Oktiabr'skoi Revoliutsii* (Rostov, 1965) 195.
80. VOVM 1862.
81. PSZ II, 8163, prilozhenie; 8172.
82. Kharuzin, 6; Krasnov, RV, Jul–Aug 1865, 343–4.
83. Krasnov, 337; *Istoriia Dona* ... (op cit.) 196–7, 203.
84. PSZ II, 8163, prilozhenie.
85. PSZ II, 32975; there was considerable variation among the voiskos.
86. Krasnov, RV, Jul–Aug 1865.
87. SVM, XI/2, 505–9; it appears that the tsar was influenced by his brother Mikhail, who as Viceroy of the Caucasus submitted a proposal for giving the Kuban and Terek officers permanent title to land.
88. Ibid., 511.
89. PSZ II, 48274; 48275; 52574; 54297; 57304; 57303.
90. The tax was to expire when the fund became large enough to carry the pensions from interest, but this never happened.
91. Khlystov, 63.
92. Ibid., 64–9; VB, Vorob'ev, *Zemelnyi vopros u kazakov* (SPB, 1908) 18.
93. Kharuzin, 12–14.
94. Ibid., 15, 19–20.
95. PSZ II, 48354.
96. Kharuzin, 17–19.
97. Ibid., 20–4, 327.
98. Ibid., 18–42; DR 22 Oct 1892; Shcherbov, 18; Zasedatel'eva, 238.
99. Kharuzin, 22–41.
100. Ibid., 52–6.

101. Korolenko, RB, 1901, no. 12, 177–8.
102. Kharuzin, 269–70.
103. Ibid., 52–6.
104. VOVM 1882–1912; in 1912 the amount of 'good' iurt land per male Cossack was: Don, 10.8 desiatinas, Kuban, 7.4; Terek, 11.7.
105. VOVM 1890–1912; in 1912 the amount of 'good' iurt land per male Cossack was: Astrakhan, 12.8; Ural, 27.1 (1907 data, last year available); Orenburg, 20.5; Siberian, 28.4; Semirechenskoe, 22.8; Zabaikal, 23.3; Amur, 25.1; Ussuri, 31.4.
106. Futorianskii, 148, shows 6 per cent of Don and 19 per cent of Kuban stanitsa land employed for 'social needs' around 1900.
107. Other reports from around the turn of the century concerning various places range from 3 to 15.8 desiatinas, most estimating 8–10. TMK, vol. 50, 312, 359; Shcherbov, 15; DR 7 May 1892; 22 Oct 1892; 17 Oct 1895; Arefin, RB, 1906, no. 12, 130–3; 'MLE', RB, 1904, no. 5, 6, 17 (on the Kuban); Serov, VS, 1910, no. 10, 361 (on Orenburg).
108. Richard G. Robbins, *Famine in Russia 1891–1892. The Imperial Government Responds to a Crisis* (NY, 1975) 8; Haimson, op. cit., 226, referring to six desiatinas per capita as peasant 'joy' in 1906.
109. PSZ II, 46996 limited rental periods to the time between repartitions; PSZ III, 7782, limited it to one year; a 1912 law raised the limit to six (*Sobranie uzakoneniia*, 1912, no. 1240).
110. Baluev (1899), Baluev (1900); Maslakovets. E.g. Maslakovets reports that 42 318 Cossacks rented out their allotment, while Baluev reports that 82 925 rented out part of their allotment, but neither could say what percentage of those renting out land rented out any particular proportion of it. Evidently overworked okrug authorities were asked to provide (if not invent) data on complex topics that they normally did not consider.
111. Baluev (1900), 25, 87, 109, 145, 179, 195, 196. This shows that 82 925 households out of a total of 154 381 (53.7 per cent) rented out at least some land. Cf. Khlystov, who states (56.17 per cent); Zolotov (1952) 48.
112. Zasedatel'eva, 237; Chistov, 236; Serov, VS, 1910, no. 9, 147; TMK, vol. 27, 67.
113. Babychev, 9; Chistov, 237; MLE, RB, 1904, no. 5, 3–4.
114. Kuropatkin, 113; Erem'ev, RV, 1880, no. 11, 67; TMK, vol. 50, 109, 134, 164; Kaufman, 119–20; DR 17 Dec 1892; Zolotov (1952) 51; Arefin, RB, 1907, no. 4, 132.
115. Erem'ev, RV, 1880, no. 11, 68; DR 17 Dec 92; 23 Jul, 17 Oct 1895; Savel'ev, 71. VOVM 1892 reports 90 kopeks per desiatina as the average rental of voisko reserve land, generally considered under fair value.
116. See below, pp. 199–20.
117. Babychev, 9.
118. Khlystov, 275.
119. Ibid., 274; Arefin, RB, 1907, no. 4, 135; Shcherbov, 33.
120. VOVM 1882; VOOVD 1900, 14.
121. TMK, vol. 50, 108–9; DR 24 June 1893; Erem'ev, RB, 1880, no. 11, 64.
122. VOOVD 1902, 12; Kaufman, 427.

123. SPRKV 1898, no. 141; Erem'ev, RB, 1880, no. 11, 63.
124. Ivanov, VS, 1866, no. 9, 68–72; PSZ II, 8163.
125. Anon., VS, 1895, no. 5, 75, 77, 79, 97; Ivanov, VS, 1866, no. 9, 78–84; SPRKV 1872, no. 40.
126. SPRKV 1872, no. 40; 1877, no. 66.
127. PSZ III, 18809.
128. SVM, XI/2, 558–63, 694; VDVM 1893, 236.
129. DR 19 Jul 1894, 14 Dec 1895; SVM, XI/1, 694.
130. Korolenko, RB, 1901, no. 11, 183.
131. SVM, XI/1, 695–6; Kaufman, 447.
132. SVM, XI/1, 695.
133. E.g. Cossacks listed among former owners of intestate properties, DOV 21 Dec 1891.
134. Maslakovets, 46–7.
135. Among Soviet studies that stress the class differentiation, Futorianskii, Zasedatel'eva, Zolotov (1974), Babychev; Khlystov.
136. Erem'ev, RB, 1880, no. 11, 68; TMK, vol. 27, 67; Arefin, RB, 1906, no. 12, 135.
137. Khlystov, 91.
138. The number of cattle in all voiskos, whether the owner was Cossack or not, grew from 2.8 million in 1872 to 6.5 million in 1902; sheep from 5.6 million to 13.7 million; pigs from 0.3 million in 1892 to 4.3 million in 1902 (VOVM, years indicated).
139. Khlystov, 72–3; Maslakovets, 57.
140. From four million chetverts in 1862 to 65.8 million in 1912 (VOVM), the 1862 figure does not include voiskos that were closed before 1914.
141. VOVM, years indicated.
142. Khlystov quoting a contemporary, 73, 83; PVSS, 4; Kriukov, RB, 1907, no. 4, 43; Kuropatkin, 43; TMK, vol. 52, 692; Kharitonov, NS, 1896, no. 1, 181; Isk', NS 1892, no. 6, 13; Serov, VS, 1910, no. 10, 359; Zolotov (1952) 2.
143. RI, 1903, no. 193.
144. Khlystov, 73.
145. TMK, vol. 50, 164.
146. DR 7 May, 21 Jul 1892; Kuropatkin, 114; Kharitonov, NS, 1896, no. 1, 178.
147. Above, p. 182.
148. TMK, vol. 50, 167; Kharitonov, NS, 1896, no. 1, 181.
149. Khlystov, 80.
150. VOVM 1870, 1890, 1910.
151. VOVM 1890, 1910; in 1910 only about 9 per cent of the land planted with tobacco was in Cossack hands.
152. Maslakovets, 46–7; Arefin, RB, 1906, no. 12, 128.
153. Futorianskii, 152.
154. Zasedatel'eva, 284; Chistov, 237; TMK, vol. 50, 337; Kharuzin, 374.
155. Zasedatel'eva, 283; the average annual wage of such a worker was around 100 rubles, bare subsistence (Isk', NS, 1897, no. 6, |134).
156. Khlystov, 27–8, 76, 97; Maslakovets, 55.
157. TMK, vol. 52, 694.

158. Khlystov, 81–2, 238.
159. See above, p. 10.
160. SVM, XI/1, 526.
161. Khlystov, 224–5.
162. SVM, XI/1, 526–8; SPRKV 1870, no. 121.
163. PSZ, II, 45758.
165. PSZ II, 47056.
165. Savel'ev, 71, 160.
166. PSZ III, 3268.
167. Savel'ev, 75–8.
168. VOVM, years indicated; Khoroshkhin', 210–11.
169. *Iskra*, 1903, no. 61; Khoroshkhin', 179–81; PSZ III, 10395; SVM, XI/1, 673; SPRKV 1914, no. 77.
170. VOVM, years indicated.
171. Korolenko, RB, 1901, no. 10, 165–77.
172. Kharuzin, 368–70; Kuropatkin, 114.
173. VOVM 1881.
174. Kuropatkin, annex XXIII.
175. Shcherbov estimates 200–250; Kuropatkin 200–250; Medvedev 250–300; Maslakovets 250–300; Erem'ev, RB, 1880, no. 11, 300; 'Ne kazak', VS, 1888, no. 5, 135, 250. The equipment price list is in PSOGD, IV/1, no. 279, 2.
176. TMK, vol. 52, 695; 'MLE', RB, 1904, no. 5, 6; 'Doklad o rezultatakh komandirovki sostoiashchago gen.-letenanta Maslakovetsa v 1903 g. v zabaikal'skoe kazach'e voisko', 82, shows only 60 rubles for a horse there.
177. Maslakovets, 13–14; Kuropatkin, annex XXXII, which estimates the cost of horse at 120 rubles in the 1860s.
178. F. A. Shcherbina, *Krest'ianskie budzhety* (Voronezh, 1909) 337.
179. Maslakovets, 14, 113; Shcherbov, 33, 53; 'MLE', RB, 1904, no. 5, 1; Kuropatkin, 113.
180. See above, pp. 183–4.
181. Maslakovets, 60; Kuropatkin, annexes XXII, XXIII, XXV, XXXIV.
182. Serov, VS, 1900, no. 9, 163.
183. Maslakovets, 47; 'MLE', RB, 1904, no. 5, 7.
184. PSOGD, III/5, no. 125, 7–8; RI, 1903, no. 191, GSSO 26 Mar 1914, 1340.
185. Robbins, op. cit., esp. map, 5.
186. VDVM 1892, 161–3; 1893; 198–204; DR Mar-Apr 1892, passim.
187. VDVM 1892, 161–3; 1893, 198–200; 1894, 201–4; 1895, 224; 1896, 212–13.
188. SPRKV 1892, no. 286; VDVM as noted above.
189. VDVM 1893, 200.
190. VDVM 1894, 201–2.
191. VDVM 1895, 225, which also applied to non-Cossack parts of the Empire. This was calculated at 2 358 000 rubles as a gift to the Orenburg, Don, Siberian and Astrakhan voiskos.
192. SVM, XI/1, 670; VDVM 1894, 203; SPRKV 1893, no. 180.
193. VDVM 1893, 201.

194. John R. Fisher, 'The Witte Conference on the Needs of Agriculture in Russia; 1902–1905' (University of Toronto dissertation, 1978).
195. See above, pp. 73–4.
196. Manning, op. cit., 47, shows an increase from 30 in 1890 to 422 in 1905.
197. Kuropatkin, 114; PSZ III, 19758, 26137; TMK, vol. 50, 26–7; SVM, XI/1, 754.
198. Kaufman, 421.
199. *Postanovleniia okruzhnykh Voiska Donskago Komitetov* ... (op. cit.) 9; the idea was not included in the final report of the Maslakovets inquiry.
200. VDVM 1902, 88; PSZ III, 29767 elaborated the scheme and included the Astrakhan voisko.
201. TMK, vol. 50, 35–7.
202. Khlystov, 78–9.
203. Ibid., 68.
204. TMK, vol. 50, 9, 36, 140, 313; vol. 52, 684.
205. VOVM 1890.
206. VDVM 1883, 221; 1884, 190–1; 1885, 229; 1895, 229; 1896, 217; 1897, 205.
207. VDVM 1880, 176; PSZ II, 60970.
208. SPRKV 1892, no. 202; 1902, no. 175.
209. VDVM 1899, 71; 1902, 88.
210. VDVM 1914, 60.
211. SPRKV 1902, no. 137; VDVM 1902, no. 119.
212. SPRKV 1906, no. 223.
213. GDSO 2 June 1906, 963, 1079, 1326. Also 13 June 1907, 1313, 1317–18; 12 Apr 1970, 1969–70.
214. Only Astrakhan and Zabaikal had small harvests, Amur and Ussuri not reporting. VOVM 1904–6.
215. VOVM, years indicated: SPRKV 1906, nos. 236, 257, 532; VDVM 1907, 124; OZSM 1908, no. 75. No single source appears to contain consistently full data.
216. Denisov, 61; SPRKV 1906, nos. 104, 275, 370, 371, 394, 399, 432, 436, 494. In the cases of the Astrakhan, Ural, and Orenburg voiskos, it seems to have been necessary to issue a second charter because the wording in the first failed to make specific reference to land.
217. Arefin, RB, 1906, no. 12, 150; Kriukov, RB, 1907, no. 4, 26; GDSO 13 Jun 1906, 1315; Vorob'ev, op cit., 17–18.
218. VRKV, 18–23; VOVM 1906, 1910; PSZ III, 28887.
219. GDSO 9 Dec 1909, 3275–9; SPRKV 1910, no. 77.
220. PVSS, 3–4; Zolotov (1952) passim.
221. SPRKV 1910, no. 77; PVSS, 70; PSZ III, 33143.
222. PVSS, 79–270.
223. PVSS, 15.
224. PVSS, 6; Zolotov (1952) 14–15, 32; Khlystov, 66–8. In 1913, Cossack Duma deputies introduced a bill to give all voiskos access to the Peasant Bank, but nothing came of it (PSGDO, IV/1, no. 632).
225. PVSS, 15; Zolotov (1952) 40.
226. Zolotov (1952) 40–1.

227. VOOVD 1913, 16–17.
228. PVSS, 258–63.
229. Zolotov (1952) 45.
230. Ibid., 44–5; DOV 14–15 Aug 1912.
231. PVSS, 97.
232. Ibid., 206–10; Zolotov (1952) 45–7.
233. SPRKV 1909, nos. 70, 122. There was a proposal on the ministerial level to increase the expenditure on Don agriculture to 4.5 million rubles per year (OZSM 1912, no. 49).
234. SPRKV 1908, no. 184; PSOGD, IV/1, no. 38, 11.
235. SPRKV 1909, no. 122; 1910, no. 219; VOVM 1907–12.
236. SPRKV 1908, no. 155; 1909, no. 122.
237. SPRKV 1908, no. 63; 1912, no. 297.
238. PSZ III, 32040.
239. PVSS, 2; DOV 10, 14 Jan, 16 May 1912; Babychev, 17–18, 20.
240. GDSO 12 Jun 1913, 1920; PSOGD, IV/1, no. 38, 12.
242. VOVM 1904, 1910.
243. OZSM 1907, no. 176, 4; VOVM 1906, 1908.
244. VOVM 1913.
245. VOVM, years indicated.
246. VDVM 1911, 64.
247. VOVM 1910, 1913; VDVM 1914, 58; OZSM 1912, no. 38, 5.
248. See pp. 208-10.
249. VOVM, years indicated.
250. VDVM 1912, 59; 1913, 56, which states that at existing rates the voisko funds will be exhausted in four years. VOVM 1909–12.
251. OZSM 1913, no. 357.
252. SPRKV 1909, no. 243; 1912, no. 348.
253. SPRKV 1910, nos. 379, 389; 1911, nos. 383, 389; 1912, no. 411; 1913, nos. 388, 393.
254. SPRKV 1913, nos. 228, 255, 256, 315.
255. SPRKV 1914, nos. 39, 284; 1912, nos. 282, 309, 322.
256. Denisov, 26; GDSO 13 May 1907, 2892; 20 Mar 1910, 1330; 12 Jun 1913, 1914; PSOGD, IV/1, no. 38, 3 ff.; IV/1, no. 254, 3.
257. PSOGD, IV/1, no. 28, 4–5; no. 254, 4: GDSO 8 May 1912, 805.
258. PSOGD, IV/1, no. 254, 4; no. 38, 3; GDSO 12 Jun 1913, 1915–16.
259. PSZ III, 32238.
260. SPRKV 1910, no. 31; 1912, nos. 29, 37.
261. GDSO 12 Jun 1913, 1914–16; PSOGD, IV/1, no. 38, 5.
262. VDVM 1915, 102–10; 1916, 74.
263. PSZ III, 32238; SPRKV 1910, no. 64.
264. DOV 27 Oct 1912.
265. GDSO 31 May 1909, 2897–900; 12 Apr 1907, 1969–70; 13 Dec 1907, 970. One speaker estimated the value at 5 000 000 per year.
266. OZSM 1912, no. 49; 1913, no. 6.
267. OZSM 1912, no. 49; no. 125; 1913, no. 36.
268. PSZ III, 36487.
269. OZSM 1912, no. 49; 1913, no. 36.
270. VOVM 1905, 1912.

271.   VDVM 1907, 123; VOVM, years indicated.
272.   Babychev, 15–16.
273.   GSSO 26 Feb 1914, 1334.

CHAPTER 5

1.   Among early twentieth-century references to this process, A. A. Kaufman, 683, 687; Korolenko, RB, 1901, no. 12, 185; Lagunov, VE, 1910, no. 4, 299–300.
2.   GSSO 26 Feb 1914, 1343–4.
3.   E.g. DOV 9 May 1906; GDSO 13 Jun 1906, 1328; PSOGD, IV/1, no. 384, 11.
4.   Carsten Goehrke, 'Historische Selbstilisierung des Kosakentums: Standische Tradition als Integrationideologie' in *Osteuropa in Geschichte und Gegenwart. Festschrift fuer Guenter Stoekl zuer 60 Geburtstag* (Koln, Wien, 1977) 359–75; Peter Kenez, 'The Ideology of the Don Cosseacks in the Civil War' in R. C. Elwood (ed), *Russian and East European History. Selected Papers from the Second World Congress of Soviet and East European Studies* (Berkeley, forthcoming).
5.   Some idea of this large historical literature appears in the excerpts and bibliography in R. H. McNeal (ed), *Russia in Transition* (New York, 1976) and 'The Fate of Imperial Russia' in Samuel H. Baron and Nancy W. Heer (eds), *Windows on the Russian Past. Essays in Soviet Historiography since Stalin* (Columbia, 1979.)

Index